772 KEE

D0587246

**MAIN LIBRARY**
**QUEEN MARY UNIVERSITY OF LONDON**

Some of the greatest 20th century authors — Brecht, Kafka, Mann — wrote in German and here is an enjoyable way into their, and many others', best work.

*Babel Guides* are a new series on contemporary world fiction available in English. There are two parts; the *Database* gives useful details on every book from Germany, Austria and Switzerland translated since 1945 and the *Reviews* introduce over a hundred of the best, most representative books, with a quotation as a taster.

Great for travellers, students and the adventurous; map out a new world of reading pleasure!

'a brilliant idea, well executed'
— *The Good Book Guide*

'accessible and entertaining'
— *Traveller's Literary Companion*

# The Babel Guide
# to German Fiction
# in English Translation
## [Austria, Germany, Switzerland]

by Ray Keenoy, Mike Mitchell & Maren Meinhardt

*with*

Mark Axelrod
Petra M. Bagley
Simonetta Castello
Clara Corona
Robert Gillet
Charles Hills
Nick Jacobs
Brian Murdoch
Margaret B Sargent

Illustrations by Jackie Wrout

**BOULEVARD**

Babel Guide to German Fiction in English Translation

©Boulevard Books 1997.
First published 1997 by Boulevard Books
8 Aldbourne Road
London W12 OLN, UK
Tel/Fax 0181 743 5278
email: raybabel@dircon.co.uk

*Special thanks to*;
Clara Corona, Maren Meinhardt, Gabrielle Sonnleitner
Barbara Haanke, Mike Mitchell, Brian Murdoch, Patrick Curry,
Jackie Wrout & Robert Gillet

QM LIBRARY
(MILE END)

ISBN 1 899460 20 9

Boulevard Books are distributed in the UK & Europe by Central Books, London
and in the USA & Canada by Paul & Co. Publishers Consortium Inc.c/o
PCS Data Processing Inc, 360 West 31 St, NY, NY 10001
212-564-3730 ext. 295 Fax 212-967-0928.

Cover Art: Jackie Wrout
Typeset & Design: Studio Europa
Printed and bound by the Guernsey Press, Guernsey, C.I.

*For Chief Topo*

## Contents

9  Index of Authors reviewed

10  Reviews of selected books

186  Fiction in English Translation Database; fiction from the German-speaking world published in the UK

251  Editors & Contributors

# Index of authors reviewed

ANTHOLOGIES 11,13,14,17

ARJOUNI, Jakob 18

BACHMANN, Ingeborg 20,21

BECKER, Jurek 23

BERNHARD, Thomas 24,25,26,28,29

BIERMANN, Pieke 30

BÖLL, Heinrich 32,34,35,37,39,41,42

BRECHT, Bertolt 45

CANETTI, Elias 46

CANETTI, Veza 48

DODERER, Heimito von 50

DÖRRIE, Doris 53

ENDE, Michael 54

FALLADA, Hans 55,56

FICHTE, Hubert 57,58

FONTANE, Theodor 60

FRIED, Erich 62

FRISCH, Max 64,65

GRAB, Hermann 66

GRASS, Günter 67,69

HACKL, Erich 72,73

HANDKE, Peter 75,78

HEIN, Cristoph 79

HESSE, Hermann 80,81,83,85,86

HEYM, Georg 87

HEYM, Stefan 88

HOCHHUTH, Rolf 90

HOFMANN, Gert 91

HORVÁTH, Ödön von 93

JAHN, Hans Henny 94

JELINEK, Elfriede 96,97

JÜNGER, Ernst 99,102

KAFKA, Franz 103,107

KÄSTNER, Erich 108

KIRCHOFF, Bodo 110

KIRST, Hans Hellmut 111,113

KOEPPEN, Wolfgang 114

KUBIN, Alfred 116

KUNZE, Reiner 118

LASKER-SCHÜLER, Else 119

LOEST, Erich 122

MANN, Thomas 124,126,127,128

MARON, Monika 130

MEYRINK, Gustav 131,132,134

MITGUTSCH, Anna 135

MUSIL, Robert 136,138,140

NOLL, Ingrid 141

PAUSEWANG, Gudrun 142

PERUTZ, Leo 144,146

PIRINÇCI, Akif 147

RANSMAYR, Christoph 149,150

REICHART, Elisabeth 152

REMARQUE, Erich Maria 153

RINSER, Luise 155

ROSENDORFER, Herbert 156, 158, 160, 161

ROTH, Joseph 163,164

SANDER, Helke 166

SCHNITZLER, Arthur 167

STRAUSS, Botho 168

SÜSKIND, Patrick 169

TRAVEN, B 170

TUCHOLSKY, Kurt 172

WALSER, Robert 174,175

WEISS, Ernst 176

WODIN, Natascha 178

WOLF, Christa 180,182

ZWEIG, Stefan 184

Lukens, N. & Rosenberg, D. (eds.)

## Daughters of Eve. Women's Writing from the German Democratic Republic

A large and well-produced book covering women writers of fiction from the 1970s and 80s, edited, perhaps appropriately for a book on East German literature, on very ideological lines. It's a useful, if not very pleasurable, representative collection. The ideology of it's authors — a sort of Stalinoid Feminism — is clear from the highly skippable introduction that carries on at inappropriate length (for a literary anthology at least) on a comparison between West and East German welfare states.

The stories themselves, from twenty-five different authors, give what is no doubt a good picture of the officially-acceptable literature of the GDR, at this late stage quite preoccupied, in a fairly ploddy way, with socialist-feminist themes such as combining careers, caring, men, self-respect etc. They read somewhat predictably now but were probably very worthwhile and even perhaps controversial when first published.

The collection is a mix of short stories and novel-excerpts with one very interesting piece from a book of interviews with rural East Germans by Gabriele Eckart. Although as a whole the collection is run-of-the-mill stuff there are some better pieces too. In Helga Schütz's extract from *In Annas Namen* — which lifts off from the strange fact of the division of Germany between 1949 and 1990 and all the consequent separation of families and lovers — she demonstrates herself a real writer. The important writer Irmtraud Morgner is represented with an extract called *The Tightrope*, an unobvious bit of writing that makes the (now) obvious point that many women in the 1970s were being asked to do two full-time jobs (home and work) when employed men did one. Rosemarie Zeplin tells the sad tale of a young woman seduced by a higher-up man in a bureaucracy and executes it with the greatest irony. Other good and s ubtle stories come from Christiane Grosz, Monika Helmecke, Maria Seidemann and Maja Wiens. Christa Wolf was the GDR's most eminent woman writer but her 1970s piece included here, *Tomcat,* satirises East-block materialism with a humour that now seems ponderous.

Although a useful collection in its way, there seems in this mainly officially-sanctioned work so much left out about the life of this quiescent and isolated little republic. Perhaps people are tackling this now or perhaps life there was just too dull and restricted to inspire exciting, truthful writing. Where is the East German *Smallpiece's Day* or even *The Joke* (Kundera)? R K

'It was wartime, and we lived in Babelsberg. The bombing raids every day... finally it got so I didn't care if I died or not. I thought, it's not as bad for a young girl like me as it is for somebody who has a family. Like my uncle. He was an artist, a painter, and had two children with a third on the way. He often talked to me like a grownup, about sexuality and everything. He was killed in combat and I thought, why should I live instead of him?

After the air raid on Potsdam, Father and I went to visit my grand-parents. When we got to the station, there was a munitions train on the tracks, grenades were exploding, everything was on fire, bomb craters every-where, flames leaping over to the factory on the right, I was afraid my hair and clothes would catch fire, I stopped, my father kept going. Then a young couple came along, the husband threw his coat over my head, and we walked down the street that way.

The next day I had to report to the district headquarters where I worked. When I got to the top of the stairs I saw my co-worker, two feet tall and burned to a crisp. That's when something in me came unglued.' p251 (*Ilse, 56, Chairperson of an Agricultural Production Co-operative* from Gabriele Eckart *So sehe ick die Sache: Protokolle aus der DDR/That's How I See It: interviews from the GDR* 1984)

'As always, the baby wakes up when I push the carriage into the dark entryway of our building. I would have liked to leave it in the courtyard for a while, in the overgrown grass. But baby will cry. So I carry the things upstairs first. All of a sudden there's screaming. I forgot the older one wants to win when we climb the stairs. I went too fast. She resents that. The worst name you can be called at kindergarten seems to be Slowpoke. I go downstairs, the baby's whimpering. I'm imprisoned by my children's crying.

I start a fire in the kitchen stove. The baby needs heat. Thank God it doesn't smoke. And now the older one. "Please, please, mommy. play com-pany."

I try to distract her, suggest all the games I'd much rather play, in fact would even like to play with her: dice, chess, dominoes, or picture lotto. Or better, clay. That's what I would like to do now. Form some things. Ani-mals. The Bremen Town Musicians, or a little line of elephants that get smaller and smaller, seals balancing balls. That would be fun right now. But no. "Com-pany, please, pretty please, play Company." I curse my friend who showed her this dismal game and obey, since the last half hour, at least that much, belongs to her. So:

"Knock Knock."

"Hello."

"Hello. What's your name?"

"Mrs. Doering."

"Oh, Mrs. Doering. How nice. And what is your baby's name?"

"Yoga."

"What a pretty name." And so forth. Every evening, if my daughter had her way. Only the baby's names change, because she forgets the one from the day before.' p190 (from Monika Helmecke *Klopfzeichen* 1979)

## ANTHOLOGY

### Constantine, David (ed.)

## German Short Stories 2 [Deutsche Kurzgeschichten 2]

As a parallel text collection this is a useful kind of book for anyone trying to learn or just refresh their German. Edited by a leading scholar and translator, David Constantine, it is all done to a very high standard, with an introduction that usefully explains something of what the term 'short story' means in a German context.

It's an interesting enough collection of pieces — particularly strong on East German and Austrian writers — to read in English alone. It includes *Fedezeen* by Gunter de Bruyn, a subtle, elliptical story set in a 1930s Berlin neighbourhood where the local clothing store offers 'uniforms for all party ranks', beautifully summing up this cruel and bizarre time in Germany. From a little later in historical time Siegfried Lenz's *The Renunciation* further unravels the melancholy truth about German political extremism.

The celebrated Ingeborg Bachmann is represented with a story *The Dogs,* written with great sophistication, about a classic selfish male bastard and the loving tribe of women who suffer in his wake. It's the usual pessimistic view of humanity by this celebrated Austrian writer, a voice of the extremely disillusioned postwar generation.

For variety the important East German (and all the stories here are from the period when East Germany was still very much in existence) Johannes Bobrowski delivers a charming rural idyll *Lobellen Grove,* set in a part of Germany now split between Poland and Russia.

There are also stories by the major figures Alexander Kluge — a starkly excellent piece about a disturbed and displaced woman caught in the vice-like normality of 1960s Germany — and Thomas Bernhard, with a stunning fable of violence and greed.

This is a very potent collection and a good introduction to some fine authors, with the bonus of the chance to explore them in their own language too. R K

'She was freezing in the unheated room and felt a cold coming on as something to be welcomed and yet resented for its potential inconvenience; a bit like having a baby. She sought warmth in the body next to her, first having to accustom herself to it again. She was no longer embarrassed with him. Whatever part of her body he wanted, she gave him. She gave herself with a simplicity which simple people don't in fact have, and took care to keep her stories about the past natural. She arranged her past in such a way that it couldn't disturb him. She made no plans, content instead to await his suggestions for the next day. Through the thin cover she made sure of the body sleeping next to her. With him there, she slept outside the blanket, on the edge of the bed, lying on her side and leaning slightly against the mound under the clothes, fearing that otherwise she would disturb him with movements which at night she couldn't control.' p205 (Anita G. By Alexander Kluge)

ANTHOLOGY
Lappin, Elena (ed.)

## Jewish Voices, German Words

This collection of nineteen short stories, novel extracts, the odd essay and several poems is by young Jewish writers writing in German, in Austria and the two Germanies, and who grew up in these countries after 1945. The idea of being Jewish in post-*Shoah* ('Holocaust') Germany or Austria already starts from such a bleak premise — you're living amidst a nation of Fred Wests who've put your brothers, sisters and aunties under the Fatherland's great patio in the sky — that anything is possible.

In fact quite a variety of situations are explored and different conclusions reached, often no more or less sour about their uncomfortable homeland than are *Goyish* German writers. The book's editor — also Jewish and (partly) raised in Germany — who currently edits one of Britain's most interesting literary/ current affairs magazines, the *Jewish Quarterly*, does an excellent job posing the kind of issues that many Germans would prefer to be overlooked. As she says in her introduction while 'for most young German writers, the past appears to have been deleted... for their Jewish counterparts it is an indelible part of their consciousness of the present'. Until younger Germans wake up to the fact that Germany can only clear its name by trying, for a suggestion, to do a tenth of the good in the next one hundred years as the evil that was done in those infamous twelve years of the Third Reich, then Jews in dealing with Germans are, as Peter Jungk says in his contribution, 'obliged to forget, forget each day anew, what took place there, forty years ago', to forget on behalf of the Germans and Austrians, to spare *their* feelings.

In the actual collection a particularly interesting piece is by East German Chaim Noll who grew up as the son of faithful Party parents but writes laconically, 'The country to which our part of Berlin belonged called itself the GDR (German Democratic Republic). That name stood for three claims: Germany, democracy, and republic, none of which would bear close examination. One saw them everywhere, in block letters: on bridges, on roofs, in store windows among baby carriages and cabbages. Usually associated with promises of a brilliant future.'

Thomas Feibel in a beautiful, hilarious piece *'Gefilte Fish and Pepsi: A Childhood in Enemy Territory'* also plays it for laughs, in a long Jewish literary (and oral) tradition; 'We were neurotics in the marinade of Jewishness.' Another contributor, Katja Behrens, like a lot of young Jews from Western countries, is attracted to visit Israel in a search for roots — implicitly the roots that otherwise might have been sought in the Yiddish Heartland between Berlin and Moscow that was destroyed by the Germans under their famous Austrian leader and then further (culturally) filleted by Stalinism. Behrens' Israeli tale is poignant, funny and horribly true-sounding as she gets chased around Jerusalem by a sexually frustrated Fundamentalist dirty old man.

The identity crush, often very complex for non-religious Ashkenazi Jews because of secularism and the Shoah, is also addressed in two pieces by Barbara Honigmann where she talks of the curious 'lost' state of a creative, clever woman trapped between identities (German/East German and Jewish/World Citizen).

This confusion over identity is to some extent the condition of all Europeans, especially since the end of World War Two, but especially of the continent's Jewish citizens, 'super-Europeans', with a long tradition of presence in all European countries — amidst expulsions and exterminations — and with a common European culture. All in all the authors in this book are appropriate witnesses to the way Germany and Austria have (not) dealt with their recent past.

The book also includes many other thoughtful and well-written pieces and is a beautifully produced and translated book, a tribute to its small American publisher, Catbird Press. R K

'In the longer run the German nation will not be forgiven for Auschwitz, or for the calculated attack on humanity this word has come to symbolise. How Germany comes to terms with this is its own problem. When a people makes such a spectacle of itself, its name becomes emblematic of something revolting; for centuries that was the case with the Huns, Tartars, and Mongols.' p54 (Chaim Noll A *Country, A Child*)

'Could any people be more uprooted than the Germans?... they have lost the ground under their feet and cannot recover it with the gravitational pull of money. Abroad one gets to look at them under a magnifying glass. A German tourist enters a restaurant in Holland with his family and does not dare to say "Guten Tag", because he would not want to be identified with the Germans who invaded Holland; even so, he feels guilty. This man is the civilised façade of the same man who goes to his club with fellow Germans and sings soldiers' songs... The Germans are a schizophrenic people. The hatred they feel for their own identity comes from the lost war, forced democratisation, and the incomprehensible crimes of the Second World War... Nothing in this country's consciousness has done as much harm as the notion of collective guilt. The fascists' crimes were unloaded on the entire people, and the executioners, the fellow-travellers, the merely indifferent, and the resistance fighters were all tarred with the same brush... If Herr Krupp's chauffeur is as guilty as Herr Krupp, both may feel free to continue going about their business — or neither. Thus the Germans blocked themselves from calling their criminals by name, from distinguishing between them and the fellow-travellers, the indifferent, and the resistance fighters, and building their future on the right people.... Not guilt but shame would have been appropriate. Guilt is a religious emotion and obscures one's understanding. But a person who feels shame about something contemplates that thing and tries to get to the bottom of it, even if that means pursuing his father's crimes... Then he can purge them and live without guilt. The child who promises to be better only because of a guilty conscience is already paving the way for the next misdeed.' p35-6 (Benjamin Korn *Shock and Aftershock*)

'If you ask me whether I have a *Heimat* (Homeland), and where it is, I reply in classic Jewish style: evasively. I think I have a *Heimat*, but I can't localize it. It's the odour of gefilte fish and potato pancakes, the taste of borscht and pickled herring, the melody of the Hatikva and the sound of the Internationale, but only when it's sung in Yiddish by old members of the Bund in Tel Aviv on the first of May. It's the Marx brothers' night in Casablanca, and Ernst Lubitsch's to be or not to be. It's Karl Kraus's Torch and the autobiography of Theodor Lessing. It's a spot on the Aussenalster in Hamburg, a little stairway in the old harbour of Jaffa, and the Leidseplein in Amsterdam. Isn't that enough?' p101 (Henryk M. Broder Heimat? No, Thanks!)

Humann, Klaus (ed.)

## Nightdrive. Modern German Short Stories

This recent (1995) anthology aims to introduce younger East and West German writers. With nearly three hundred pages and almost thirty stories it's definitely a good attempt. It somewhat unusually focuses exclusively on German writers, partly no doubt because it's part of a series of country-by-country anthologies that already includes similar Italian, Spanish and Czech anthologies. This makes it glaringly obvious though how important the Austrian contribution to more recent German-language fiction has been, as one really misses Thomas Bernhard, Elfriede Jelinek and Peter Handke. However, most of the writers here haven't had any books translated into English so it's a good opportunity to discover new voices.

This is especially true as the editor has wisely included two pieces by some of his authors, giving us a better picture of their work and reducing the breathless effect of reading a small chunk by one writer after another...

The most interesting stories for this reader were the East German Katja Lange-Müller's two bleak but powerful stories of old women, particularly the story of Margot, born by the railway track to a signalman but who has to wait fifty years before she gets to go for a train ride. Another story of constrained lives is by a writer from remote East Friesland, Jochen Schimmmang, with *Laederach* a lovely, funny story, highly percipient about what to an Englishman seems an astonishingly provincial society.

One of the youngest writers here, Daniel Groller, born in 1963, provides a story, again with a Friesland connection, of gruesome gothic brilliance. This seems to be a very German story — it's hard to imagine it coming from anywhere else — in its mixture of humour and ridicule of the ignorant. There is also that authentically bitter and twisted vision that comes so often from this clever, energetic but generally unhappy people. In Groller's piece a young Friesian farmer's son has the farm sold from under him to make a motorway service station — of all unfortunate Godforsaken things — and that's when the trouble starts...

In opposition to the provincial vision is Klaus Modick with whom contemporary German introspection goes global very successfully. *Off Season*, set in the United States, has a note of J.G.Ballard or of a warmer, less intellectual Albert Camus as it speaks of a very contemporary state of mixed mild disillusionment and excitement with life in the story of a young man cracking up from an intense failed love affair.

In contrast, Katja Behrens' beautiful story or perhaps better fantasy of a woman with a much younger lover truly swims in the watery magic of its title *Love*.

Finally two writers who are, happily, published in English elsewhere (see review section and database) can be first sampled in this anthology; Cristoph Hein with his uncomfortable, Fassbinderish (R.W.Fassbinder; German new wave film director) honesty, about the politically incorrect side of reality and then Bodo Kirchoff with a five-star story of sex and words that make the dream of sex come true; pure brilliance in an enjoyable collection; full marks for its publisher Serpent's Tail, a strong force on the translation front. R K

'The elevator took him in — a mechanical, rigid embrace. On the illuminated indicator the floors slid by, the height shrivelling into numbers, 57, 56, 55, no one got on anywhere, 45, 44, 43, the lift was the vein of a sleeping body, pumping used-up blood back to the heart. He felt for the ticket in his breast pocket; tomorrow he would be flying back, back to what had been once. 38, 37, 36, yes, he was thirty-six now, and 35, 34, 33 was how old he had been when he was offered the job and took it without hesitation. Three years in New York on a good salary was a good break. It was a chance to break with boredom, with the corridors, looks and faces that were always the same. And the loneliness, too, that had had him in its grip ever since he and Lisa had separated, he wanted to leave behind him as well, like a worn-out raincoat. Here he had worn the required business suits, and here he had worked harder than ever before, 12, 11, 10 hours a day, but he accepted the demands the job made almost gratefully because it meant he scarcely had time to think about himself and Lisa, and the five, or was it six, women he had slept with here, and 3, 2, 1 — three years had sped past him.' p109 (from *Off Season*, Klaus Modick)

## ARJOUNI
Jakob

# Happy Birthday, Turk [Happy Birthday, Türke]

Much of the detective story's appeal depends on milieu, like the Oxford of British TV's Inspector Morse and the detective figure is also very often an outsider of some sort, like Sherlock Holmes, Sam Spade or Hercule Poirot in their different ways. Arjouni's detective in this first novel (filmed in Germany, and with a sequel

*More Beer* also translated) is a specific kind of outsider in a specifically German milieu. Kemal Kayankaya, a private detective working in Frankfurt, is of Turkish origin but was adopted and brought up by Germans in Germany and is quite unable to speak Turkish. Turks, of course, form a large part of the migrant-worker population in Germany, and there have been racial attacks and problems of all kinds. A German-speaking Turk as a detective outside the police force is, therefore, a multiple outsider. Working in a large industrial city, he is asked to investigate a murder in the Turkish community simply because he has a Turkish name, and because the police are not terribly interested in a dead Turk. So there is tension not only in the action, but also in the fact of his origins (and looks) and the way he is treated by the police and by the Germans he encounters. Kayankaya faces racial abuse, regular mockery and beatings-up on a regular basis as he pursues his investigation.

These indications of very sensitive social issues give an extra dimension to the detective-story format, although much of the plot-line conforms to the standard underworld novel, with drug addiction and smuggling, ladies of dubious virtue, blackmail, corrupt policemen and quite a lot of violence. The format is not the genteel English detective story but more Raymond Chandler, whose influence is unmistakable in the style, though the use of the local Frankfurt dialect (and a few other features) get unfortunately lost in translation. The story moves along rapidly, and with much incidental humour in the dry self-reflection of this Turkish-origin Philip Marlowe in the land of economic miracles and *Gastarbeiter* ('Guestworker' — name for foreign workers in postwar W. Germany). B M

'My investigations had gotten off to a flying start. I wiped the last drops of puke out of my ears and made myself a Scotch and soda...At some time, who knows when, a prostitute had yelled for Ahmed Hamul. That was what I had found out.... I wondered how much physical abuse I would have to endure in exchange for some decent information, and whether I could charge visits to brothels on my expense sheet. Slowly my second Scotch and soda anaesthetised my bruised stomach. If I really had to locate that prostitute to find out a little more about Ahmed Hamul, my search could turn out to be interminable.'

## Malina [Malina]

As well as a novelist Ingeborg Bachmann was an acclaimed poet, winning the prestigious Georg Büchner prize. As with the work of Paul Celan, the great Jewish poet writing in German, she was concerned with the problem of writing poetry in this language after Auschwitz, perceiving it as permanently soiled. She was also a prominent member of the Gruppe 47, an influential left-wing writers' association. The circumstances of her death by fire in Rome, attributed to an unextinguished cigarette, are still not entirely explained.

*Malina* was conceived as the first part of a cycle called *Todesarten (Styles of Death)*, but was the only novel she in fact completed. Although first published to great success in 1971, it was only published in English translation in 1990.

The parallels between the content of the novel and the life of its author seem like an invitation to speculate about the latter: both author and narrator are born in Klagenfurt, are strongly rooted in Vienna, and it is hinted that even their Christian names are identical.

Replying to comments that *Malina* was about her relationship with the famous Swiss writer Max Frisch — who proved to be less shy in making literary use of the relationship — she objected to a strictly autobiographical reading and wanted it to be seen rather as a 'spiritual, imaginary autobiography'.

The composition of the novel has been compared to a piece of music or a play, with different themes and variations developing and interweaving. After introducing her main protagonists, there are three 'acts'. Within these acts the structure loosens up with quotations from fairy tales, telephone conversations, letters, passages of Schönberg's *Pierrot Lunaire* floating about and eventually flowing into the stream of consciousness of the narrator's voice.

The novel, set in Vienna, involves three people. The female narrator lives together with her male partner Malina, but loves Ivan, a younger Hungarian man with two children. For the narrator, this relationship with Ivan is so important that it blanks out her real surroundings and she builds an imaginary country, the *Ungargassenland*, inhabited exclusively by the two of them. Ivan is the practical, down-to-earth type, which renders him the ideal ill-fated love object for the narrator. He is the sort of person who wants her to write a 'happy' novel and finds himself alienated by her dark, death-focused writing. Whilst Ivan retreats more and more from the relationship and the neediness of the narrator, she confides in Malina.

Malina's persona assumes clearer definition only in the later parts of the novel. Unlike Ivan, who personifies the positive and optimistic kind of person the narrator can never become, Malina is a soulmate. He is interested in art, is sympathetic, if passionless, and infallibly correct in the face of his partner's infidelity.

As the relationship with Ivan becomes more fraught the narrator feels her self split between her emotional and rational selves, seen here as female and male polarities. She attempts to harmonize her emotional obsession for Ivan with her rational thoughts, but this project is destined to fail...

Malina is about emotion made absolute, transcending everything else and leading here, in its final consequence, to the annihilation of the narrator. Maren M

"I have to watch out that I don't fall face first onto the hot plate, that I don't disfigure myself, burn myself, then Malina would have to call the police and the ambu lance, he would have to confess his carelessness at having let a woman burn halfway to death. I stand up straight, my face glowing from the red plate on the stove, where I so often burned scraps of paper at night, not so much to burn something written, but to light a last and a very last cigarette. But I don't smoke anymore, I'v e given it up as of today. I can turn the knob back to 0.

...I stare at Malina resolutely, but he doesn't look up. I stand up, thinking that if he doesn't say something immediately, if he doesn't stop me, it will be murder, and since I can no longer say this I walk away. It's not so frightening anymore, just that our falling apart is more frightening than any falling together. I have lived in Ivan and die in Malina." p223

BACHMANN
Ingeborg

## The Thirtieth Year [Das dreißigste Jahr]

Ingeborg Bachmann is a poetess and her writing has its startling, poetically powerful passages that seem to sum up wonderfully the dilapidated, uneasy postwar Austria of her youth, for example 'an estate that has crawled out tame and hidebound from under mortgages'.

In the title story of this collection The Thirtieth Year the thirty-year old in question has reached an age to step out boldly on the road and live with passion — but he's not yet toughened enough to defend himself from the love and malice his passionate self encounters. This is a rather remarkable 'how to be thirty story', an intense, inspired reflection on youth, love-affairs, on new beginnings and the betrayal of new beginnings...

Overall Bachmann's work is tinged though with a sense of the material and spiritual bleakness of postwar Austria, with its moral bankruptcy following the Nazi adventure. In one story here a group of (male) cultural types, a journalist, a radio director etc., gather for a convivial get-together but after some drinking the cultural side sloughs off as they excitedly start on war stories which come to an abrupt halt 'when the dead Slovenian nuns were lying naked in the wood outside Veldes'. The story serves for an effective metaphor for contemporary Austria, which likes to present itself as the home of high culture — a little Beethoven to distract us from the stink of the crematoria? Or all the looted valuables carefully piled up out of sight until all the (Jewish) victims are completely forgotten?

Alongside the title story the best piece in the collection is probably the archly-titled *A Step towards Gomorrah*, the very well-captured start of a love-affair, in this case a woman's first lesbian relationship. When Ingeborg Bachmann is good, she is very very good, capturing the emotional, the subjective, concisely and with great artfulness. R K

'A waitress appeared in court, in a case concerning the disputed paternity of an illegitimate child, I think; she had difficulty expressing herself, and then again she uttered sentences of such candour, such bluntness, that I, who at that time was still unaccustomed to the speech of alien milieus, had to take a grip on myself in order to appear cold, friendly and impartial. I remember the case only in general outline and should have forgotten it long ago if the in-eradicable picture of Wanda were not still there: her loose black hair, her moist, fabulous mouth, her hair tossed over her breast, her hair tossed behind her, her hair in the way everywhere, out of the way, in the way of a body that wanted to experience every possibility of expanding, bending, moving, that can possibly exist; the picture includes her arms that wanted at every moment to be arms, her fingers that really were ten fingers and each single one of them could set fire to the skin...' p166

## Jacob the Liar [Jakob der Lügner]

Becker was a Jewish Pole who settled in East Germany and became a leading author there. Jakob the Liar is set in one of the ghettos created by the Nazis in occupied Poland by stuffing thousands of Jews into a barricaded part of a city with very little food and under various harsh regulations. Eventually nearly all the surviving inhabitants would be transported to extermination camps.

Extraordinarily enough in this setting Becker creates a story with a good deal of humour and warmth. The ghetto denizens are, after all, ordinary people only recently torn from everyday lives and in their conversations emerge poignant details of their pre-deluge lives; their little shops selling potato pancakes, haircuts or tobacco; the tricky loose ends of love-affairs and marriages, all evoked by a particular kind of sardonic Yiddish wit and warmth. In fact, although writing in German, Becker draws on a Yiddish oral storytelling tradition.

One of the conditions of ghetto life was that any contact with the world outside was forbidden, including the possession of any radios. Jakob, the former proprietor of a potato pancake (*latke*) and ice-cream shop, claims one day to have a radio and this story of the imaginary radio rapidly develops under its own strange logic bringing in the hopes for survival of various very different individuals including a eight-year-old child that Jakob looks after, one of the stray children of exterminated parents who often died of starvation in the Ghettos. The relationship of these two is at the emotional centre of this tremendous and humane book. This tenderly described odd couple and the light shed by their human warmth only goes to illuminate the monstrous crime of the Shoah or Holocaust, leaving open all those questions still unanswered as to how should the nation that perpetrated it be thought of today. R K

'Come on, lean back and close your eyes, let's not spoil the pleasure by talking, let's take a few puffs and dream of old times, which will soon be back again. Come on, let's think of Chaim Balabusne with his thick steel-rimmed spectacles and the tiny shop where we always bought our cigarettes, or rather the tobacco to roll our own. His shop was closer to yours than mine was, it was between our two shops, yet we never became real friends with him, but that was his fault. Because he wasn't interested in pancakes and ice-cream, or in a haircut or a shave. Many people said he let his red hair grow so long out of religious piety, but I know better, it was out of stinginess, nothing else. Ah well, never mind, mustn't speak ill of the dead, Balabusne always had a good selection, cigars, pipes, cigarette cases with little flowers, gold-tipped cigarettes for the rich, always tried to persuade us to take a more expensive brand but we stuck with 'Excelsior'. And the stand with the little gas flame and the cigar cutter on the counter, the brass stand he was always polishing when one went into his shop, it's that brass stand one always remembers in thinking back to the old days, though we only bought tobacco from him once a week at most and never used the stand.' p91-2

BERNHARD
Thomas

## Concrete [Beton]

Thomas Bernhard's work has been labelled 'gloomy' or 'bilious' or 'pessimistic' and not out of keeping with a tradition of what the Germans call *Weltschmerz* or 'world despair', a notion with roots in Goethe's *Sorrows of Young Werther*. But this denies the value of Bernhard's work because he is also preoccupied with the notion of perfection and his characters not only exhaust themselves with the relative absurdity of the human condition, but also obsess about perfecting something which they perceive is dear to them. This tack is found in much, if not all of Bernhard's work, and *Concrete* is no exception.

In *Concrete* the protagonist, a wealthy yet sickly forty-five-year old independent scholar, steeped in Austrian angst, suffers dreadfully from his mid-life crisis and insists on producing the 'penultimately perfect' work on Mendelssohn. What we discover is his total inability to ever begin this book on Mendelssohn let alone complete it. While he is attempting to discover just how to begin the work, which he has begun and abandoned numerous times, he is constantly 'digressing' on things that annoy him — most of which concern the social manners of the Austrians — and also on whether or not to take a trip to Spain to avoid the chill of an Austrian winter. In a manner not unlike Thomas Mann in Death in Venice, Bernhard finally takes his protagonist to Palma, a place he has visited before, at which point he meets a woman who tells him the most tragic story about her life and how her husband, whom she convinced to quit his job as a civil engineer and begin an independent business, was found dead, lying on the concrete sidewalk of their hotel the apparent victim of either a suicide or an accident. At that point, concrete itself becomes a kind of character and is constantly referred to in relation to death. The protagonist muses about this woman and whatever became of her and the climax of the novel reveals that in her despair and guilt over her husband's death, she committed suicide and was buried, in concrete, along with her husband in the Palma cemetery.

This book, like many of Bernhard's novels, is written in the first person, as a reminiscence, and in one long paragraph which lends a kind of raving, 'mad' quality to the work, something which Bernhard often alludes to. Certainly, Bernhard is not reading for the 'faint of heart or spirit' as his work can be both a diatribe and didactic, but the writing is superb and his vision of the human condition is exceedingly persuasive. M R A

'And above all we always overrate whatever we plan to do, for, if the truth were known, every intellectual work, like every other work, is grossly overrated, and there is no intellectual work in the generally overrated world which could not be dispensed with, just as there is no person, and hence no intellect, which cannot be dispensed with in his world: everything could be dispensed with if only we had the strength and the courage'. p28

BERNHARD
Thomas

## Cutting Timber [Holzfällen]

Bernhard is magnificently sour and in a self-confessedly 'artistic' milieu of Vienna, a city that grew to be far too big for its boots, provincialism piles upon pretension and Bernhard etches it all down with the acid of his gaze. In this extraordinary novel, set almost entirely over two succeeding events; a funeral and a dinner-party, he utterly takes apart a little world of idlers who exist on the fringes of any professional achievement but who nevertheless espouse enormous artistic and social snobbery. The curious and fascinating thing about Bernhard's work is how he puts over his profoundly bilious viewpoint with such an enjoyable humour and narrative drive — he's been called 'both repellent and addictive' for this accomplishment.

Unfortunately though the dinner party at the salon of the shiftless Auersbergers — who live entirely off the proceeds of inherited money — is also an accurate microcosm for the larger world and these 'perfidious social masturbators' with their false lives and false goals seem quite a widely spread type anywhere money, laziness and snobbery coexist. Amongst the guests at this awful soirée are 'the Viennese Virginia Woolf' a female writer of very moderate achievement (but superbly talented at getting government handouts) who wallows in deeply unattractive egotism as she baits the principal guest, an actor of the Burgtheater which Bernhard excoriates as 'an infirmary for dramatic dilettantism'. The eventual showdown after the gradually rising tension of the dinner party as potato soup, two fish courses and cream tarts are consumed is a marvellous moment when the mirror dissolves and suddenly we are through into the looking-glass world, better and nobler than our own and yet also our own if we were equal to it.

Vienna, as the ex-Imperial metropolis of a small country has something in common with London, and the cynicism (and boredom) of *Cutting Timber's* would-be creative giants seems refracted too in the reigning cynicism of the British capital.

Perhaps though it's better to take a pretentious interest in art than spend all day watching Schwarzenegger (to mention a famous Austrian) videos... In any case it must be said that *Cutting Timber* is beautiful stuff, written with great skill, an entrancing and unique narrative rhythm as well as a highly disabused honesty. R K

'...to walk down the Graben is just to walk straight into the hell of Viennese society and meeting these very people whom I do not wish to meet, whose appearance to this day causes me all kinds of bodily and mental cramps, I reflected, sitting in the wing chair, and it was for that reason that during my visits to Vienna from London in recent years I had avoided the Graben and chosen other routes, just as I had not taken the Kohlmarkt, nor, needless to say, the Kärtnerstrasse, and I had avoided the Spiegelgassse as much as the Stallburggasse and the Dorotheergasse, or the Wollzeile, which I had always feared, and the Operngasse, where I had so often walked right into the trap of the very people I had always hated most.' p4

BERNHARD
Thomas

## Extinction [Auslöschung: Ein Zerfall]

This sustained and excellent work, with Bernhard as stylistically light-footed as ever, is a kind of Family Saga but an anti-Family saga. Giving us all the opportunity for a bit of Family Therapy, i.e. granting us permission to hate some people in our own family — 'the awfulness of my family, to whom, when I come to think of it, the words *shame*, *sensitivity* and *consideration* meant virtually nothing. And who never felt the slightest need to improve themselves, having stopped in their tracks decades ago and been content to stay put ever since.' Know anyone like that?

In this book Bernhard reveals a great secret about himself, he is, as the Italians have it, *un esagerato* ('an exaggerated one'), one who likes to emphasise their feelings and reactions, partly to pull in more attention to themselves but also as something of a daily art-project, a way of making life feel more lived... His exaggeration fuels him to all kinds of heights of bilious wiseness and *Extinction* is a treasure-trove of his reflections on humanity. For example, he defines for us 'wilful ignorance' — something that the 1980s adulation of money and mass culture made so fashionable — as the condition of those who have no excuse to be uncultivated but are nevertheless. Of course in Austria, 'land of High Culture', he unearths plenty of these, especially at rural Wolfsegg, the family seat the protagonist stems from and where much of the anti-Family Saga is played out. He also reflects wisely for instance on solitude: 'the highest condition is solitude, yet I know very well that solitude is the most fearful punishment of all ... total solitude ultimately means total madness'. He has thought through his own condition of having a highly critical view of the world — Bernhard's books are about himself but become interesting because he has dissected himself and the world that created and surrounded him so carefully...

This story of a family of idle rich, tortured by the problem of how to make the dinner party conversation flow while busy covering up their past enthusiasms for Nazi Austria, is vintage Bernhard, thoughtful, sarcastically humorous and rewarding.

The book ends with a wonderfully spleenful attack on the German bureaucracy — quoted below — an insensate, status-obsessed and useless coterie ever-ready to inflict suffering on anyone who has to deal with them. But blessed are the exaggerators, for they shall inherit the Kingdom of Truth. R K

'No, this won't be my office, I thought. I won't let myself be tyrannized by the three-ring binders. Millions are tyrannized by three-ring binders, and the tyranny is increasingly oppressive. Soon the whole of Europe will be not only tyrannized but destroyed by them. I once told Gambetti that it was above all the Germans who had let themselves be tyrannized by three-ring binders.' p313

## On the Mountain [In der Höhe]

The unforgettable first words of this unusual, powerful work are 'Fatherland, *nonsense*', appropriate words to kick off a rebel's eye view of 1950s Austria. This first book, completed when he was 28, by the great beast of postwar Austrian literature, Thomas Bernhard, is a complex but highly readable collage of trains of thought and snatches of conversation from the life of a young court-reporter in provincial Salzburg. It is a very inspired collage, sometimes reminiscent of Ezra Pound's masterwork *The Pisan Cantos*; things seem to come up from nowhere — scenes of piggish criminals and policemen in the courtroom, a walk and an unsuccessful seduction in the woods with 'the Fräulein' — all in a breathless continuity of writing but all making perfect sense without the usual tricks of narrative... Bernhard is telling the story of his life in Salzburg but not egocentrically; with his 'gravedigger thoughts' (this is a dark vision of post-Imperial, post-Nazi Austria) he is 'on top of the mountain and looking down on the rain-soaked, scurvy city'.

The rich psycho-panorama Bernhard produces is difficult to describe because of its uniqueness and originality and this early work is not significantly different in style to his later books. He writes with musical rather than traditional prose structures in mind. There is a sense of breath held, regulated, the sentences controlled in the way a flautist controls musical phrases, reaching to their end effortlessly because well-practised and completely aware of the composition. Reading Bernhard, grim as he can be — 'dead sun, dead angels over the dead cities'— is as stimulating as Schoenberg, and as refreshing as Mozart. Bernhard is a master who has to be read by anyone interested in contemporary writing that pushes the possibilities of writing itself forward, and one could as well start with *On the Mountain* as anywhere. R K

'...in the afternoon my fatigue rapidly gets the better of me, reaching its high point in the evening, the fatigue that comes from looking at people, from looking at commotion; people, the world, there's always commotion: the torment of commotion: once darkness falls and my fatigue lessens, the fatigue goes away: those who don't see anything don't get tired...' p76

## Wittgenstein's Nephew [Wittgensteins Neffe]

*Wittgenstein's Nephew* reads like one of Bernhard's novels, yet it is an autobiographical piece. Unlike in the novels, the point-of-view is not that of an invented character but of Bernhard himself, which keeps the usual unpleasantness of Bernhard's protagonists at bay and the reader gets to hear Bernhard's voice directly, which is a great pleasure.

The book starts with Bernhard and his friend Paul Wittgenstein in hospital. It is a twin institution, housing tubercular cases in one part, and mental patients in the other. Bernhard is there with lung problems, whilst Paul is there for his mind. The fact that they are both there at the same time provides a starting point for a reflection on their friendship.

Bernhard develops the idea that both he and Wittgenstein got to their respective destination through the parallel course of their lives. As he sees it, they have both been brought down to earth by a chronic overestimation of themselves as well as the world.

At the end of the book, though, the parallel falls away as Paul dies of his condition while Bernhard lives on. With the degeneration of his friend's health, Bernhard elaborates his thoughts on illness — how those who are well can never really do justice to the ill, how the well are afraid of the ill because they remind them of their own mortality, and how those convalescing from life-threatening illnesses are not wholeheartedly welcomed back into the community of the living.

As in his work *Extinction*, in *Wittgenstein's Nephew* there is the theme of running away from a wealthy but oppressive and uncultured family. This escape is facilitated by the example of an older member of the family, here Wittgenstein's uncle, the philosopher Ludwig.

The book is a homage to his friend and his extraordinary existence. As a member of the rich Wittgenstein family, Paul had lived in grand style for the first half of his life. In the second half, he spent or gave away most of his inheritance and had to depend on his relatives, in what was a rather undignified situation. Whenever his extravagant gestures got too expensive or too embarrassing, he was turned over to the mental hospital by the aggrieved relatives. Two and a half years before his death he undertook to write his autobiography, but actually managed only ten to fifteen pages of it, a great pity according to Bernhard. He reasons that Ludwig, Paul's famous uncle, was known to be at least as mad as Paul, but concentrated on his philosophy, while Paul put most of his expressive power into his madness, instead of writing down his vision of the world...

The book becomes painful when Bernhard recounts how he avoided the old and frail Paul, for fear of being confronted by a friend so clearly marked by death, and he is not quite sure if he does it to spare himself or his friend.

"Two hundred friends shall be at my funeral, and you must make a speech at my grave", Paul Wittgenstein had told his friend. In fact Bernhard didn't go, but has made up for it here in this beautiful and very likeable book. Maren M

'...for let us not deceive ourselves, the heads which are most often accessible to us are uninteresting, we do not profit from them much more than if we were in the company of overgrown potatoes eking out a miserable but alas not at all pitiable existence on top of complaining bodies in more or less tasteless clothes.' p30

BIERMANN
Pieke

## Violetta [Violetta]

*Violetta* is a crime novel set in Berlin in 1990, the year of German reunification and a year after the wall had come down. Berlin had been a strange enough place even before that: geographically closer to Poland than to the rest of West Germany, you could not leave the city by surface routes without passing through East Germany and obtaining a transit visa. Buses terminated right in front of the wall. It felt special and strangely significant to be there, having history, in the shape of the wall, right in your face.

The collapse of the wall came, amongst other things, as a bit of an anticlimax: with East and West Berlin rehearsing the reunification of the rest of Germany, political significance made way for problems of a socioeconomic and, reportedly, emotional nature, all in all resulting in quite a mess. Berlin is in a position without historical precedent, but at the same time conscious that the way it develops will have an influence on the identity of the whole of Germany.

Considering this setting, it is not surprising that *Violetta* strays from the conventional path of the crime genre. We don't get the usual pattern of a murder, followed by a subsequent identification, chase and capture of the baddy, with perhaps a motive and a psychological profile thrown in. *Violetta* is less akin to traditional crime novels than to the more sophisticated brand of TV crime series like *Homicide*. In fact 'Homicide and Organised Crime' is the name of the police department headed by Chief Inspector Karin Lietze. Returning from holiday, she finds to her dismay that none of the cases have cleared themselves up during her absence, instead, they seem to have become more insoluble than ever.

There is the 'rubberstamp' murderer, a serial killer who prints a letter on the forehead of each of his female victims, according to their nationality: *P* for Polish, *T* for Turkish and so on.

But men have no reason to sleep quietly either in Biermann's Berlin: several of them are found dead in their beds, killed after having had sex with their murderer.

How does the violent women's organisation, the 'JoAnne Little Brigade' fit into all this? And who is the mysterious Violetta, who wears the tightest trousers in Berlin and does not come over as exactly ordinary, to say the least?

'Black! The stretch pants. No t-shirt, no slogan. But? The patent leather bodice. The transparent blouse over it like a jacket. Open. *Trompe l'oeil*. No jewellery. No violet. Just the shoes. The open-toed high heels that obscenely reveal the cleavage between big toe and the next one. And her fingernails. Each a different shade of purple, and one in red and one in blue.'

All these cases link up, but that doesn't mean everything falls into place, and although at the end of the book things clear somewhat, they still feel far from resolved.

But how can everything be explained, resolved, especially in Berlin A.D. 1990? Just as the characters in Pieke Biermann's book, especially Chief Inspector Lietze, grapple with the fact that the restoring of order might be an impossibility per se, this is only appropriate for a story set in Berlin, a city that, in 1990 as well as today, has not found a concept of normality. Maren M

'And at some point, at some point all the knots will come undone. At some point, all the scraps of evidence will fall into place and the puzzle will be solved. And then you'll see, Lietze Karin, that the only connection between all these cases which have been wearing out your last ounce of grey matter all these months is this city, these times and this weather! The Zeitgeist — the spirit of the age — pure shit! These times don't have spirit. This city is a pressure cooker in the middle of a sea, in which a few waves ripple and spill over. It's time for the lid to come off.' p222

## Children Are Civilians Too [part of 1947 bis 1951]

These are the early, startling and powerful stories of Heinrich Böll, the one German writer apart from Bertolt Brecht and Günter Grass that most people have heard of. And it is these stories, dealing with the long defeat of the German army between 1942 and 1945 and the aftermath in a ruined and hungry Fatherland, that made Böll famous.

His subsequent popularity and success obscures just how extremely good the early work was. Even if there was tremendous material at hand providing the human details of the story of Germany's war against Europe, Böll was also up to the enormous challenge of writing about such bitter, cataclysmic times in a way that doesn't traduce them. He discovered a style of short, stripped-down pieces, flashgun images of the lurid landscape created by 'total war', by Nazi mass murder and Allied saturation bombing.

This collection contains twenty-six stories that collate the obsessions, feelings and reflections wrested out of his personal experience as a young footsoldier serving in 'Hitler's great and glorious army' and of then returning in 1945 to his shattered hometown of Cologne. To tell the story of this war, with its massive mobilisation of German men and subsequent enormous losses is to tell the story of many deaths and Böll doesn't flinch from that. In *Broommakers* a plane full of screaming soldiers plunges to extinction over the Crimea; *In the Darkness* describes the wet and freezing dugouts on the (collapsing) Eastern Front inhabited by 'soldiers who had to wish for the war to be lost' and who lose their lives in useless sacrifice while perhaps the most painful and resonant story on this bitter theme is *Stranger, Bear Word to the Spartans We...* where a mortally wounded boy soldier becomes groggily aware that he is in his old *Gymnasium* (High School) building, now in use as a war hospital, and sees the inspiring and bellicose quotation of the title on the blackboard above him, written in his own hand a short while previously... Böll's stories of war fill one with anger at the psychopathic politicians and military fatheads who perpetrate it for their personal gain and prestige.

For the return home to the devastated Fatherland there is *Across the Bridge*, as simple and bleakly powerful as Raymond

Carver and using the same subtle but soulful technique as the celebrated Hebrew writer S.Y.Agnon, confronting the unconfrontable fact of immense losses by consciously, precisely, leaving things unsaid so that they loom up behind the story, shuttering the light to a single harsh flare across a 'normalised' landscape which is completely abnormal. The normality here is the enormous loss of an entire settled way of life (the essence of German civilisation) while the protagonists scratch a living amongst the rubble and corpses of a bombed-out city. Many other pieces show us this dispiriting world; in *Breaking the News* the sad task of telling a comrade soldier's wife the bad news about her husband's death has to be carried out in a benighted (and brilliantly described) neighbourhood; 'where infinity seems to have congealed over a handful of dirty houses and a dilapidated factory'. The survivor eventually finds the widow in a cramped and grim one-room house where 'Even the cheap sentimental prints seemed to have been stuck on the walls like indictments'.

But there is more to Böll and Böll's book than photo-realistic gloom; he poignantly discovers some shoots of hope and renewal amongst the ruins. In *My Pal with the long hair*, in a key locale for Böll — the railway — two lost people find each other, a sort of reverse German *Brief Encounter*, with a more positive ending if equally romantic. One of the last stories in the collection *Candles for the Madonna* prefigures something that emerges more in Böll's subsequent longer works than those included in this collection; the celebration, by a left-wing Catholic, of the possibility of *grace*. A man at the far end of his tether struggling unsuccessfully to rebuild his life in a ruined city somehow manages to step into a magical and revitalising moment of grace; a fitting end for a book that takes the reader on a profound journey to contemplate the worse moments of our century. R K

'...suddenly she stopped. It was under a street lamp. She fixed me with a long, wide-eyed stare and said in a strained voice: "If only I knew where I was going." Her face moved slightly, like a scarf stirred by the breeze. No, we did not kiss... We walked slowly out through the town and eventually crawled into a haystack. I had no friends here, of course: I was as much a stranger in this silent town as in any other. When it got chilly towards morning, I crept close beside her, and she covered me with part of her thin, skimpy coat. And so we warmed each other with our breath and our blood.

We have been together ever since — in these hard times.' p19 (*My pal with the long hair*)

## And where were you, Adam? [Wo warst du, Adam?]

An early work, a novella set in wartime, in this case in Hungary. This is a fascinating extended portrait of the *Wehrmacht* (German army) in retreat, told episodically. The main protagonists are Lieutenant Greck with his bad stomach and punishingly narrow-minded upbringing, the young romantic Feinhals who falls in love with Ilona, a Hungarian Jewish teacher and the Nazi fanatic SS Captain Filskeit who runs a minor extermination camp in the woods with exemplary Teutonic precision and nurses a passion for choral music.

The episodes with Greck and Feinhals are, to begin with, relatively lighthearted, which only serves to set off a description of the transportation and murder of a group of Hungarian Jews (the last Jewish population to survive in Nazi Europe). No punches are pulled in this, nor should they be.

This is a salutary brief work because given the (generally healthy) human tendency to forget painful and horrifying things time is covering the traces of all this suffering, and all these prematurely ended lives (the circa 80 million deaths of World War Two). We get left with an enormous casualness about the most screamingly obvious lessons of that conflict; the dangers of nationalism, the need for European political unity and cultural understanding to forestall conflict... R K

'She walked slowly up the steps to the hut, pulling Maria along; she glanced up astonished when the guard jabbed the muzzle of his machine pistol into her side and shouted, "Faster — faster." She walked faster. Inside sat three clerks at tables; big stacks of index cards lay in front of them, the cards as big as cigar-box lids. She was pushed towards the first table...Another half hour, she thought. Maybe she would still have a chance to be alone for a bit after all. She was astonished at the casual atmosphere in this place given over to the administration of death. Everything was done mechanically, somewhat irritably, impatiently; these people were doing their job with the same lack of enthusiasm they would have brought to any other clerical work, they were merely doing their duty, a duty which they found tiresome but did anyway.' p117-118

## The Clown [Ansichten eines Clowns]

Hans Schnier is the son of a father who has made an honorary doctorate out of brown coal and a mother who is President of the Executive of the Committee for the Reconciliation of Racial Differences. Although he comes from Protestant stock, his brother Leo is in training for the Catholic priesthood. His sister, who, like himself, was endowed with apparently mystical tendencies and a penchant for calling spades spades, died in the last days of World War Two, after being sent out by her mother to help defend the Fatherland against the Bolshevik Jewish Yankees.

Schnier himself suffers from depression, headaches, laziness, and the ability to detect smells through the telephone. He is also fatally inclined to monogamy. By his own admission, he lives almost exclusively on soft-boiled eggs, consomme, meatballs and tomatoes. His private vices consist of evening papers, cigarettes, and the trivial game of parchesi. Just before the beginning of our story, he has fallen badly, literally, metaphorically and professionally, and is physically and psychologically wounded. His girlfriend Marie has left him in order to marry a Catholic called Züpfner, ostensibly because of his refusal to regularize their relationship.

The gestures made and the opinions expressed in the novel are crucially affected by these few salient facts. Schnier spends much of the novel on the telephone, and the smells he detects on the other end of the line tell us a great deal about his attitude to his interlocutor. In many of these conversations, he is asking for money — a fact which, given the financial position of his family, gives rise to a pervasive irony. We see him making a mess of a meal (even preparing a cup of coffee is apparently beyond him) and badly mismanaging an interview with his father. We hear him reminiscing about the good times and the bad times, about acts of friendship and instances of despicable small-mindedness, about genuine charity and sounding brasses. We are party, too, to a marvellous series of verbal exchanges, ranging in tone from the bitterest conflict to the most heartwarming sympathy. But we are never allowed to forget that the person orchestrating them, whose antics actually constitute the novel, is, after all, a clown.

Seen as a series of routines, which are by turns unashamedly exaggerated and unrestrainedly sentimental, which we have to laugh at because otherwise the sadness of them will overwhelm us, which over the years have again and again aroused the mirth of the right people and the anger of the right people (sometimes, of course, the same people), this book is, without a doubt, a virtuoso masterpiece. And although it does not pull any punches, and despite its pervasive air of melancholy, the ultimate effect, as with any good piece of clowning, is oddly life-affirming. R G

*The Clown* is a novel that stands out in Böll's work; not as strongly preoccupied with reappraising the war as the early novels, it still shows a Germany that is deeply marked by the effects of the war. Most importantly, though, *The Clown* is a very intimate, personal story, told from the perspective of Hans Schnier, the clown of the title.

Hans personifies many of the ambiguities of postwar Germany; he comes from a rich family, but rejects their wealth and bourgeois attitudes, and is in turn rejected by them. He is repulsed by the hypocrisy of a society stuck in a pathetic attempt to justify itself and chooses for himself the role of all innocent, a clown, with its professional demand of absolute truth to yourself.

It is not altogether surprising that Böll, when writing about Germany in the 1950s, chooses the figure of the clown as narrator. We can imagine there must be a lot wrong with a country if the only position the author can assume is that of the misfit. It seems to suggest that it is impossible to have a position of any decency in such a guilt-stained country, and therefore only the complete innocence of the clown, free of all prejudices and societal assumptions can offer an answer — albeit only a temporary one, as the eventual downfall of Hans proves.

Hans' gradual decline is linked to a fixed point in time: 'Since Marie left me'. Hans does not manage well without her and behaves as if he needed to prove it. Against his better judgement he cannot let go of the hope that by wrecking himself he will make her come back to him. He takes to drink, which does nothing for his career. He rings up Marie's friends, unfairly accusing them of hiding her from him. He imagines his own funeral. In the end, he makes a sentimental spectacle of himself by sitting in front of Cologne station playing his guitar, waiting for Marie to return from her honeymoon.

But all this does not make him a lesser person, it makes him more human, and therefore something close to a hero, a Böll-hero; while everybody else behaves in an unfailingly correct manner, he has the courage to expose himself and render himself vulnerable to the point of ridiculousness. The clown has thrown his whole existence in the scales, he has been true to himself and fought an honest battle, and he has lost on all fronts; not only Marie, he also becomes a social outcast, while hypocrites and opportunists seem to make a successful living.

By refusing to play by the rules of society, he exposes the hypocrisy of German society at that time. More than that, he proves that personal integrity is worth maintaining, although the price may be high. Maren M

'My knee felt as fat and round as a gasometer. Without opening my eyes I groped my way around the chair, sat down, groped for the cigarettes on the table like a blind man. My father cried out in alarm. I can pretend to be a blind man so well that people believe I am blind. I felt blind too, maybe I would stay blind. What I was acting was not a sightless man but a man who has just lost his sight, and when I had finally got the cigarette into my mouth I felt the flame from Father's lighter, felt, too, how violently it trembled. "Son," he said anxiously, "are you ill?" "Yes," I said softly, drew on the cigarette, inhaled deeply, "I am terribly ill, but not blind. Pains in my stomach, my head, my knee, a rapidly proliferating depression — but the worst thing is, I know perfectly well Genneholm is right, about ninety-five per cent, and I even know what he went on to say. Did he mention Kleist?"

"Yes," said my father.

"Did he say I must first lose my soul — be totally empty, then I could afford to have one again. Did he say that?"

"Yes," said my father, "how do you know?"

"Hell," I said, "after all I know his theories, and where he gets them from. But I don't want to lose my soul, I want to get it back."

"You've lost it?"

"Yes."

"Where is it?"

"In Rome," I said, opened my eyes and laughed.

My father had really gone quite pale and haggard with fear. His laugh sounded relieved and yet annoyed.

"You rascal," he said, "was the whole thing put on?"'

BÖLL
Heinrich

## Irish Journal [Irisches Tagebuch]

Here is a piece where fiction, travel writing and joyful fantasy meet in a witty and sympathetic picture of the Ireland of the

1950s. As Böll warns us at the very beginning 'This Ireland exists: but whoever goes there and fails to find it has no claim on the author'. There's more here than the straightforward traveller's account of land and people it seems to be at first look. *Irish Journal* is in fact a highly constructed work of art, an odyssey touched by grace to find the soul of a country and we move in the wake of a beautiful myth; for this is a *journey*, a voyage, a discovery...

Even so, to this visitor, protective friend and semi-descendant of Ireland, *Irish Journal* seems exceptionally understanding of the character of the place and people. In his Irish journey Böll notices so many important but not immediately obvious things; for example the frequent gentleness/diffidence of the Irishman in a position of authority, so humane (and humorous) compared to his opposite numbers in England or Germany. Encountering a policeman 'Reluctantly the Irish policeman raises his hand to stop the car...'

He also senses the physical realities of Ireland in a very direct way, as a strange little territory at the edge of a great ocean, watery, damp and mysterious, a kind of borderland to Atlantis, where normal conditions do not always apply... He celebrates the beauty of a turf fire in the grate and simple, good food ready on the table warming his children after a long and hungry train ride. He feels more keenly the hardness and joys of life in what was then a very poor country by travelling — with difficulties but warm welcomes — accompanied by his family.

He sees just as foursquarely the strange air of temporariness, the spirit of improvisation that reigns amongst a people when, because of continuous massive emigration, nobody really expects to stay, or for that broken door to have to last more than a year or two. He has grasped how that historical experience has made the Irish peculiarly fluid and restless, sometimes pushing them into a kind of forced extended 'adolescence' and living-for-the-moment compared to their neighbours in richer and more economically stable societies...

Altogether *Irish Journal* proves the early Böll to have been the sweetest of storytellers for, in short, here he discovers the great Ireland in its small things and makes what must be one of the finest and most enjoyable books written in German since 1945. R K

'One thing is certain, and that is that of Mrs. D.'s nine children five or six will have to emigrate. Will little Pedar, now being patiently rocked by his oldest brother while his mother makes fried eggs for her boardinghouse guests, fills jam pits, cuts white and brown bread, pours tea, while she bakes bread in the peat fire... .in fourteen years, in 1970, on October 1 or April 1, will this little Pedar, aged fourteen, carrying his cardboard suitcase, hung about with medallions, supplied with a package of extra-thick sandwiches, embraced by his sobbing mother, stand at the bus stop to begin the great journey to Cleveland, Ohio, to Manchester, Liverpool, London, or Sydney...?

These farewells at Irish railway stations, at bus stops in the middle of the bog, when tears blend with raindrops and the Atlantic wind is blowing; Grandfather stands there too, he knows the canyons of Manhattan, he knows the New York waterfront, for thirty years he has been through the mill, and he quickly stuffs another pound note into the boy's pocket, the boy with the cropped hair, the runny nose, the boy who is being wept over as Jacob wept over Joseph; the bus driver cautiously sounds his horn, very cautiously — he has driven hundreds, perhaps thousands, of boys whom he has seen grow up to the station, and he knows the train does not wait and that a farewell that is over and done with is easier to bear than one which is still to come.' p94-95

BÖLL
Heinrich

## The Silent Angel [Der Engel schwieg]

*The Silent Angel* is the first novel Heinrich Böll wrote, and yet the last one to be published. When he wrote it his financial situation was so desperate he had to put it aside frequently to earn his keep with more profitable short stories.

When the manuscript was finished, his publishers were reluctant to go ahead with it, even after Böll had agreed to many changes. Finally, he resigned himself to never seeing this novel in print (it was published posthumously, on what would have been his 75th birthday). Consequently, he incorporated much of the material and the plot in his next novel, *And Never Said a Single Word*. His criticism of bourgeois Catholicism, which he attacks and exposes as hypocritical, is also later developed in *The Clown*, reviewed above.

Overall there is Böll's contempt for those types who know all too well how to look after themselves and who after the war carried on as if nothing had happened, turning the restoration of democracy to their own advantage and brushing off the chance for a truly new beginning.

On the day of Germany's capitulation, Hans, a young soldier, has just returned to a destroyed Cologne. He has nowhere to go and does not even possess valid papers. Carrying the testament of a fallen fellow soldier with him, he searches for his widow. She, in turn, is cheated of her inheritance by her brother-in-law, the successful, (and catholic) Herr Fischer. When Hans tries to ask for support later, the same Herr Fischer turns him away.

Later, Hans meets Regina, in whose house he looks for shelter. Regina, who has lost her baby only days before, lets him recuperate with her, and after a while, they start a relationship. Hans tries to get himself work on the black market to support the two of them. He finds help with an unorthodox priest who lets him have some of the church offerings and who turns a blind eye when he learns that Hans and Regina are not married.

The melodrama that such a plot suggests is avoided by Böll's matter of fact descriptions of the dying, the despairing, the unjustly treated. Although there is a love story, it is not enough to redeem a very harsh reality, and, as the title suggests, if there are any angels, they are mostly made of plaster.

*The Silent Angel* does not discuss the war, and hardly touches the later postwar era. Really it is about what normal people felt just after the war had finished. The historical significance of the capitulation disappears in the tiredness of the people, too preoccupied with the necessities of living to feel anything but a vague sense of relief.

The novel can be regarded as an important document of the state of Germany in May 1945, and is one of the best examples of *Trümmerliteratur* — 'rubble literature'. It shows the human condition, stripped of all pretences, of the 'lost generation' — in Böll's words 'a generation which has "come home", a generation that knows there is no home for them on this earth'.

Maren M

'He gave her five marks and saw the coupons lying in his hand, tiny scraps of printed paper. "Are they any good?" he asked softly. She raised her eyebrows indignantly and blinked her eyes like a doll. "Of course," she said "don't you know we're at peace now?" "Peace," he said, "since when?"

"Since this morning," she said. "We've been at peace since this morning... the war's over..."

"I know," he said. "It's been over for a long time, but peace?"

"We've capitulated; don't you believe it?"

"No..."

She called to an amputee who was sitting a few steps away in the remnants of a wall, holding an open packet of cigarettes before him. He hobbled over. "He doesn't believe we're at peace," she said[...]

"Yes, it's true, the war's over, really over. Didn't you know?"

"No," said Hans. "Where can I buy bread with these coupons? Are they good?'"

p 45

# BÖLL
## Heinrich

### The Train Was On Time [Der Zug war pünktlich]

This early novella successfully expands themes of the short pieces published in *Children Are Civilians Too*. It is the compelling narrative of one World War Two German soldier's journey from occupied Paris to occupied Poland and it is simultaneously the bitter account of a generation whose life was destroyed or poisoned by the workings of an enormous and inescapable war-machine.

As the title suggests the young Andreas traverses the entire purgatory of Böll's wartime railway universe; sleeping amongst heaps of grimy and exhausted fellow-soldiers on troop trains, the ghastly soup of wartime buffets, the desperate drinking to forget their fate as the cannon-fodder of an army in retreat. Throughout his long journey to the killing-fields of the Eastern Front Andreas is convinced that he is riding just to meet his death in a place 'between Lvov and Cernauti'. But he is simultaneously seeking to recapture the one moment of feminine tenderness he has ever experienced, which, being a very young man facing death, inflates to enormous significance for him. In the succeeding days of brutality in the cruel world of 'Hitler's great and glorious army' he experiences, at the climax of the novella, a night of transfiguration through a pure, lustless passion for a Polish girl, Olina. In this one highly-charged and unforgettable night everything inside is changed while the unutterably harsh world of 'Greater Germany' remains unchangeable outside.

There is something rawly and unsentimentally convincing in all this that makes this one of the great works to deal with the wartime period. R K

'Life is beautiful, he thought, it was beautiful. Twelve hours before my death I have to find out that life is beautiful, and it's too late. I've been ungrateful, I've denied the existence of human happiness. And life was beautiful. He turned red with humiliation, red with fear, red with remorse. I really did deny the existence of human happiness, and life was beautiful. I've had an unhappy life... a wasted life, as they say. I've suffered every instant from this ghastly uniform, and they've nattered my ears off, and they made me shed blood on their battlefields, real blood it was, three times I was wounded on the field of so-called honour, outside Amiens, and down at Tiraspol, and then in Nikopol — and I've seen nothing but dirt and blood and shit and smelled nothing but filth... and misery... heard nothing but obscenities, and for a mere tenth of a second, and twelve hours or eleven hours before my death I have to find out that life is beautiful. I drank Sauternes... on a terrace above Le Tréport by the sea, and in Cayeux, in Cayeux I also drank Sauternes, also on a summer evening, and my beloved was with me...' p215

BÖLL
Heinrich

## The Lost Honour of Katharina Blum [Die verlorene Ehre der Katharina Blum]

*The Lost Honour of Katharina Blum* is the opposite of a newspaper report. To be more specific, it is designed to counter the sort of report which might appear in a tabloid newspaper like Rupert Murdoch's British tabloid *The Sun*, but worse. The only certain murder in it is that of a journalist. The perpetrator is a completely blameless young woman who not only cares about the precise meaning of words, but has views on sex which are the exact reverse of those implied by newspapers like *The Sun*. Attempts to seduce her, even on the part of an enormously wealthy and influential married Catholic industrialist, fail miserably. Instead she falls in love at first sight with a young man who had foolishly relieved the army not only of his own conscripted presence, but also of considerable amounts of cash and a weapon — and that with the apparent collusion of officers and their wives. Since it is possible that the two lovers will serve similar sentences, there is some hope for them. But since in the process their lawyer — who harbours an unreciprocated Platonic passion for the lady — and his admirable but sharp-tongued architect wife, seem certain to be all but ruined, it cannot be said that the novel has a happy ending, or indeed that it affirms the status quo in the way one would expect from, say, a right-thinking tabloid.

Worse than that — there is a deliberate deployment in this novel of all those stylistic devices not available to such newspapers: irony for instance (whereby the scrupulous insistence on objectivity turns out to be the exact opposite), or satire (whereby great concern is expressed for the psychological well-being of telephone tappers, subjected through no fault of their own to material ranging from the utmost triviality to the direst pornography). There are flashbacks and there is understatement (the description of blood on white sheets and tomato ketchup on immaculate walls is particularly delicate). There is altogether too much disguise in the novel, and not only because it is set at the time of carnival. All the names are clearly fictitious, and the events described are an obvious mixture of wishful thinking and anxiety nightmare. Yet behind it all there is without any doubt a passionate concern for the truth; if the description of certain journalistic practices in this novel bears any resemblance to those of a certain famous German newspaper, these similarities are, according to an epigraph not translated in the English version, neither deliberate nor accidental, but inevitable.

In short, this novel is concerned to depict the reality of life in West Germany in the 1960s and 1970s by subjecting its leading public figures, its ordinary citizens, its priests and its police force, and above all its press and its vocabulary to remorseless satire. The result is perhaps overdone, perhaps rather uneven, perhaps smells slightly of special pleading. But at its best it is brilliant — and the success of the book, and of the film based on it, bear eloquent testimony to its importance. R G

'Before embarking on our final diversion and rerouting maneuvers we must be permitted to make the following 'technical' interjection. Too much is happening in this story. To an embarrassing, almost ungovernable degree, it is pregnant with action: to its disadvantage. Naturally it is to be deplored when a self-employed housekeeper shoots and kills a reporter, and a case of this kind undoubtedly has to be cleared up or at least an attempt must be made to do so. But what is to be done with successful attorneys who break off their hard-earned skiing vacations for the sake of a housekeeper? With industrialists (who are professors and politicos on the side) who in their callow sentimental way simply force keys to country homes (and themselves) on this housekeeper, in both cases unavailingly, as we know, and who want publicity, but only of a certain kind; with a whole raft of objects and people whom it is impossible to synchronize and who continually disturb the flow (i.e. the linear course of events), because they are, shall we say, immune? What is to be done with crime commissioners who continually, and successfully, demand 'little plugs'? In a nutshell: it is all too full of holes, and yet, at what is for the narrator the crucial moment, not full enough, because, while it is possible to learn of this or that (from Hach, maybe, and a few male and female police officials, nothing, absolutely nothing of what they say holds water because it would never be confirmed by or even stated in a court of law. It is not conclusive evidence! It has not the slightest public value.'

**Böll**

**Brecht**

## Short Stories [*from* Geschichten 1967; Kalendergeschichten 1949; Geschichten und Prosa I 1965]

The short story was not of course Brecht's main activity as a writer and both his enormous success as a playwright and relative failure as a Hollywood screenwriter conspired to keep him too busy to write very many or revise the ones he did write. However, this is nevertheless really an excellent collection of pieces, divided into the three groups *Bavarian Stories* by the young Brecht written before he moved to Berlin and great success in the theatre, *Berlin Stories* written 1924-1933 and *Exile* stories written in his various lands of exile from Hitler's accession to power in 1933 until 1948 when he returned to live in East Germany.

The Bavarian stories are already full of the bluff tough-guy stuff we know from *Mahagonny* or the *Threepenny Opera* that Brecht loved so much but they are also shot through with his startling originality in theme and language. The very first story *Bargan gives up* explores a favourite Brecht theme: perverse self-defeating attraction. Bargan, although a ferocious buccaneer, is betrayed by his best friend time and time again but he just can't help letting him get away with it and eventually brings utter ruin down on himself. This unsentimental acknowledgment of the awkwardness, the perversity of human character was one of Brecht's great strengths. There aren't really any heroes in Brecht's human drama because he was too aware that the heroic is not quite human.

Almost all of the thirty-seven short stories and the included biographical fragment *Life story of the boxer Samson Körner* show that other great strength of Brecht — the stripped-down narrative drive that helps push his plays across the stage with such force.

But there's a lot here too that isn't reflected in his theatre work; like the story *North Sea Shrimp* which is an extended and funny grouse about inane people who live in designer flats surrounded by designer objects, a grave malady in our times but already apparently a problem in 1920s Berlin; then there are 'entertainments' like the breathless *Barbara* or the Runyonesque *The Good Lord's Package* set in a Chicago bar. To add to the package are some cool and thoughtful explorations of Brecht's most admired historical figures; great rationalist thinkers of the past — Lucretius, Francis Bacon and Giordano Bruno.

As well as being enjoyable in themselves these stories also clarify themes and techniques in Brecht's larger theatre work, by reproducing them in miniature in a less overwhelming form, thus making this altogether a very desirable book. R K

'My grandmother used to say when it had rained for a long time, "Today it's raining. Will it ever stop? I hardly think so. At the time of the flood it did not stop." My grandmother would say, "What has happened once can happen again — and so can what hasn't". She was seventy-four years old and totally devoid of logic.

On that occasion all the animals went into the Ark quite peacefully. That is the only time when all the creatures on earth have been peaceful. And all of them really did go in. But the icthyosaurus stayed away. He was told in a vague sort of way that he should get in, but he had no time during the days in question. Noah himself drew his attention to the fact that the flood was coming. But he said placidly, 'I don't believe it.' He was generally unpopular by the time he drowned.... That particular animal was the oldest of all the beasts, and given his long experience he was fully capable of telling whether anything like a flood was possible or not.

It is quite possible that I myself might not go in in similar circumstances. I think that on that evening, as the night fell in which he perished, the icthyosaurus saw through the corruption and chicanery of providence, as well as the unspeakable stupidity of all earthly creatures, the moment he realised how necessary these things were.' p59-60

CANETTI
Elias

## Auto-da-fe [Auto-da-fe]

*Auto da fe* is an extraordinary and acerbic book in which Canetti illustrates his ideas about the relationship between individual and community, and between men and women through an array of grotesque and absurdly inhumane figures and settings, and all with acute and savage wit.

Although originally conceived as a sort of *Comédie humaine* of madness along with eight other books, between 1929 and 1930, where each was to have revolved around one radical figure, isolated by experience, in language and in thought, *Auto da fe* was in fact a solitary work, Canetti's first and only novel.

The novel is about two fundamentally contrasted characters, united only by their refusal to allow anything else into their world; the forty-year-old sinologist Peter Kein and his housekeeper, an ignorant, grasping and uneducated woman, Therese, nearing 60, whose only thoughts are about how the price of potatoes continues to rise and how young people are becoming increasingly ill-mannered.

Kein, whose name means 'pine wood', an allusion to the fire in which he will burn alongside his books, is the personification of the *Head without a World* — the title of the first part of the novel. He seeks to grasp at the immortal via his absolute dedication to the pursuit of scientific knowledge. He hides from life behind his 25,000 volumes and the 40,000 characters of the Chinese alphabet. Under this tremendous burden of knowledge however, he adopts an inhumane attitude towards others and is doomed to suicide, and in his own end he also destroys his books, and along with them the very truth he sought.

Canetti saw the other — and equally destructive — path before the individual of his time (Europe in the 1920s and 30s) as the antheap collectivism represented by the mob-worship of 'the masses' or *'das Volk'* of Fascism and Stalinism.

It is in the second part of the book, *World without a Head,* that Canetti really reveals his rich and florid imagination. Foolish enough to marry the awful Therese, Kien is then catapulted into the outside world as she proceeds to rob him of everything and forces him into the street. He then begins his descent into the underworld of the metropolis, becoming involved in ever more surreal situations that accentuate his obsessive, frantic need to be alone.

The last part of the work, *The World in the Head* is less satisfying because it seems more didactic, and features George, Kien's brother the psychiatrist, who fails, despite all his efforts, to save his brother's life.

*Auto-da-fe* is an epic story of moral disintegration and generally read too as an account of the rise of the fascist mentality. C C

'Professor Peter Kien, a tall, emaciated figure, man of learning and specialist in sinology, replaced the Chinese book in the tightly packed briefcase which he carried under his arm, carefully closed it and watched the clever little boy out of sight. By nature morose and sparing of his words, he was already reproaching himself for a conversation into which he had entered for no compelling reason.

It was his custom on his morning walk, between seven and eight o'clock, to look into the window of every shop which he passed. He was thus able to assure himself, with a kind of pleasure, that smut and trash were daily gaining ground. He himself was the owner of the most important private library in the whole of this great city. He carried a minute portion of it with him wherever he went. His passion for it, the only one which he had permitted himself during a life of austere and exacting study, moved him to take special precautions. Books, even bad ones, tempted him easily into making a purchase. Fortunately the greater number of the book shops did not open until after eight o'clock. Sometimes an apprentice, anxious to earn his chief's approbation, would come earlier and wait on the doorstep for the first employee whom he would ceremoniously relieve of the latch key. "I've been waiting since seven o'clock," he would exclaim, or "I can't get in!" So much zeal communicated itself all too easily to Kien; with an effort he would master the impulse to follow the apprentice into the shop. Among the proprietors of smaller shops there were on of two early risers, who might be seen busying themselves behind their open doors from half past seven onwards. Defying these temptations, Kien tapped his own well-filled briefcase. He clasped it tightly to him, in a very particular manner which he had himself thought out, so that the greatest possible area of his body was always in contact with it. Even his ribs could feels its presence through his cheap, thin suit. His upper arm covered the whole side elevation; it fitted exactly. The lower portion of his arm supported the case from below. His outstretched fingers splayed out over every part of the flat surface to which they yearned. He privately excused himself for this exaggerated care because of the value of his contents. Should the briefcase by any mischance fall to the ground, or should the lock, which he tested every morning before setting out, spring open at precisely that perilous moment, ruin would come to his priceless volumes. There was nothing he loathed more intensely than battered books.' p10-12

CANETTI
Veza

## The Yellow Street [Die gelbe Straße]

*The Yellow Street* contains five interconnected stories, all set in the same street, with the same characters reappearing, sometimes at the centre of the tale, sometimes on the periphery. These pieces first appeared in the socialist *Arbeiter-Zeitung* in Vienna in the 1930s, and are filled with the atmosphere of that prewar period.

The inhabitants of the street range from the middle-class — a rentier, a businessman, a 'fine lady' — through various shop-owners, to workers and servants. They are very much ordinary people, but their foibles and idiosyncrasies are exaggerated, or perhaps just more clearly revealed than we usually allow. Canetti has an ironic eye for human weaknesses, especially self-deception, and that gives *The Yellow Street* an underlying tone of humour, in spite of the misery and exploitation it often records.

Each section focuses on women as victims: the wife who is bullied and tricked out of her inheritance by her husband, maidservants desperate for work sent by the employment agency to dubious establishments where they are expected to prostitute themselves in various ways, including sexually. But Canetti is no blinkered socialist feminist, mechanically measuring society by an ideological yardstick. Victims and oppressors are both regarded with the same ironic eye. Women are, largely, the exploiters as well as the exploited (the men, it must be admitted, are a rather pathetic bunch), and most of the figures are realistically two-sided: full of goodwill when it is only a matter of expressing sympathy, but weak and backsliding when it comes to action.

In *The Monster*, the title figure is herself disadvantaged, a cripple known as Runkel, owner of two shops in the street, who has to rely on others to get about. In a fit of despair, she tries to commit suicide by engineering a road accident. It is, however, her maid who is killed, trying to protect her mistress. Runkel recovers to continue her life of domineering those dependent on her. Her newspaper and tobacconist's shop is run by a young girl, Lina, who is everything Runkel is not: blonde, pretty, lively, helpful. She has increased trade considerably, not least because of the men she attracts, but not only because of that; the women also like her, she seems to be a kind of blond, blue-eyed doll to them. However, despite the increased profits she is making, Runkel uses the complaints of two men as an excuse to dismiss Lina. The whole street is up in arms and determined to do something about it. But when they each, individually, confront Runkel to demand she withdraw Lina's notice, their indignation crumbles, and they find themselves automatically agreeing with the employer's trenchantly expressed, but very vague 'reasons' for the dismissal. Lina herself is left as a sad, but rather limp victim; abandoned by others, she does nothing to fight for herself.

One victim who does do something for herself is Emma, the out-of-work maid who throws herself into the river so she can get looked after in the home for girls who have tried to commit suicide. It is typical of the strength of Canettis's narration, that the effect of this is neither mawkishly sentimental, nor depressingly doleful, but comic, as Emma has to wait and wait for the right moment, when the policeman on traffic duty is likely to see her, before she can jump. Proof, if proof be needed, that socially committed writing can also amuse and entertain the reader. M M

'She could not lie still, her bruises burned into her like fire. Then she noticed him edging towards her, She wanted to leap out of bed, but he seized her battered arms. She struggled with him, she thrashed around and bit him.

And that was how she conceived her second child.

Next morning, as she rose, the dark blood coursed through her face. She left the house before her husband. In the lawyer's office she was so insistent that he had to be called from a case.

He examined the bruises, which reached as far as her neck, and the police report, in which everything was laid out.

"Yes, these are grounds for divorce with the husband as sole guilty party." He took it all in with satisfaction. "So far everything seems in order. Your dowry is safe, you are bound to get it back. The child will of course be given into the custody of the mother, just one further question I must ask, dear lady, you must forgive me... After the quarrel, did intimacy take place?"

The young woman flushed deeply.

"Then I regret very much, dear lady, I cannot, in that case, implement the divorce." p45-6

# DODERER
Heimito von

## The Demons [Die Dämonen]

*The Demons* is Doderer's great (some 1300 pages) panoramic novel of Viennese society between the two world wars, charting the rise of the forces — the 'demons' — that were to destroy it in the *Anschluß* (absorption by Germany) of 1938, and also charting the recognition of those demons by the author, who was himself a member of the Austrian Nazi Party from 1933 to 1938. Doderer does this not by attempting a comprehensive survey of political events, but by focusing on the development of attitudes leading up to the burning of the Palace of Justice in 1927, which forms the grandiose climax to the novel, a climax in which the threads of many personal lives come together in the glare of the fire in the centre of the city. An orderly Socialist Party demonstration against the verdict of not guilty on two right-wingers who had shot dead a worker and a child, gradually develops into a riot, while the police are transformed from a group of humane individuals into an armed unit. It is this self-destruction, rather than the invasion by Hitler's Germany over ten years later, that signified for Doderer the end of Austria's freedom. 'Kaleidoscopic' rather than 'panoramic' would be the way to describe the technique Doderer uses. He weaves his tapestry from many small subplots involving people from all areas of society: the aristocracy, the high bourgeoisie, the middle classes, workers, prostitutes and criminals. It is a packed canvas, full of life, rich in character and detail. The nucleus around which the novel initially crystallises is a collection of men- and women-about-town in the somewhat rootless 1920s who coalesce into a group which thinks of itself as 'our crowd'. Some of the leading members of this crowd have covert fascist tendencies (anti-semitism, authoritarianism), which come to dominate the thinking of many, but then also contribute to the group's disintegration. In the second and third parts the novel's scope expands to encompass a wider range of character and milieu.

Many of the subplots are rather novellettish in character, and the book ends with a plethora of marriages. The most extreme, perhaps, involves the illegitimate daughter of a wealthy nobleman, a suppressed will, a dastardly financial adviser, and the recognition of the daughter by a trusty family retainer. However, the strands of these rather improbable and potentially sentimental plots are so interwoven with the rich texture of the book that the reader only grasps the connections in retrospect, when the effect is ironic rather than sensational. In context, they are subservient to the more serious aspects. The attempt to suppress the will, for example, is just one part of the machinations which reflect the economic and financial instability of the newly born republic of Austria in the years after the First World War.

Despite the inclusion of events like the burning of the Palace of Justice, and of characters with Nazi sympathies, such as the narrator's nephew Körger, the main portrayal of fascist tendencies is not a direct presentation of political attitudes, but is done on the psychological level. For Doderer, ideology — any ideology — is a pair of psychological blinkers. A number of characters have set, preconceived ideas, which make the openness to reality which is Doderer's ideal impossible. These private 'ideologies' usually have little direct connection with politics, and are more usually sexual in nature. One such is the novelist Kajetan von Schlaggenberg's obsession with fat ladies, whom he pursues, with tape-measure and card-index, through various cafés specialising in cream cakes, until the encounter with Mary K., who does not at all fit his conception of the ideal woman, explodes the delusion.

Another delusion is the narrator's assumption he can write a chronicle of the doings of 'our crowd' contemporaneously with the events. Two thirds of the way through, he realises this is impossible (as does the narrator of the novel which gave Doderer the initial impulse, Dostoyevsky's *The Possessed*, also sometimes translated as *The Demons*). This allows Doderer to give his book a triple perspective: Geyrenhoff's original chronicle and subsequent notes are written up by Geyrenhoff himself twenty-eight years after the events (i.e. in 1955), which allows him the advantage of hindsight, especially the knowledge of the fascist dictatorship which will follow the events of the story. On top of this, Doderer himself, ('the author') appears, to add another perspective, not a time perspective, but a stylistic (he mocks Geyrenhoff's occasional pompousness) and intellectual one (some things Geyrenhoff just does not understand).

Despite the intricacies of the narrative perspective, however, *The Demons* is a great example of the realist tradition of the novel. Written in a style which ranges from baroque metaphor to gossipy chitchat, it teems with life and illuminates Doderer's ideal of *Menschwerdung*, the realisation of the full human potential in each individual. M M

'After the heat of the cabin, it felt cooler outside, in spite of the blazing sun... Right beside the end of Lea's path stood Hubert K.. He was brown and slender as a pencil, more boy than youth. The upper part of his body was feebly developed. He had crossed his arms over his chest and was looking at Lea, without making the slightest movement, or smiling, or attempting to make any contact with her as she approached him down the path. He studied her. His eyes wandered slowly down along her body... He looked first at her shoulders, which were as white as her arms, then at her hips, and finally at her bare knees and legs. What Hubert succeeded in doing would have been extremely difficult for a young man differently constituted: he remained completely outside the situation... He seemed to feel no need to establish a connection. By this coolness he converted the partly undressed woman on the flagstone path to a pure object. It was a monstrous performance. Lea could not endure it... At that moment Fella Storch came by, thin as a rail, fragile as an insect. Hubert calmly turned his gaze away from Lea, took Fella's arm and sauntered to the pool with her. There he unexpectedly threw her backwards into the water, and plunged in himself.' p1240

## DÖRRIE
Doris

## Love, Pain and the Whole Damn Thing [Liebe, Schmerz und das ganze verdammte Zeug]

'"Make a schedule for each new day," her mother's advice. How humiliating the way humankind whitewashed the meaninglessness with a precise daily schedule.' This passage, damning everyday practicality and its let's-get-through-life-without-fuss-and-bother philosophy gives us the flavour of Doris Dörrie's book; a woman writing from a feminist-influenced perspective and with a mordant view of modern consciousness rather like that of Peter Handke.

The first of the four long short stories of this collection *Straight to the Heart* is a hilarious, cynical but perceptive fable about a rich dentist who 'adopts' a student mistress with blue hair and a saxophone to provide the sparkle and beauty his life lacks. Exactly as a fable should be, it is simple with a flattened narrative but underlying it is a sharp picture of a craven feminine psyche that allows itself to be overwhelmed by an emotionless but decisive male. Dörrie wants us to ask why this sparky female creature allows herself to be, in effect, purchased by this male monster.

The story *Men* shows us an 1968 vintage rebel now in his forties who, like the male dentist in *Straight to the Heart,* has become a soulless emotion-free zone. The plot is an elegantly effected *pas de deux* of couples, amusing and highly cynical about conventional aspirations.

*Money* rather than a fable is a farce, a delicious and funny story of mature suburbanites-become-bank-robbers that would probably make a brilliant film. The last story *Paradise,* unfortunately, is an unsuccessful and overblown affair about a femme fatale that was probably included to bring the book up to size. Nevertheless *Love, Pain and the Whole Damn Thing* is well worth reading, enjoyable if caustic. R K

'...she walked through the plant while conveyor belts of toy pistols, tanks, robots and plastic soldiers rolled past her..."Your husband? You me an you don't know?" Carmen shook her head, and Frau Busch choked on her next sentence as if on some indigestible lump:"He doesn't work here any more, hasn't for two months now... Orders are way down.. more than fifty people were let go... I'm really very sorry, but what can we do. Our speciality is war toys, after all, and orders have been ...this whole peace movement thing has played havoc with us. We're going to rethink things, here, look at this" — she pointed to small plastic men meant to look like policemen, while down the belt next to them little barbarians rolled — "These are the demonstrators, and there are the police. The game'll be called Battle at the Reactor, and if that doesn't sell, we can close up shop...' p82-83 from *Money*

ENDE
Michael

## The Neverending Story [Die unendliche Geschichte]

*The Lion, The Witch and the Wardrobe* (C.S. Lewis) meets *Lord of the Rings* (J.R.R. Tolkien) but with postmodern touches — this is a fable for children but with adult intent.

*The Neverending Story* is set both in our world and in the unreal world of the imagination Ende calls 'Fantastica'. These two worlds touch intimately in the book 'for a serious purpose' — just as they do in real life. Fantasy, paradoxically, as Ende tells us, is in fact one of the things that makes life real, for without it the vitality and colour in life just drains away.

His parable, based around this quite simple idea, is extended to startling complexity in a classic quest story where the quest-seeker is a little boy who passes from the prosaic world of school and home into marvellous Fantastica, a land with a superabundance of different creatures all living together tranquilly in a sort of anarchist federation.

At the centre of the book is the idea of 'following your dream' as an essential part of achieving a happy or tolerable existence when childhood dreaming and wishing become instead adult life. It's not unlike the message of many of Hermann Hesse's books or the ancient injunction 'To thine own self be true'. What Ende achieves is to explore in an easy-to-read way the connections between the imagining that comes before any act of creation, between permitting oneself to have wishes and desires and the finding of a purpose in life. Conversely he warns about the effect of curtailing the dreaming side of our natures.

Perhaps Germany's (or is it Prussia's?) rather strict, disciplined culture is bound to produce writers like Ende who kick against its restrictions and *Neverending Story* has been a cult book for rebellious young Germans. In any case it's a book to be recommended for anyone who needs to open up to the voice of the heart. There is also a very nice dragon, who sings. R K

'Throughout the day they were joined by new adherents, not only those Atreyu had sighted the day before, but many more. There were goat-legged fauns and gigantic night-hobs, there were elves and kobolds, beetle riders and three-legses, a man-sized rooster in jackboots, a stag with golden antlers who walked erect and wore a Prince Albert. Many of the new arrivals bore no resemblance whatsoever to human beings. There were helmeted copper ants, strangely shaped wandering rocks, flute birds, who made music with their long beaks, and there were three so-called puddlers, who moved by dissolving into a puddle at every step and resuming their usual form a little farther on. But perhaps the most startling of all was a twee, whose fore and hindquarters had a way of running about independently of one another. Except for its red and white stripes it looked rather like a hippopotamus.' p262-263

## FALLADA
Hans

### The Drinker [Der Trinker]

*The Drinker*, the most extraordinary of Fallada's many novels, was written in a few weeks in an asylum for the criminally insane in North Germany where Fallada had been confined in September 1944 after a domestic incident involving his firing a gun at his wife. In the novel which — as John Willett says in his introduction — 'has a plan and a shape like a Gadarene slope', Fallada, a morphine addict and an alcoholic, once a world-famous author, then touching rock-bottom in Nazi Germany, disguised himself as Herr Erwin Sommer, a rather pedantic, petty-minded small businessman, to describe what had happened.

Sommer leaves his wife Magda then falls in love and has a squalid affair with Elinor, a barmaid whom he calls his *reine d'alcool* ('Alcohol Queen'). After a series of alcoholically-induced blackouts and behavioural breakdowns, the still outwardly respectable and soberly pedestrian Herr Sommer finds himself in an asylum after apparently trying to murder the long-suffering Magda.

The effect of all this is like reading about Mr. Pooter (the risibly conventional householder in the Victorian masterpiece *Diary of a Nobody* by the Grossmith Brothers) in Kafka-land, and the denouement is horrific. To conceal the work from the asylum authorities, Fallada seems to have feigned madness. He produced a manuscript which appeared to consist of tiny lines of scribbles, turning each page round and continuing between the lines, and then across them. Deciphering it under a microscope actually took longer than had the writing, but the result was a work of faultless narrative prose. This is a novel with the fluency and inevitability of automatic writing, as seen in the following quote with its obvious disingenuousness, a harbinger of the disasters to come. N J

'Of course I have not always been a drunkard. Indeed it is not very long since I first took to drink. Formerly I was repelled by alcohol, I might take a glass of beer, but wine tasted sour to me, and the smell of schnapps made me ill. But then the time came when things began to go wrong with me. My business affairs did not proceed as they should, and in my dealings with people I met with all kinds of setbacks. I have always been a sensitive man...' p1

FALLADA
Hans

## Listen Little Man [Kleiner Mann — was nun?]

A set of colourful and sympathetic characters from the Weimar Republic period in Germany are assembled in one of the most successful books of its era. Although it deals with a society besieged by mass unemployment and political strife it's humorous and positive in tone; enjoyable and often tender in its story of a young, hard-up couple trying to survive — with a baby on the way — in a harsh economic climate.

*Listen Little Man* is full of fascinating detail of urban life in this important and, in retrospect, disastrous period. It shows, no doubt realistically, how the German working class were divided between Nazi, Socialist and Communist viewpoints as well as the more minor but interesting details of apartment-block life, of Weimar fads like Naturism, of the pornography business in that time and the ins and outs of how department stores operated.

The 'Little Man' of the title is a well-meaning but timid character surrounded by magnificent larger-than-lifes; his mother, a sympathetic ageing trollop living it up for all its worth, his courageous young wife Lammchen, the veteran nudist and salesman Joachim Heilbutt and his mother's fancy man, the jolly Mr. Jachmann.

Together they people an animated and enjoyable picture of Germany in the 1930s just before all hell broke loose under the great Austrian leader. First published in 1932, *Listen Little Man* has been recently retranslated and published in a beautiful new edition by a small publisher, Libris, who specialise in forgotten German classics. R K

"'What a good idea of yours to come. Look around. It's just the usual sort of den, hideous really but I don't mind. It doesn't worry me. It's nothing to do with me."

He paused.

"Do you see the nude photos? Yes, I've got quite a collection. Thereby hangs a tale. Whenever I move in anywhere, and put the pictures up on the wall, the landlady is always horrified. Some want me to move out on the spot."

He paused again. He looked around him. "Yes, there's always trouble to start with," said Heilbutt. "These landladies are mostly incredibly narrow-minded. But then I convince them. One simply has to reflect that in itself nudity is the only decent state. That's how I convince them." Another pause. "My landlady here for example. Mrs. Witt. She was in such a state! 'Put them in the chest of drawers,' she said, 'excite yourself with them as much as you like, but not in front of me...'."

Heilbutt stared earnestly at Pinneberg: "I convinced her. You must realize, Pinneberg, that I'm a born naturist, so I said to Mrs. Witt: 'All right, sleep on it, and if tomorrow morning you still want me to take the pictures down, I will. Coffee at seven please.' So at seven o'clock in the morning she knocks on the door with the coffee tray, and I'm standing there, completely naked doing my morning exercises. I say to her: 'Mrs. Witt, look at me, look closely at me. Does it disturb you? Does it excite you? Natural nakedness is without shame, and you aren't ashamed either." She's convinced. She's stopped grumbling about them. She thinks I'm right." p201-202

FICHTE
Hubert

## The Orphanage [Das Waisenhaus]

Detlev is eight. Uprooted from the home of his Protestant grandparents in Hamburg, he has been surreptitiously deposited by his mother in a Catholic orphanage in Bavaria. As he waits for his mother to deliver him, he gets bird droppings on his hands. This provokes, at least in his mind, the derision of the orphans and the disapprobation of the nuns. And the accompanying feelings of terror, shame, and loneliness give rise to and connect the apparent jumble of memories which constitute the novel.

The year is 1942/3. Detlev is the object of the hostile gaze of two allegedly subordinate, but mutually supporting, hierarchies. He is the victim of a totalitarian microcosm headed by a certain Albert who shares an 'A' with Adolf. It feels as if the mother who should comfort and protect him has abandoned him, and would prefer him not to exist. The prayer promised to make him an unexceptionable Catholic has not yet been received, and may prove impossible to learn. Hence there is an ever-present danger of his going to a Hell that is structurally equivalent to Auschwitz.

When, towards the end of the novel, his mother explains that his father is a Jew, Detlev does not understand. He does not understand Catholicism either, with its insistence on martyrdom, pain and punishment. He is at once puzzled and fascinated by that process of dismemberment which puts dummies in coffins and relics behind altars. He is confused by the prurient sexual ethics inculcated in the orphanage. And because the explanations of the adults are all ideologically tainted, they only make matters worse. Detlev is eight. By writing as it were from his perspective, Fichte is able to present a dislocated and devastating view of the continuum of terror and torture which links the nuns and Albert with nativity plays and policeman Kriegel. In the process he presents Nazism not as something monstrous, not as something silly, not even as something shabbily opportunistic, but as something endemic to the structures of Western thought. It is a rare achievement, and the resulting novel, painful though it is, demands to be read. R G

'In the Protestant Church near the town wall there was a painted Christ. The colours were pale. The paintwork showed up every irregularity of the plaster. The Christ there had no ribs under his skin. His toes weren't spread apart like here. The blood there wasn't black at the edge of the wounds. His mother looked at Christ too. She turned Detlev away from the wooden figure. Sister Silissa drew a sweet out of one of the many folds in her habit, held it in front of Detlev's face by a corner of the red wrapping paper. Detlev looked up at the cross again. He felt a pain across his shoulders. His ribs pressed against his skin. He thought he would have to stretch out his arms, like the white-coated traffic police on Stephan's Square — his grandfather had been a traffic policeman before the First World War.

Detlev shut his eyes tightly. He was afraid that the whole rose hedge would be pressed down on him. Detlev didn't see his mother looking at Sister Silissa, Sister Silissa nodding slowly once, his mother quickly handing the brightly coloured Bavarian jacket to Sister Silissa, Sister Silissa quietly opening the dining room door for his mother.

When Detlev turned away from the green face again, his head came up against the black cloth of Sister Silissa's habit. His mother had disappeared.' p21

FICHTE
Hubert

## Detlev's Imitations [Detlevs Imitationen]

In narrated time, one night divides *Detlev's Imitations* from *The Orphanage*. For Fichte, the two works were separated by the popular success of his 'beat' novel *Die Palette*, in which a seedy

Hamburg bar is seen through the eyes of a bisexual art critic called Jäcki. *Detlev's Imitations* juxtaposes the main characters of the two previous novels, and hence the dates 1943 and 1968, the fire bombing of Hamburg and the student revolt. It is the opposite of an anniversary: it is an attempt to come to terms with the past.

Such attempts are very common in postwar German literature. But this one is as subtle, tightly structured and as fiercely intelligent as any, and it goes a good deal further than most. As in *The Orphanage*, Fichte here insists that structures of persecution are everywhere, underlying not only the infamous anti-gay legislation which the Federal Republic took over from the Nazis, not only the humdrum cruelty, hypocrisy and power-play of everyday life (and everyday speech), not only the whole fraught business of education, especially sex education — but also such apparently harmless or even edifying branches of learning as natural science, history, poetry, philosophy.

Inspired by his psychedelic experiences in the gay bars of Hamburg and his intimate knowledge of European mannerism, Fichte is concerned to suggest alternatives to all polarized and polarizing systems of thought. At the same time, the novel tells a familiar story of unrequited sexual obsession, examines in detail a problematical mother-son relationship, and constitutes an act of mourning. And repeatedly, in various forms, it asks the question which is a touchstone for the consciences of protagonists and readers alike: would you torture?

As well as doing all these deep things, though, *Detlev's Imitations* is a wonderfully sardonic evocation of the postwar period in Germany. The over-earnest mimicry of a naïve but precocious child exposes the speech and behaviour of the adults in all its preposterous absurdity. Jäcki, though older and altogether more knowing than his younger imitator, continues the same attack on different levels — by parodying Wittgenstein, for example. And his observation is every bit as sharp and merciless as that of his counterpart. The result is a novel which is by turns both extremely accessible, and inexhaustibly rich: a *tour de force* which will make you laugh and cry in (almost) equal measure. R G

'There's been an assassination attempt on our Führer, shouts granny. It's been announced on the radio. I almost got a heart attack.

The people's radio.

Detlev used to believe that dwarves live, fiddle and sing, inside the black igelite box. He looked in by the side of the dial to see them working.

Zarah Leander sings out of the box.

The Führer's friend, says grandad.

She sings like a bear.

Zarah, the vodka queen, at whose feet the devil's general, O.E. Hasse, sits in 1968 at the premiere in the Operetta House.

The whole scene is there and admires the queens from all over the world in their brightly coloured coats.

Zarah in 1943 out of the people's radio.

Now out of the people's radio the attempt on our leader's life. Granny says it again and again, to all the neighbours.

I almost got a heart attack.

But for Detlev something's missing.

She could say: With fright. Because I'm shocked. Because I don't know, what will become of our nation and the movement.

Granny says I almost got a heart attack!

The neighbours want to calm her:

But nothing happened to him.

And granny says nothing.

# FONTANE
## Theodor

## Effi Briest [Effi Briest]

The great novel of German realism. Like *Anna Karenina* and *Madame Bovary*, the story revolves round a woman's adultery, the focus through which a whole society is illuminated.

The events are set in the *Junker* class, the Prussian landed gentry and minor nobility that provided much of the personnel to run the new German Empire (Innstetten, Effi's husban d, is one of Bismarck's protégés); the three locations reflect three aspects of society: Hohen-Cremmen, the estate where Effi's family live, in the Mark of Brandenburg, the cradle of Prussia; the Baltic port of Kessin, with its mixture of German and Slav populations; and Berlin, the dynamic capital of the new, Prussian-dominated Empire.

The seeds of the story are contained within the opening section: Effi, a lively, impulsive young girl, with a touch of the arrogance of her class, is playing in the garden with her friends, talking about their visitor, Geert von Innstetten, many years ago a suitor for her mother, who could not marry her because he was too young, and still had to make his way in the world. For the girls this is a delightfully sad love story with a hero and a heroine who gave each other up. Effi is called to the house and told Innstetten has asked to marry her. She accepts: although over twice her age, he is good-looking and has prospects of a glittering career, and Effi's mother does not have to apply much pressure to get her to make the match she was denied.

Innstetten is a model of propriety and decency, but lacks, not the passion, but the human warmth that Effi needs. (The honeymoon, on which he takes her on an exhaustive conducted tour of Italian art treasures, is characteristic of his lack of understanding of her needs.) Living far from her home in the, from the perspective of Brandenburg, almost exotic Baltic port of Kessin, with Innstetten often absent on business, lonely and occasionally slightly frightened, and with no close friend in the rather straitlaced society of the local aristocratic families, she slides into a halfhearted affair with Crampas, who has an invalid wife and a reputation as a ladies' man. It is a relief when she discovers that her husband has been promoted and they are to move to the capital.

It is six years later that the adultery is discovered, by the standard device of old letters concealed in Effi's sewing box that Innstetten comes across by chance while she is away at a spa for infertility treatment. As he wonders what to do, Innstetten realises he loves his wife and has no strong feelings against Crampas. And yet he goes through the motions prescribed by his class code, challenges and kills Crampas, and sends Effi away. Her parents also feel they cannot take her in (her mother writes that they must show the whole world that they condemn her actions) and she is left to live out a lonely life, cut off from society, and with no useful function in the world.

As in many of Fontane's novels (e.g. *Cécile*, *The Woman taken in Adultery*) it is the female characters who are at the centre of interest and through whom the inadequacies of society are revealed. It is not the tragedy of a life destroyed that informs *Effi Briest*, but the sadness of a life wasted. All the characters feel compelled to act as society insists, even if they do not accept these principles as absolutes. Fontane's criticism of Prussia, moderated by his irony and gentle humour, is not political or even, in the strictest sense, moral, but humanitarian, directed against a social order whose rigidity leaves no room for a truly human dimension. M M

"'This boring old embroidery. Thank goodness you're here," and she put her elbows on the table.

"But we've driven your mamma away," said Hulda.

"Not really. You heard her, she was going anyhow, she's expecting a visitor you see, some old friend from when she was a girl, I'm going to tell you about that later, a love-story complete with hero and heroine, and ending in renunciation. You'll be amazed, you won't believe your ears. I've seen him too, Mamma's old friend, over in Schwantikow. He's a Landrat, and very handsome and manly."

"That's the main thing," said Hertha.

"Of course it's the main thing, 'women should be womanly, men should be manly' — that's one of Papa's favourite sayings, as you know. Now help me tidy this table, otherwise I'll be in trouble again."

In a trice all the skeins were packed into the basket, and when they were all seated again, Hulda said, "Well then Effi, it's time now, let's have this tale of love and renunciation. Or is it not really that bad?"

"A tale of renunciation is never bad." p11

FRIED
Erich

## Children and Fools [*pieces from* Kinder und Narren, Fast Alles Mögliche, Das Unmaß aller Dinge, Mitunter sogar Lachen]

*Children and Fools* is an extraordinary collection of thirty-four short prose pieces by a Jewish Austrian poet who was exiled from Vienna as a teenager. Fried settled in England and some of the best pieces in the book are sad/amusing vignettes of Austrian exile life set in North London.

This is a poet's book, with a poet's sudden unexpected swooping down onto bright fragments of truth; sometimes found in minor but illuminating objects or moments; the day (*The Green Suite*) when the green sofa, the Viennese grandmother's lifetime pride and joy, is finally ignominiously lugged up into the attic (prefiguring her own end) or the little handful of damp 'sand' picked up at Auschwitz (in *My Doll at Auschwitz*) that, casually pocketed, turns out, back at the hotel, to be composed of human bone fragments; the sole remains of millions of exterminated people.

There is no avoiding the shadow of Nazism that passed over Fried's life — his father was beaten to death by a Gestapo officer who, he notes, later pursued a successful career in West Germany, and the Grandmother touchingly described in *The Green Suite* was 'transported' at the age of 76, blind and frail, to be executed by other good citizens of Greater Germany. The charming, humorous tales of pre-1938 Vienna are mixed with pieces about the succeeding barbarism and bittersweet stories of exile — of love and friendship but also desperate attempts to get relatives out of Nazi Austria.

There are also some satirical pieces about the postwar world concerning different kinds of terror. *Tortoise Turning* is an ironic fantasy about contemporary power brokers like the oil companies, destroying the planet while distracting us with adverts featuring the odd wild animal they are 'protecting' and *The Real* which is on the final perfection of the extermination Hitler started piecemeal through the deployment of nuclear weapons.

It is however the most autobiographical pieces, mainly at the end of the book, including *My Heroic Age*, *The Unworthy Families*, *Three Library Users*, *Läzchen* and *Fini* that demand to be read and which provide an impeccably artistic and sympathetic account of times and people close enough to touch and far away enough to forget. R K

'One day a few of those who were not taken to the gas chambers right away are said to have called out at the end, "Watch out, we don't burn well! More will be left of us than you bargained for! Our smoke will suffocate you!"

These were their last words before they were burned. Their predictions have not, however, come true. They burned well, very well even, care had been taken of that. Although petrol was already in short supply then, it had not been spared, and had been poured or sprayed on most shortly beforehand. "Emergency baptism" it was called by the others, who drove them into the fire, the last part with long poles, in order not to come too close to the flames themselves.

Not one of the drivers and commanders of the drivers were suffocated by the smoke of those burning. From experience they knew very well how far back they had to stand and also that they had to take account of the wind. And since these burnings, which they used to call "Minor Resettlement Without Special Facilities", were basically an insignificant, little noticed episode which was not to be compared to the simultaneous so-called "Major Resettlement Action" with the Zyklon-B crystals manufactured by Degesch, the German Pest Control Company [Deutsche Gesellschaft für Schädlingsbekämpfung], they also did not attract much attention, and some of the burners who later returned to their homeland, still live today as respected elderly gentlemen in their postwar professions, or as pensioners, loved by their grandchildren. The last words of the burned were therefore mistaken at best.' p59-60

## Homo Faber [Homo Faber]

In *Homo Faber,* as in his preceding works *Gantenbein* and *I'm not Stiller*, Frisch examines the problem of individual identity in an increasingly impersonal and alienating world. *Homo Faber* achieves this through the form of a psychoanalytic diary that tells the strange story of a middle-class intellectual called Walter Faber. The name 'Faber' means 'artisan' in Latin and suggests the practical vision of life — he is an engineer — that marks the limits of his convictions and psychology. As an ideal-typical representative of technocratic civilisation he is ascetic, unimaginative and lives in a well-organised black-and-white world, where everything is quantifiable and comprehensible and from where all 'superstition' and 'mysticism' is excluded.

The chance landing of his aeroplane in the desert and the suicide of his childhood friend Joachim in the Mexican jungle doesn't sway him in his sternly rational image of the world. But destiny, in the shape of a proliferating series of extraordinary events, erupts darkly and inexorably into his life, sweeping away the citadel of his ingenuous security.

He meets and falls in love with a young woman who turns out to be his daughter — whose existence he was unaware of. She dies in Greece, land of myth, land of Oedipus, because of a snake bite, not from the poison but because of a concussion that the doctors hadn't noticed. Faber himself becomes ill with cancer and an operation can't help.

Frisch's precise writing, flattened and unsentimental unseats the technocratic delusion of defeating death, a delusion that, for the writer, paradoxically extinguishes the chance of really living. C C

'My mistake lay in the fact that we technologists try to live without death. Her own words:"You don't treat life as a form, but as a mere addition sum, hence you have no relationship to time, because you have no relationship to death." Life is form in time. Hanna admits that she can't explain what she means. Life is not matter and cannot be mastered by technolo gy. My mistake with Sabeth lay in repetition. I behaved as though age did not exist, and hence contrary to nature." p166

## Man In the Holocene [Der Mensch erscheint im Holozän]

A highly original and post-modern work written in 1980, *Man In the Holocene* is (as is the case with many translations) wrongly titled. Early on into the novel we read that 'the geological present is termed the Holocene.' But the original title, *Der Mensch erscheint im Holozän* (Man emerges in the Holocene) renders the novel much more evolutionary than the English title would imply.

The protagonist, Herr Geiser, is found at the beginning of the novel building a pagoda out of crispbread. This project appears to be a rather foolish, if not futile undertaking since it's been raining for days in the village where he lives, in the valley of Ticino, in southern Switzerland. Throughout the narrative an assortment of other narratives are embedded within the main narrative; definitions, encyclopedia citations, references to rain and water, dates of geologic interest, biblical passages and historical entries all of which relate, in one way or another, to the weather, the climate, Geiser's and/or man's relative state of evolutionary progress.

In an attempt to 'wait out the rain' Geiser reads whatever he can from which he takes excerpts which he posts all over his house. As one reads Geiser's story and the clippings which he most often uses, one discovers the link between the evolution of man and Geiser's evolution; that one not only discovers when and where man 'emerges' from his evolution, but the diametric constituent of 'extinction'; his regression. To that extent, one sees how Frisch incorporates elements of the historical, of those elements than seem to be incorruptibly accurate, with the relative nature of his protagonist. As the rains continue, Geiser plans for his survival, checking to see if he has enough food, firewood, fuel; but, in effect, the task is futile. In a state of human and climactic evolutionary regression, in an age of expanding ozone layers, the problem is not to be solved with the prescient hoarding of consumer goods. There is little value to those things if the planet is in a state of decay and the interminable state of decay, above all, appears to be the crux of Frisch's parable. M R A

'While Geiser is wondering why he wanted a candle in the middle of the afternoon, he remembers having intended to seal a document, his final instructions in case anything happened. His resolve, as he searches for a pan, is to clean out his closet one of these days. But the pan, the little one, is already standing on the hot plate, the water in it bubbling, though the hot plate is no longer glowing. He forgot, while thinking about the untidiness of his closet and about his heirs, that he had already drunk his tea; the empty cup is warm, the tea bag dark and wet.' p57

GRAB
Hermann

## The Town Park [Der Stadtpark]

Hermann Grab, like Franz Kafka, was a 'Prague Jew', part of a German-speaking group of great cultural importance. As a Jew Grab was forced to leave Prague and emigrated to the United States were seven of the eleven pieces in this book are set.

In one of the American stories *Wedding in Brooklyn* he captures the unsettled awkward world of those whose settled, established lives in Prague, Vienna or Berlin were thrown on the table like dice. They were then doomed to try to eke out a living, starting from scratch in their forties or fifties, in a foreign country. And these of course were the lucky ones! Just one of the many crimes on the chargesheet of the Germans under Hitler was the virtual crippling of European intellectual life as a result of their domination of Central and Eastern Europe.

In the title piece, a novella, we discover quite what a loss Hermann Grab's exile was to literature in German. His writerly gift is immediately apparent as the young boy passes through early morning city streets: 'Renato would notice how one or other of the shop windows would already be illuminated at that hour, thereby transplanting an interior into the midst of the cold streets'. There is a powerful visual imagination here that recalls the master, Proust, especially as this is a story of childhood and youth constructed from memories of school (where reigned the quirky Dr. Wanka) and Mama ('Visiting Mama in her bedroom, Renato would look at the elongated glass drops which were always just on the point of falling from the chandelier'). With the other stories in the section 'Early Tales' there is a wonderful evocation of the atmosphere of Austria-Hungary (of which Prague was a part) in its last years.

Whether reminiscence unfolded out of the unforced logic of childhood or the intelligent naïveté of adolescent thwarted love — 'I probably am fond of her, he declared and immediately reflected how strangely it was arranged that one was fond of people who seemed quite indifferent to one.' — Grab is strange, original and striking.

He can also be tender and humorous as in *The Lawyer's Office* which, set in Prague between 1920 and 1938, evokes in the petty existence of minor office staff a vivid human world, just like our own with its office politics, lonely people and claustrophobia; but different in that by the end of the story Jewish or Communist employees are starting to disappear into thin air...

The Nazis tried to write Grab and his fellows out of history so congratulations to the small transatlantic publishing house (Verso) that has restored this excellent writer to the English-speaking world and the present day. R K

'Her betrothed sometimes remained away over a Sunday. Then Fräulein Lange would ask whether Fräulein Kleinert would like to spend the afternoon with her. They would go to a picture theatre, to a promenade concert or to the big pastry shop. Here they would sit at one of the little gilt tables with their princely ornamentation and, when they had consumed the plump doughnuts with coffee-flavoured or chocolate icing and scraped up every last remnant of whipped cream from their plates, they would watch the families slowly endeavouring to forge a way between the close-packed tables, they would see the Sunday bustle of the waitresses, the impassive faces of the customers who had found a place and the cigarette smoke which hung in the teatime air. Fräulein Lange always spoke only about her betrothed and his dazzling prospects and, if he were not travelling, Fräulein Kleinert would say she was quite content on a Sunday afternoon to alter a dress, brush her carpet or rearrange her cupboards. In her room in the high-lying suburb, which afforded her fresh air and also a view over a small children's playground, she would hear the occasional radio and sometimes piano-playing too, since, like her, a few families in the building would be spending the afternoon at home.' p149 (from *The Lawyer's Office*)

GRASS
Günter

## Cat and Mouse [Katz und Maus]

Poets are usually lovers and their lost loves make the best poetry, and if the novelist is often someone who bears witness to his or her homeland, then lost homelands inform the best novels. This is certainly the case of Günter Grass, the most critically and popularly successful German novelist of the postwar world.

The lost homeland is Danzig, a port city on the Baltic today Polish and called *Gdansk* but which was an important German city from the middle ages to 1918. For Grass it is lost in three senses; the more usual one of being the city of childhood and adolescence, then because much of its historic fabric, the tall old Hanseatic houses and fine public buildings were destroyed in fighting and bombing 1944–5, and finally because it was ethnically cleansed of Germans at the end of the war and resettled by Poles, some of them themselves resettled from Eastern Poland which had been taken over by the Soviet Union.

This loss of place and the need to somehow recapture it to feel whole is one of Grass' great themes and *Cat and Mouse* is his most poignant and achieved work on it. On the one hand there is a sustained recreation of the world and sights of prewar Danzig; a workaday world of little suburbs and their gardens with 'glazed garden ornaments; frogs, mushrooms or dwarfs', church halls with tarred tarpaulin roofs, rusting ships in the port, neighbourhood stores with potato cellars and herring barrels. A workaday, petty-bourgeois youth's eye view of the city but also with a certain exotic tinge — this is a city where Poles, Germans and Kashubians (a Slav minority) mingle and clash, sometimes in the same family. It's also a political oddity, an independent Free City State under a League of Nations (forerunner of the UN) commissioner and its own governing senate which eventually, to the Danzig Germans undying shame, elected a Nazi majority.

All this is also just the background to an evocation of the book's central figure, the unforgettable Mahlke, a kind of awkward and gangling German James Dean. With his screwdriver hung permanently around his neck and the stuffed owl left to him by his absent father he is a hero to his boyish contemporaries he seems to possess the secret of style and individuality and the courage to be daring and different.

He must be one of the most sympathetic portrayals of an adolescent in world literature. Mahlke is a kind of oddball saint, with his own cast-iron sense of ethics which stays untainted by the degenerate behaviour and ideology of the Nazis.

Written with immense nostalgia, or as the Portuguese say, *saudade*, *Cat and Mouse* is one of the great unmissable books, a wartime German (and hence somewhat terrifying) *Catcher in the Rye* or *Le Grand Meaulnes* (see French Babel Guide). R K

'The principal's speech went on and on. Boredom spread from the lush green plants to the oil painting on the rear auditorium, a portrait of Baron von Conradi the founder of our school... In this lofty hall Klohse's cool peppermint breath, which suffused all his mathematics classes, substituting for the odour of pure science, wasn't much of a help. From up front his words barely carried to the middle of the auditorium: "Thosewhocomeafterus Andinthishourwhenthetravellerreturnsbuthistimethehomelandand letusneverpureofheartaslsaidbeforepureofheart andifanyonedisagreesletandinthishourkeepcleantoconclude withthewordsofSchillerif yourlifeyoudonotstakethelaurelneverwillyoutake Andnowbacktowork!'" p72-3

GRASS
Günther

## The Tin Drum [Die Blechtrommel]

Grass' masterpiece and the greatest single work of postwar German literature, is a sustained series of quasi-odd events — magical realism in fact — that unloads all the living detail of life in a great city. The city is Danzig, a fascinating, once-beautiful city on the Baltic shore, now a part of Poland and renamed *Gdansk*. Part of the fascination is its mixed ethnic character, part Low German (a Northern German language similar to Dutch) part Polish and part Kashubian (a Slavic minority people). Partly the book is about the tensions around who the city belongs to that eventually lead (in World War Two) to its ethnic and physical destruction as a predominantly German city. It also reveals a world of affectionate or competitive interaction between different groups of the sort we see in any of the great multi-ethnic cities of today like London, New York or São Paulo.

The focal point of the saga of Danzig is Grass' greatest leap of imagination, the character of the dwarfish 'tin drummer' Oskar, who unites in himself the different ethnic strains and takes no active part in their rivalry; more than anything he observes a world slowly slipping into chaos around him. He is a classic outsider-witness and perhaps his 'dissassociatedness' is what a German writer needs to look at his or her own recent history.

Later on Oskar, in retirement from life, 'drums up' for himself the past and it is Grass' magnificent achievement that this book so graphically and wittily evokes the city's vibrant past in its nearly 600 gripping pages. Reading the *Tin Drum* does almost feel like having been there, in Danzig, Grass' city, bombed, ruined, then finally thoroughly ethnically cleansed. A place in fact taken to oblivion from where this master storyteller and 'rememberer' has rescued it... R K

(An officer, Bebra, is inspecting fortified pillboxes on German sea defences —

ed.)

'LANKES: See! There's always something cockeyed. Every real artist has got to express himself. If you'd like to take a look at the ornaments over the entrance, sir, I did them.

BEBRA (after a thorough examination of them): Amazing! What wealth of form. What expressive power!

LANKES: Structural formations I call them.

BEBRA: And your creation, your picture, or should I call it a relief, has it a title?

LANKES: I just told you: Formations. Or Oblique Formations if you like that better. It's a new style. Never been done before.

BEBRA: Even so, you ought to give it a title. Just to avoid misunderstandings. It's you work, after all.

LANKES: What for? What good are titles? Except to put in the catalogue when you have a show.

BEBRA: You're putting on airs, Lankes. Think of me as an art lover, not as an officer. Cigarette? (Lankes takes it) Well then, what's on your mind?

LANKES: Oh, all right, if you put it that way. This is how I figure it. When this war is over - one way or another, it will be over someday — well, then, when the war is over, the pillboxes will still be here. These things were made to last. And then my time will come. The centuries... (He puts the last cigarette in his pocket.) Maybe you've got another cigarette, sir? Thank you, sir... the centuries start coming and going, one after another like nothing at all. But the pillboxes stay put just like the Pyramids stayed put. And one fine day one of those archaeologist fellows comes along. And he says to himself: what an artistic void there was between the First and the Seventh World Wars! Dull drab concrete; here and there, over a pillbox entrance, you find some clumsy amateurish squiggles in the old-home style. And that's all. Then he discovers Dora Five, Six, Seven; he sees my Structural Oblique Formations, and he says to himself, Say, take a look at that, Very, very interesting, magic, menacing, and yet shot through with spirituality. In these works a genius, perhaps the only genius of the twentieth century, has expressed himself clearly, resolutely, and for all time. I wonder, says our archaeologist to himself, I wonder if it's got a name? A signature to tell us who the master was? Well, sir, if you look closely, sir, and hold your head at a slant, you'll see, between those Oblique Formations...

BEBRA: My glasses. Help me, Lankes.

LANKES: All right, here's what it says: Herbert Lankes, anno nineteen hundred and forty-four. Title: Barbaric, mystical, bored.'

BEBRA: You have given our century its name'. p329-330

## Aurora's Motive [Auroras Anlaß]

The novels of the young Austrian writer, Erich Hackl, use individual characters to examine themes from recent history. He appears particularly interested in the struggles of the 1930s, and his books reveal a sympathy for the downtrodden and those committed to the fight against bourgeois conventionality.

'One day Aurora Rodríguez was compelled to kill her daughter', is the opening sentence, and the novel looks back over her life and that of her daughter in order to reveal 'Aurora's motive'. Born in pre-World War One Spain, Aurora is an unconventional woman. She suffered the harsh Spanish upbringing of the time, tempered by her close relationship with her father, a sensitive but ineffective idealist with sympathy for 'simple folk', but who has a low opinion of women. After the death of his wife, Aurora becomes his conversation partner, reads his library, and develops advanced ideas. The day she reaches legal maturity she advertises for a man to father her child, whom she brings up independently, according to her own ideas rather than convention.

The child, Hildegart, responds to her mother's emphasis on healthy, free physical development, and the encouragement of her intellectual and emotional faculties. She is a prodigy who is far in advance of her age in all things (except perhaps socially; her mother does not let her play with other children because 'wrong upbringing is contagious'). At thirteen she goes to the university to study constitutional law, and at seventeen she is lecturing to socialist meetings and writing articles for left-wing newspapers.

Aurora feels she is beginning to lose Hildegart to her political activities and her ideological friends, and also suspects she is tempted to give in to the 'flesh'. Her daughter asserts her independence and accepts a job working with Havelock Ellis (turn of the century writer and sexologist), arranged by H.G. Wells. Then, in a sudden volte face, she returns to her mother and pleads for help to stop her 'going off the straight and narrow', asking Aurora to kill her.

Hildegart, quotations from whose writings on the situation of women punctuate the text, is a kind of nun of secular enlightenment. Her upbringing has fostered a sense of vocation which is so ingrained that when she feels she may not be strong enough to maintain it in the face of the world she chooses to escape rather than succumb.

Hackl's sober but not humourless narration ensures that the story of Aurora and her daughter, which, with its rigidly uncompromising rejection of convention, might easily descend to the comic grotesque, engages both the readers' sympathy and their understanding. In answering the question of Aurora's motive, he raises many more about the nature of society. M M

'Look, the maid said, how funny, the bees are flying round.

They're working, Hildegart answered. They're bringing the male pollen to the stigma. Then a tube goes down to the egg and then it's fertilized.

You certainly know a lot.

I know a lot more.

Julia Sanz was only half listening. She was watching the photographer in front of them, who was leisurely unpacking his tripod and setting up his box camera...

Why is that man staring at you? Hildegart asked.

Maybe he likes me.

Maybe he wants to fertilize you, the little girl said.

Not so loud.

Why are you turning red?

I'm not turning red.

Yes you are.

Julia tried to change the subject. I've never been photographed.

But fertilizing people is different from fertilizing plants.

Hildegart! Be quiet. The man. He can hear us.

He has a penis, Hildegart said, and he sticks it in your vagina. And then semen comes out and fertilizes an egg and then a child begins to grow in your stomach." p55

## HACKL
## Erich

## Farewell Sidonia [Abschied von Sidonie]

An infant is abandoned outside a church. The local authorities try to pass it on to the next town to avoid having to pay for its upkeep, but eventually find a working-class couple to foster it. The couple and their own children, despite economic difficulties, come to love the child, which they name Sidonia, and feel it is part of the family. She starts to grow up happy, wanted, protected.

The authorities, however, under the motto of 'A child's best with its real mother, isn't it?' continue to search for Sidonia's biological parents. Ten years later they find them, and Sidonia is sent to join her presumed mother, to the desolation of her foster family, who never see her again.

But this is Austria, the year is 1933, and the abandoned Sidonia is a gypsy child whose swarthy complexion proclaims her racial difference to everyone. Her 'black' colour automatically arouses prejudice, but that often disappears in her presence, dissipated by her charm and vivacity, and, before the German invasion of 1938, the locals are often half ashamed of their feelings. The doctor, for example, although regarded as a 'soft touch' who treats the poor for free, refuses to take Sidonia because 'she doesn't belong here', and then afterwards he regrets it and offers to help.

After the Nazi takeover the situation does not change radically. Although the prejudice against her has official sanction and the authorities' search for her parents is now racially motivated, there are still neighbours who are not afraid to show they care for her. The decision to send Sidonia back to them is shown to be as much the result of an uncaring attitude on the part of individual officials, who take what seems the most straightforward course, as the direct implementation of racialist policies. Immediately Sidonia has rejoined her parents the whole gypsy clan is deported to Auschwitz.

Sidonia's foster-parents, Hans and Josefa Breirather represent a side of Austrian history often ignored, especially in the picture presented abroad. They are active socialists. Hans spends eighteen months in jail after the abortive uprising against Chancellor Dollfuss' authoritarian state in 1934; the couple are blackmailed and browbeaten into joining the Catholic church; after 1938 they secretly collect for the families of comrades who have been imprisoned by the Nazis, and Hans is involved in resistance sabotage; Josefa is denounced for giving food to forced labourers.

For the English-speaking reader, *Farewell Sidonia* presents a picture of Austrian society which evokes the poverty of the early 1930s, and the atmosphere of menace and suspicion of the Nazi period. In the Breirathers Hackl has created two figures who have the strength of character to act according to their beliefs and who refuse to join the majority of the population in cringing acquiescence, yet do so not with heroic declarations, but as a matter of course. In this portrait of a working-class society under great economic and political pressure Sidonia is not so much the main focus of the story as the touchstone which brings out the attitudes of those around her with particular clarity.

After the war Hans Breirather is briefly elected mayor of the town, but then suffers from the anticommunism of the incipient Cold War. After he has discovered how she died, he wants Sidonia to be remembered, but he is regarded as a troublemaker. Sidonia has been forgotten and is never mentioned; it is as if she never existed. Besides being a vivid evocation of the 1930s, *Farewell Sidonia* has much to say about attitudes to the past in the Austria of the Waldheim affair (Kurt Waldheim became secretary-general of the UN and in 1986 Austrian President although accused of involvement in genocide during World War Two). M M

'There were new developments in the apartment house. The Krobaths moved in, national comrades from the Sudetenland in their mid-forties... Neither ever tired of stressing how happy they were to be on German soil, at which Frau Krobath would point to the linoleum at her feet. They were childless, the woman would not have the opportunity to earn a Mother's Cross, and he was unfit for duty at the front, so a Medal of Honour was a long way off. Lux, the cell leader from next door, helped them move in and introduced them to their neighbours that evening... In the name of all your neighbours, I heartily welcome you. And what is that? Frau Krobath asked in a shrill voice, that black thing? And into the silence that followed, as all eyes were fixed on Sidonia: Heinz, I think we've fallen among negroes. She laughed affectedly, her husband and Lux laughed with her.' p59

# HANDKE
## Peter

## The Left-handed Woman [Die linkshändige Frau]

Peter Handke's *The Left-handed Woman* grew out of a film script he wrote (the film appeared under the same title) and the novel's technique is very filmic. There is no narrator going inside the characters to tell us what they are thinking or feeling. Apart from the husband, the main characters are simply referred to as 'the woman', 'the child', 'the teacher', and we only know their names from when they talk to each other. Everything and everyone is seen from outside in a very visual manner, the author acting like a film director shifting his camera from shot to shot. What guides the reader's experience of the characters and events is the literary equivalent of the camera angle, the light in which the figures are shown, the parallels and contrasts, the repeated motifs. The overall effect of this technique is to create a central character who is mysteriously self-contained and through this exerts a fascination on the reader.

Marianne ('the woman') and Bruno spend the night after he returns from a business trip in a nearby hotel. The following morning, suddenly and without explanation, she asks him to leave her. He does, and moves in with her friend, the feminist and woman's group organiser, Franziska. The story then follows the minor events of her day-to-day existence — shopping, collecting her child from school, having coffee with Franziska, working as a translator — in what appears to be a downward spiral of depression. This reaches its lowest point in a trip to the town with her son when the ordinary features of city life — the lights, the noise, the traffic, other people — gradually intensify and merge into a nightmare.

From then on Marianne seems to regain control over herself and her life, in particular retaining her independence of other people, all of whom seem to want something from her, although it is often disguised as the offer of help. Bruno offers her money; her publisher, as soon as he hears she has thrown her husband out, appears at the door with flowers and a bottle of champagne; an out-of-work actor falls in love with her just from seeing her in a café; Franziska wants her to join the women's group as an example of a woman who has 'woken up'.

The novel is very carefully structured, with similarities to a musical composition, and the final scene brings all the figures together in an impromptu party as they turn up unannounced at Marianne's house. The scene becomes noisier and noisier and more and more chaotic, as the various characters interact with each other. The only exception is Marianne, who is a calm at the centre of the bedlam. When everyone has left she can say to her reflection in the mirror, "You have not betrayed yourself. And no one will humiliate you again." The final coda, the final visual 'comment', is a picture of Marianne, alone, sitting in her rocking chair looking out of the window.

The way Handke concentrates — on externals and allows his central character to be herself is the major factor in the effectiveness of this portrait of a woman who succeeds in asserting her independence. M M

In this bleak but brilliant book Handke puts some everyday souls under the microscope. It's an operation done with Teutonic precision; there's something of the same disillusioned stare as in the cinema of Fassbinder or Wim Wenders (before he got religion).

There's a wonderfully acid vision of the city of market progress most of us are forced to live in where 'The roar of the traffic was so loud that a long-lasting catastrophe seemed to be in progress'.

In this world, deliberately modern, of executive housing estates and shopping malls — the instant utopia of consumerism — a woman chooses solitude (self-knowledge?) over her officially-sanctioned state of married-with-one-kid bliss. Is it because she has seen herself like this; 'you lounge around your tidy homes like narcissistic photos of yourselves'. For whatever reason she makes her journey out of her 'major relationship' because 'Everything seems so banal with people around'.

Perhaps Handke is rather obviously projecting his own vision onto his female protagonist, his feeling of cold compassion towards ultramodern suburban lives in a country where a citizen can think 'he himself had no image of his native land'. This seems to be the flattened historical perspective of the contemporary Austrian, unable and unwilling to face up to a criminal past and so prone to exist in the perfect vacuum of a Fake America of supermarkets and tract houses... One of the most celebrated postwar Austrian novels. R K

'She sat rigid in the living room while the child and his fat friend jumped from a chair onto a pile of pillows, singing at the top of their voices:"The shit jumps on the piss, and the piss jumps on the shit, and the shit jumps on the piss..." They screeched and writhed with laughter, whispered into each other's ears, looked at the woman, pointed at her, and laughed some more. They didn't stop and they didn't stop; the woman did not react.

She sat at her typewriter. The child came up on tiptoes and leaned against her. She pushed him away with her shoulder, but he kept standing beside her. Suddenly the woman pulled him close and grabbed him by the throat; she shook him, let him go, and averted her eyes.

At night the woman sat at the desk; something rose slowly from the lower edge of her eyes and made them glisten; she was crying, without a sound, without a movement' p46

## Short Letter, Long Farewell [Der kurze Brief zum langen Abschied]

Peter Handke appeared on the literary scene when as a completely unknown twenty-two year old he attacked the members of the *Gruppe 47*, the most influential group of post-1945 writers, in what was then an unprecedented act of disrespect. Among his broad output, *Short letter, Long Farewell* is one of the most successful and popular of his novels, probably due to its accessibility. It also marks the beginning of Handke's turn to 'inwardness', an introverted and introspective way of writing typical of his later style.

*Short Letter, Long Farewell* deals with the aftermath of a failed marriage and is about as romantic as a Peter Handke novel gets, which is not very. The narrator, an unnamed Austrian writer, travels through America. In the first hotel he stays at, a letter from Judith, his estranged wife, reaches him; 'I am in New York. Please don't look for me. It would not be nice for you to find me.' Now a strange sort of chase ensues. Strange, as the narrator acts as an accomplice to his own pursuit by Judith: He makes sure to leave details of his next destination whenever he leaves a hotel, and even checks by telephone if Judith has picked up his tracks and followed. His flight leads the narrator from the East to the West coast of the USA. Because of a longing to be more like the Great Gatsby, he chooses, in homage to F. Scott Fitzgerald, to stay at the Algonquin hotel in New York.

The novel heads towards its natural conclusion, which is a final confrontation between Judith and the narrator. Dilettantish death threats lead to a scene where she finally confronts him with a pistol in the street. The narrator knows that the outcome of this confrontation will be determined by the progress he will have made in his quest for his identity.

The narrator spends long stretches of the novel thinking about himself, and subjecting his character to painstaking analysis. At one point, the reader finds an unexpected ally in the narrator when he brilliantly diagnoses himself with a 'thinking cramp'. Parts of the novel indeed read like a study in self-consciousness as when the narrator does not even seem be able to walk down a street naturally.

Its very straightforward plot makes *Short Letter, Long Farewell* ideal for getting a first taste of Handke's writing and the almost esoteric pleasure of his introspective focus, but if you are put off by 'navel-gazing' you probably won't much enjoy the rest of his work. Maren M

'I walked east on Forty-fourth Street. "No, west!" I turned around and went in the opposite direction, thinking I would come to Broadway. I had crossed Fifth and Madison avenue before I realized that I had not really turned around. I must only have imagined that I had turned around and gone in the opposite direction. However, because I felt turned around, I stood still and thought it over until my head was spinning. Then I went down Madison Avenue to Forty-second Street. There I turned, proceeded slowly, and actually reached Broadway at Times Square.' p25

# HEIN
Cristoph

## Distant Lover [Der Fremde Freund]

A very well-written piece of disillusion by a successful East German playwright. As one might except from a dramatist the brief encounters of the protagonist, a solitary woman doctor, are particularly well portrayed. Brief, limited encounters with her 'distant lover' whose very (emotional) distance she welcomes after the painful collapse of her marriage — 'The distance between us gave our relationship a cool familiarity that I found pleasant. I had no desire to reveal myself completely to another person again. I enjoyed caressing another's skin without wanting to crawl inside it.' Further brief encounters are with other lonely denizens of her apartment block; like old Frau Ruprecht living alone with a menagerie of cagebirds who become the only witnesses to her death.

The key relationship of the book between the doctor — whose hobby is photographing ruins — and her lover Henry, a nihilistic and bored architect whose hated work is designing nuclear power stations is well delineated, catching the predicament of people existing in a fundamentally unsympathetic human environment. To some extent this is the world of East Germany, as there are references to the persecution of Christians as potential dissidents, to the suppressed East Berlin workers' uprising in 1953 as well as to the prevalence of neighbour spying on neighbour on behalf of 'the authorities'; but it is also the prim, competitive world of the North German middle class that is being exposed.

More to the point perhaps, is that this is finally a very *European* book, full of the boredom and sense of empty lives lacking adventure that are found everywhere amongst the moderately well-off in settled, well-organised societies. R K

'To be sure, I didn't understand why it was so bad that he'd had an affair with a student. When I said this to my mother, she decided to enlighten me. Alarmed by the goings-on at school, she did it with a vengeance. Along with my illusions she destroyed my loveliest dream, the hope of growing up quickly. I didn't want to marry any more, or at least, I wanted to marry very late. I knew now you absolutely had to avoid getting involved with a man too soon, that it took years to be sure of his love, that every woman was allowed to love only one single man, for whom she had to save herself. Terrible diseases, wasted figures covered with scabs and pus, a life whose only desire was death — these were the stern, insistent ghosts that pursued me for years. I was sixteen before I let a boy kiss me. And I rushed home afterwards to scrub myself from head to foot.' p120

HESSE
Hermann

## The Glass Bead Game [Das Glasperlenspiel]

First published in 1946, *The Glass Bead Game* was Hermann Hesse's last novel, the final step in the author's search for the self, the same theme present in *Demian, Steppenwolf, Siddhartha* and *Narziss and Goldmund*. In the same year, Hesse was awarded the Nobel Prize for Literature.

*The Glass Bead Game* is the chronicle of the ascent of the shy and modest Joseph Knecht to the highest hierarchy of the Castalian Order, keepers of the Glass Bead Game, and reflects Hesse's constant interest in Oriental philosophy and religion. Here, much stress is set on classical Chinese culture and on the practice of meditation as a mean of refreshing and energising the body and the mind. The Glass Bead Game itself is 'the quintessence of intellectuality and art' a game that combines all known disciplines in elaborate patterns to achieve a kind of universality.

A gifted music pupil, Joseph Knecht at first rejects the Game and the ordained purpose of his life. In a painful adolescent crisis, partly relieved by the affectionate guidance of the old Music Master, his mentor and benefactor, Knecht finally experiences his vocation as a player by discovering the true nature of the Game, which is not in fact recreational but a practice of self awareness.

As a boy, Knecht was chosen to renounce the world and devote his life to Castalia. The militant friendship with Plinio Designori, an outsider allowed to attend the Order's school by a special privilege, exposes Knecht to the outside world, a place that fascinates and frightens him. While Plinio is bound to choose a career, marry and get on in life, Knecht must abide by the rules of the Castalian Order, among which are poverty and chastity.

Knecht's rise to power runs parallel to his emotional and intellectual awakening. At barely forty years of age, he is the youngest Master of the Game, the high priest of the Order. In spite of his young age, Knecht proves to be an excellent Master, concerned about the well-being and reputation of a Castalia surrounded by hostile forces.

To the external world, Castalia is an expensive appendage and Knecht is so troubled by these threats that he decides to leave the Order to convert the outside world to the importance and the aesthetic beauty of the Glass Bead Game. S C

'The Master had never heard him speak so fervently. He walked on in silence for a little, then said: "There is truth, my boy. But the doctrine you desire, absolute, perfect dogma that alone provides wisdom, does not exist. Nor should you long for a perfect doctrine, my friend. Rather, you should long for the perfection of yourself. The deity is within you, not in ideas and books."' p83

HESSE
Hermann

## The Journey to the East [Die Morgenlandfahrt]

Everybody — hopefully — has at least one book that they can read and reread, enjoy again and again and draw heart and energy from, like the company of an old friend. *The Journey to the East* is one of those very special books. A book too, that seems to be a perfect use of its particular medium, the brief novella based around the reminiscence of a single narrator. It would be hard to imagine it as a film; such is the air of exciting and mysterious insubstantiality Hesse weaves around a seemingly concrete argument — a journey.

It's a spiritual journey, the spiritual journey of a cultivated European traveling through his own culture, who doesn't set off merely to discover newness and wonder elsewhere but who, as an educated, reflective journeyer carries wonders within himself as well. *Journey to the East* is a magnificent travel book because it relates a journey to nowhere that never took place and yet continues through every day that passes. It's a journey outside the 'world deluded by money, number and time', a journey into the wonderful possibilities of life, of life rich in grace and enchantment, where the best things of the human spirit and natural beauty combine. The fellow-pilgrims on Hesse's journey are people who have detached themselves from the noisy, ratcheting world of contemporary routines and absorbed something of what is profound and eternal.

Hesse's traveller is a man like any other, so that just as he reaches the attainment of his quest he allows it to slip from him and the book then becomes a story of the shattered idealism of youth and the long subsequent search to recover or replace it. In fact the narrative is a very sophisticated interweaving of the pursuit of the grail of truth and of the delusions, contumely and dissent around that pursuit.

The book can be read as a beautiful story of a crisis of (creative) faith and the struggle to retain it. Although one of Hesse's shortest works it stands alongside the more famous *Steppenwolf* as his best; subtle, sketched rather than spelt out, wonderfully wise, a good investment for every traveller on the planet. R K

'What life is when it is beautiful and happy—a game! Naturally one can also do all kinds of other things with it, make a duty of it, or a battleground, or a prison, but that does not make it any prettier.' p72

'I looked for and found the place in the archives. There lay a tiny locket which could be opened and contained a miniature portrait of a ravishingly beautiful princess, which in an instant reminded me of all three thousand and one nights, of all the tales of my youth, of all the dreams and wishes of that great period when, in order to travel to Fatima in the Orient, I had served my noviciate and had reported myself as a member of the League. The locket was wrapped in a finely-spun mauve silk kerchief, which had an immeasurably remote and sweet fragrance, reminiscent of princesses and the East.' p94-95

'despair is the result of each earnest attempt to understand and vindicate human life. Despair is the result of each earnest attempt to go through life with virtue, justice and understanding and fulfil their requirements. Children live on one side of despair, the awakened on the other side.' p106

## Klingsor's Last Summer [Klingsors letzter Sommer]

*Klingsor's Last Summer* is a set of three short novellas that build in intensity to the title story; the blazing last summer of an artist possessed by a such an irresistible sense of life and beauty he extinguishes his own flame.

In the first piece, *A Child's Heart*, Hesse shares something of his childhood with us, a world overshadowed by the stern Protestant moralism of his father, a pastor. The child trips up trying to behave according to his excessively black-and-white moral code; then absolute trust in the parent is lost and, because this is a world of absolutes, a rebel is born. In the second piece, *Klein and Wagner*, a rebel is *not* born or rather born far too late, as a man in early middle age feels impelled to kick over the traces, defrauds money from his employer and flees to the glamorous and sensual Southland... In an accelerated few weeks of following 'the secret intentions of the heart' he experiences for the first time real solitude and the self-reflection it makes possible, real affinity with a woman and finally a sense of immersion in nature, a stripping away of his old self... In other words he experiences a rebirth. Although it sometimes seems a little forced and obvious *Klein and Wagner* might also be an excellent little guide to spiritual liberation.

The title story *Klingsor's Last Summer* itself is much more of a work of art, and one of Hesse's favourites. Partly autobiographical — Hesse fled from his early writing success and marriage to Ticino in Switzerland — it's also perhaps a fantasy version of the life Hesse would have liked to have lived himself if he'd been able to escape the narrow psychological bounds of his strict Protestant background. As an old man he said he had set out to live 'a real, personal, intensive life', and finally had become 'a writer, but not a human being'.

Klingsor is a larger-than-life artist, a heroic walker, drinker, painter, womaniser, boon companion... We see him at the height of his powers, aged forty or so as was the author, in the middle of his most creative period as he reaches a crescendo of joyous activity, living a splendid life in an artist's colony in southern Switzerland. Klingsor has embraced the Southern dream; 'We need so little for happiness.... eight or ten hours work a day, a bottle of Piedmontese, a half pound of bread, a cigar, a few girls, and of course warmth and good weather.'

*Klingsor* is beautiful and hopeful, celebrating a sensual and creative life, more than anything a life lived with attention and outlining possibilities of existence far from the dreary slavery to the comfortable and conventional most of us 'voluntarily' end up in. R K

'When he had painted for hours, restlessness drove him to his feet. Uneasily, unsteadily, he paced his rooms, the door slamming behind him, pulled bottles from the cupboard, pulled books from the shelves, rugs from the tables, lay on the floor reading, leaned out of the windows, breathing deeply... Everything blew about sadly when the rain-filled wind entered the windows. Among old things he found the picture of himself as a child, a photograph taken at the age of four; he was dressed in a white summer suit and under his light blond, almost white hair a sweetly defiant boy's face looked out. He found the pictures of his parents and photographs of old sweethearts of his youth. Everything occupied, excited, tensed and tormented him, pulled him back and forth. He snatched up everything, threw the things away again, until his arm twitched once more and he bent over his wooden panel and went on painting. Deeper and deeper he drew the furrows through the clefts of his portrait, broadened the temple of his life, more and more forcefully addressed the eternity of all existences, louder and louder bemoaned his transitoriness... Then he sprang to his feet again, a hunted stag, and tramped the prisoner's walk through his rooms. Gladness flashed through him, and the deep delight of creation, like a drenching joyous rainstorm, until pain threw him to the floor again and smashed the shards of his life and his art into his face. He prayed before his picture and spat at it. He was insane, as every creator is insane. But with the infallible prudence of a sleepwalker, in the insanity of creativity he did everything that furthered his work. He sensed with a deep faith that in this cruel struggle with his self-portrait more than the fate and the final accounting of an individual was involved, that he was doing something human, universal, necessary. He felt that he was once again confronting a task, a destiny, and that all the preceding anxiety and his efforts to escape and all the tumult and frenzy had been merely dread of his task and attempts to escape it. Now there was neither dread nor escape, nothing but pushing on, cut and slash, victory and defeat. He conquered and was defeated, he suffered and laughed and fought his way through, killed and died, gave birth and was born.' p332

## Steppenwolf [Der Steppenwolf]

Harry Haller, whose initials are suspiciously like the author's, is a cultivated, sensitive outsider, a fifty year old having a kind of giant mid-life crisis. It's not that he's suddenly decided his life, or the world in general ('this ravaged earth, sucked dry by the vampires of finance') is crapulous but that his violent internal contradictions are completely crushing his will to live. He feels that he has two beings inside him, the wolf of the steppes (the *Steppenwolf* of the title) and Harry the man, who each constrain and torment the other; neither allowing him to run free as wolf or live comfortably as a man. The wolf has made him resist the snares of bourgeois gentility but then he finds himself at the age of fifty a lonely man pottering around with his books, diaries and pictures stuck on the wall of his rented room...

*Stepppenwolf* is the extremely unpredictable and gripping story of how he gets out of this existential cul-de-sac, learns to tango, smoke dope, have the joy of beautiful women, become a real *mensch*. Obviously, it's a trick worth learning and has made this one of Hesse's cult books.

It's also Hesse's most structurally unorthodox book, getting away from his usual straightforward biographic narration. The Oriental, Freudian/Jungian and psychedelic paths to self-knowledge and self-liberation that *Steppenwolf* alludes to are represented in the structure of the story itself; Harry Haller's personality is disassembled and reassembled before us in the climactic final section, the famous 'Magic Theatre'. Because of this one could perhaps say that *Steppenwolf* is a book that is experienced as well as read.

The promise of the book to the reader is that if a stuffy, diffident albeit highly *simpatico* fifty year old can change his skin and discover the art of living then we should all listen up, instead of resigning ourselves to looking at life through grey-tinted spectacles. R K

'The few capacities and pursuits in which I happened to be strong had occupied all my attention, and I had painted a picture of myself as a person who was in fact nothing more than a most refined and educated specialist in poetry, music and philosophy; and as such I had lived, leaving all the rest of me to be a chaos of potentialities, instincts and impulses which I found an encumbrance and gave the label of Steppenwolf.' p643

## Strange News from a Another Star [Märchen]

This is a small collection of moral fables, simple and enjoyable, even when printed in Penguin Books' penny-pinching format of tiny type and cheap see-through paper.

*Augustus* is a clever and wise story about the problems of those gifted with an excess of charm and beauty when it is untempered by sympathy for others... *The Poet* treats a frequent theme of Hesse and is a beautiful myth-story, told in lyrical, elegiac storytelling, on the theme of artistic vocation, while the title story *Strange News from Another Star* is an odd but inspired science fiction piece about a youth visiting a version of our world from a better future. It is the Hermann Hesse version of the visionary novella *News from Nowhere* by the great English radical, designer and author William Morris.

The story called *Faldum* is also rather curious, full of magic and moral and no doubt meant to provoke endless reflection.

The collection ends with a very powerful story, *Iris*, which demonstrates Hesse's awareness of the enormously important, entrancing process of seasonal change, 'the lovely multiplicity of things' that nature unerringly delivers. A young boy immerses himself in this while playing in his family's beautiful garden. Then he grows up and becomes an academic and leaves his 'naïve' absorption with simple things far behind but eventually he hits a mid-life crisis 'It was no real happiness to be a professional... it was all stale and commonplace. Happiness once more lay far in the future and the road looked hot and dusty and tiresome'. *Iris* is really something of a warning — 'Was this life? Was this all?' and 'Whole years were missing, and when he thought back they stood there as empty as blank pages' — a story about remembering oneself and thereby coming into existence in a real sense. The collection ends with this piece, a clever and stimulating compilation of the themes of childhood sensuality, adult materialism, the mystery of love and the greater mystery of transcendent unity. R K

'...I demand a great deal from the man I marry. I make greater demands than most women... one thing I cannot and will not do without: I can never live so much as a single day in such a way that the music in my heart is not dominant...' *Iris* p 1 1 3

## The Thief [Der Dieb. Ein Novellenbuch]

Here is a writer you've probably never heard of who had a highly original, unpredictable use of words — 'the long hours on the dark tree' — as well as the sharpest humour; writing of the Louvre gallery in Paris for example — 'And suddenly she was only the ordinary Mona Lisa... which droves of English and Americans were herded past every day like swine.'

Heym was a brilliant but very short-lived Expressionist poet, working in this passionate, mercurial school of painting, poetry and film that astonished the world in the first quarter of this century. What this collection of stories show is that Expressionism can also work in prose, with extraordinary results, in the hands of a twisted genius.

Appropriately enough, the title story *The Thief* is about a man who is literally a maniac — his passionately mad view of the world, schizophrenia seen from the inside, is a perfect Expressionist vehicle. The second story *The Fifth of October* sees Heym make another huge imaginative leap, this time into the world of the poor at the time of the French Revolution, telling a tale of the mob storming the palace of Versailles with astonishing and powerful imagery — 'High above them in the cold October sky went the iron plough of time'.

Another story of madness is *The Madman,* which is frighteningly vivid, tragic and tremendously affecting, with echoes of Georg Büchner's play *Woyzeck.* Also startling is *The Autopsy* set in 'the cruel sobriety of the operating theatre' where there are 'giant needles like crooked vultures' beaks forever screaming for flesh'. Heym makes the supposedly creepy (Edgar Allan) Poe look more like (Winnie the) Pooh!

In fact this must be some of the most extraordinary stuff ever written, transgressive visions in an amazing language, inventive but true, exploring grim but real states of consciousness... The reason most of us haven't heard of Georg Heym must only be because of his death at the age of 24. Now in a sparkling translation and an elegant paperback edition there is no excuse to not explore these outer limits of literature. R K

'The door opened, the nurse came in from the neighbouring room with a lamp. While the door was open, he caught a glimpse inside. Up till midday it had been empty. He had seen the bed, which was a huge iron one like his, standing open like a mouth ready to snap up a new patient. He could see that the bed was no longer empty. He had caught sight of a pale head lying in the shadow of the big pillow. It looked like a girl, so far as he could make out in the dim lamplight. Someone who was ill like him, a companion in suffering, a friend, someone to hold onto. Someone who like him had been ejected from the garden of life. Would she answer him, what might her trouble be?

She'd seen him too; that he could tell. And their glances met in the doorway, a swift, transitory greeting, a short sign of happiness. And, like the soft wing beat of a little bird, his heart trembled with a new and mysterious hope.' p69

HEYM
Stefan

## The King David Report [Der König David Bericht]

Stefan Heym has been a thorn in the side of several regimes in the course of his long life. He left Germany for Czechoslovakia in 1933, and went to America in 1935. In the Second World War he fought in the American Army, but during the McCarthy period he returned his medals and went to live in East Germany, where he quickly fell foul of the authorities, keeping out of prison through a combination of his international status as a writer and his experience of dealing with secret services. After reunification in 1990 he won a seat in the German parliament as a representative of the PDS, the reformed communist party, to the dislike of a number of politicians who tried to discredit him as a Stasi (E. German secret police) collaborator. Since his years in America he has written most of his novels in both German and English.

Much of this experience informs Heym's best-known novel, *The King David Report*. Through an account of how the story of David in the Bible might have come to be told, the book provides a profound and witty examination of the relationship between the writer and the authoritarian state (also the subject of *The Queen against Defoe*), with many insights into the establishment and exercise of absolute power.

The historian, Ethan of Ezra, is ordered by King Solomon to produce the official version of the life of Solomon's predecessor David in *The One and Only True and Authoritative, Historically Correct and Approved Report on the Amazing Rise, God-fearing Life, Heroic Deeds, and Wonderful Achievements of David the Son of Jesse, King of Judah for Seven Years and of both Judah and Israel for Thirty-three, Chosen of God, and Father of King Solomon*. The sting is in the tail, of course: the purpose of the Report is not to publish the truth, but to legitimise Solomon's rule. Ethan, the scholar in the halls of power, has to perform a delicate balancing act. He pursues his researches among the state archives, and with David's soldiers and concubines, with Zadok the Priest, Bathsheba, and the rest, even taking a drug-induced trip to the witch of Endor. In spite of his awareness of the danger, he is driven by his historian's natural desire to find out what 'really' happened, but he knows that the report must contain what Solomon wants, while appearing to be the work of an independent writer. He cannot win. At the end he is banished, the king takes his concubine, and even appropriates his own poems, which we know today as 'the Song of Solomon'. History is not written by the Ethans of this world, but by those in power.

Solomon's Israel has all the appurtenances of the modern totalitarian state: secret police, show trials, agents provocateurs, citizens disappearing without trace or becoming 'non-persons', various factions jockeying for power, especially the priesthood and the military (a reflection, this, of the frequent conflict between the ideological and executive branches of the Communist state). Particular understanding of the situation of the writer is shown in the clever way that Solomon, who knows well what is going on in Ethan's mind, makes him into an accomplice. Ethan's moral refuge (besides the fact that he feels he has no choice if he wants to stay alive) is the traditional scientist's defence that it is his duty to gather the material, not to make value-judgments about it.

As well as the writing of history, *The King David Report* also throws light on the historical processes themselves. The Israelites under David are a nation at a key point in their development, at the time of transition from the bronze to the iron age. David begins their transformation from a group of nomadic tribes into a settled nation. David's empire, with its centralised bureaucracies, especially the army and the priesthood, is a response to historical changes to which a tribe must adapt or disappear. This is a further complication of the moral maze the novel presents, without providing a neat way out: if David's ruthlessness is simply a response to historical necessity, does that mean it is justified; and if it is historically justified, does that mean it is morally justified?

The language of the novel is a brilliant mixture of Biblical pastiche and modern phraseology, the latter often being used to reveal the naked truth behind the fine exterior of Solomon's public image. Heym's examination of questions of history, politics and morality in *The King David Report* is more serious in fundamental conception and also wittier in execution than the American writer Joseph Heller's use of much the same material in *God Knows*. M M

'I saw that Solomon had thought of practically everything, and that there was no escaping his favour. I also saw that I might end, as some writers did, with my head cut off and my body nailed to the city wall, but that, on the other hand, I might wax fat and prosperous if I guarded my tongue and used my stylus wisely. With some luck and the aid of our Lord Yahveh, I might even insert in the King David Report a word here and a line there by which later generations would perceive what manner of man David ben Jesse was: who served as a whore simultaneously to a king and the king's son and the king's daughter, who fought as a hired soldier against his own blood, who had his own son and his most loyal servants assassinated while loudly bewailing their death, and who forged a people out of a motley of miserable peasants and recalcitrant nomads.

So I rose and said to King Solomon that in his boundless wisdom he had persuaded me to accept the position...' p11

# HOCHHUTH
Rolf

## A German Love Story [Eine Liebe in Deutschland]

For those subjected while growing up to endless black-and-white, Sunday afternoon films on TV of the official Anglo-American view of the Second World War here is a fascinatingly other version of that conflict. Not from the 'German' point of view but from the perspective of the war against Nazi barbarity, a more profound struggle than the apolitical crescendo of purely military campaigns and actions from defeat at Dunkirk to victory in Berlin that our cinema mindlessly celebrates.

In fact Hochhuth's book is one of the most important postwar attempts by a German author to deconstruct the question of the individual and collective responsibility of German and Austrian citizens for the Nazi assault on the people of Europe.

*A German Love Story* is the romance between a young Polish forced labourer and a lonely German farmer's wife, that ends in the execution of the Pole and with the German woman going to a concentration camp. In telling this story from the point of view of all the participants, including the city authorities responsible for organising the execution, Hochhuth raises a series of issues about public participation in the crimes of the Nazi period. Amongst these are; the enormous popularity of Hitler in Germany and Austria; whether the armed forces who fought for Hitler can disassociate themselves from what Hitler stood for by claiming to be simple soldiers defending the Fatherland and finally, the soft treatment given to Nazi officials like the 'Peoples Court' judges who sent many innocent people to death or imprisonment in an anti-judicial process but who have subsequently received generous state pensions in West Germany and Austria. A surprise amongst Hochhuth's accusations, at least to this reader, an admirer of Switzerland's democratic tradition, was the discovery that Switzerland regularly returned escapees from Germany to the Nazi authorities.

Like the Austrian Thomas Bernhard, Hochhuth is a leading postwar novelist and playwright, and like Bernhard he speaks with a kind of sustained disgust and bitterness at his own nation, not so much for what was done in the name of Germany but at the way that subsequently most Germans have sought to avoid and evade responsibility for these profoundly barbaric acts or behaved as if they are part of a distant past. While the Jews famously have, amongst the 316 Talmudic commandments, the obligation of a 'Day of Atonement' once every year, the Germans as a nation have yet to manage five minutes of atonement in the fifty years since the war ended. Perhaps that is the meaning of Hitler's 'Thousand Year Reich'; as long as there is no demonstrable national repentance (either by the guilty generations or, failing that those that succeed them and bear the name 'German' — because who else?) it will take a thousand years before the adjective 'German' ceases to conjure up images that make the blood run cold. R K

'Those words — "I had nothing to do with it" — are the most overworked of any uttered in Germany since Hitler's death.' p167

# HOFMANN
## Gert

### The Film Explainer [Der Filmerzähler]

*The Film Explainer* is the sixth and last novel of Gert Hofmann to be translated into English before his death in 1993. The English translation has been done by the author's son, Michael Hofmann, a poet and literary critic who lives in London. The novel stays in the family even more as it tells the story of the author's grandfather, Karl Hofmann, the 'film explainer' of the title, to whom the book is also dedicated.

Film explainers used to, in the era of the silent film, play the piano, attired with tail coats or smoking jackets and equipped with a pointer tell the audience things like "Watch out, don't nod off, here comes a wonderful sequence, maybe the most wonderful in the whole film".

Karl Hofmann perfects his profession to what he fondly imagines is an art form. Especially when he takes his grandson, the narrator, into his confidence, it seems to be the most heroic, grand and glamorous occupation possible. The narrator, who huddles up in the front of the screen and watches his grandfather, is thereby introduced to the world of the cinema. For the grandfather, the cinema provides an escape from a life that is too prosaic for him, as well as a great excuse to avoid all other work, which he deems mundane.

Life is also made more bearable through his talks with Cosimo, an old friend of supposedly circus-like origins, who prides himself on his descent from a family of horse-knackers, and who always carries what he says is an 'authentic' used rope with him.

In order to widen the horizons of his grandson, his grandfather takes him on educational trips. So the little boy gets to see most of the cinemas in the area, which are then inspected. He also acquires a good knowledge of the silent movies of that time (neatly giving year and principal actors in brackets whenever a film is mentioned).

The book evokes a bygone era, where artists are still seen as suspicious creatures and closely associated with fairgrounds or the circus. But an era that is doomed from the beginning; at the time the little boy is initiated to the cinema, the world of his grandfather is already on the decline: many cinemas have closed down, and all of the ones they visit together have seen better days. While less people turn up each evening to see a film and have it explained to them by him, it is the arrival of the sound film that spells the end of Karl Hofmann's employment: his profession has died out. After losing his job, he gets depressed and then ill. Even after his convalescence he fails to find another job, most importantly for lack of trying. He does not contribute to the rent and makes himself a nuisance in the house.

Things start really to take a turn for the worse when Nazism finds its way into the village. Grandfather is befriended by two local party members, who buy him beer and let him drone on about his films whilst listening to his complaints about what he sees as his unfair dismissal. Shortly afterwards, Herr Theilhaber, the owner of the Apollo cinema, leaves the village, having sold the cinema and his other property fast and for very little. When grandfather brings his party career to a premature ending, it is not for ideological reasons. His new chums take him along to a Nazi rally in Berlin, where he is supposed to carry a flag with the other veterans. Unfortunately, he misses the rally because he steals away to watch the highlight of his cinematic experiences up till then, a showing of *Gone with the Wind*.

The book is beautifully written, evocative of a long lost era of silent films accompanied by piano music. Nazism creeps up on this atmosphere nearly imperceptibly until it permeates the atmosphere — films like *The Cabinet of Doctor Caligari* are succeeded smoothly by the likes of *Hitlerjunge Quex (Hitler Youth Quex)*, and the rupture we feel in retrospect passes nearly unnoticed. The book is not a nostalgic view of times gone by — there are no reproaches, no direct judgements, and the unerring voice of the child narrator keeps any hint of sentimentality at bay. Maren M

'As an artist, grandfather stood above Herr Erblich, yes, higher than any of us. He could look down on us. And it wasn't just that Grandfather was an artist, he also walked like one. Everywhere, even on the road to Mittweida, his artist's walk caught the eye. Farmers in their fields stopped to watch him. With the piano music he devised every evening, he felt his way into the plot, for instance in the Alpine drama, *The Blue Light* (1932, with Leni Riefenstahl and Matthias Wiemann). In that one, Junta is a young girl living in a village in the Dolomites as an outsider. (Grandfather does some girlish trills on the piano).' p39

## HORVÁTH
### Ödön von

## The Age of the Fish [Das Zeitalter der Fische]

Von Horváth was a successful young writer in Austria when it went Nazi in 1938 and then he had to flee. He died very shortly after but left this short, very readable novel which tackles head-on the vital question of what an individual can and can't do in the face of an evil political system.

It also, in telling the story of Austria under the Nazis from the viewpoint of a liberally-minded, not particularly enthusiastic schoolteacher, leaves us with fascinating and frightening material on the brutalisation and militarisation of youth under the Hitler regime.

As to the question posed by the book 'What good can one man do?' it arrives at a kind of answer — to seek and defend truth and justice — that is very much worth reflecting upon today because many of us are implicated in or connected to some kind of evil, to unjust, damaging goings-on and we can either take or let slip the opportunity to be a voice for the better, cleaner direction although it may be at some personal cost or loss of advantage. For the Austrian government authorities who secreted the household goods and valuables of murdered Austrian Jews in a warehouse for fifty years in the hope that eventually there would be no persons or descendants to claim them left alive, that would be a good reflection to make or for their Swiss banking friends sitting on millions of murdered people's money and concealing that from their heirs, and finally, when pressured, demanding to see death certificates for individuals exterminated in Auschwitz... R K

'...I knew I'd got to get on with my task of correcting twenty-six essays... I must be careful: I'm a state employee. It wouldn't do for me to venture the tiniest criticism. Even if silence irks me — what good could one man do? He must keep his anger to himself. I mustn't lose my temper.

Get on with your correcting. You want to go to the cinema tonight.

Well, what's this that N.'s written? I found myself reading: "All niggers are dirty, cunning, and contemptible." What rubbish! Cross it out.

I was on the point of writing in the margin "An unsound generalisation", when I pulled myself up. Hadn't I recently heard this very opinion of niggers? Where was it? Yes — it came out of the loudspeaker in a restaurant where I was having dinner — and quite took my appetite away.' p9

JAHN
Hans Henny

### The Ship [Das Holzschiff]

Hans Henny Jahnn is one of the great unknown writers of German literature. His most important work is the unfinished trilogy *River without Banks (Fluß ohne Ufer)*, now seen as a major twentieth century novel and which has even been placed alongside Proust's *A la récherche du temps perdu*.

*The Ship* is the first part of this trilogy. While it shows traces of Jahnn's involvement with Expressionism, it is still more traditional than the later parts of the trilogy, especially the middle part, the *Niederschrift des Gustav Anias Horn* (*Notes of G.A.H.*), with its more complicated narrative structure and heavy use of interior monologue.

Jahnn was the son of a ship's carpenter, grandson of a shipbuilder while he himself had a great passion for music and restored Baroque church organs for a living. He was in fact involved in various unusual sexual and religious explorations. After a rapid political and moral disillusionment from his experiences in World War One, Jahnn got himself released from the military on medical grounds and went to Norway for the rest of the war.

Formally, *The Ship* follows the structure of the traditional crime novel. It is set in the claustrophobic environment of the ship of the title. Gustave is on the ship as a stowaway, to be near to his fiancee Ellena, the captain's daughter. It transpires that the captain himself does not know about the content of the coffin-shaped crates in the cargo hold. Even before the departure, an unexplained fight breaks out so that some of the crew are dismissed as a consequence. There is the ominous figure of the supercargo, whose motives are completely unclear. He seems to know the secrets of this labyrinthine and mysterious ship and also be informed about the content of the cargo. All this secrecy spurs rumours in the close-knit community of the ship, and in his quest to find out more, Gustave too becomes entangled in a web of deceit, conjecture and panicky curiosity. When finally Ellena vanishes, the crew of the ship mutinies. After a while, Ellena is assumed to be dead, but what happened to her is never resolved.

The novel is sometimes reminiscent of Conrad's amazing *Heart of Darkness* with its search for the unknown and its half-expected horrors awaiting the travellers. A prevailing feeling of obscurity and uncertainty permeates the novel. We are never quite clear if the obscurity results from the complexity of the plot or the general unfathomability of the human soul... Maren M

'He had measured the various rooms on the ship by pacing them off, so as to be able to box them into the wooden hull according to a plan. He had almost succeeded in impressing on his mind their distribution and arrangement on the ship. The sealed hold, that forbidden ground, lay like a surveyable solid, sometimes above, sometimes under, sometimes beside him. It lost the mysterious attraction of the unknown once Gustave found out that it was limited and could be surrounded from the outside.

Then, suddenly, the blinding light of the supercargo's lantern was in front of him, the single eye of a dragon guarding his treasure, and at once Gustave was sobered and discouraged. He wasn't even able to put up a faint-hearted defense; he was defeated. [...] The lantern — it could have been the shipowner or Alfred Tutein, but it wasn't — it was the supercargo. No doubt about that. But from now on Gustave felt that he was being watched, even into the farthest corners, even if he went around on tiptoe [...] It was as if he were being pursued by erratic, pernicious powers.' p157

JELINEK
Elfriede

## The Piano Teacher [Die Klavierspielerin]

At the centre of this novel is the destructive and pathological relationship between a mother and her daughter. Erika has been moulded by her mother from earliest youth to be a famous concert pianist. Failing to satisfy this ambition she now works as a piano teacher in Vienna.

The mother-daughter relationship described by Jelinek is monstrous: mother and daughter live in the same apartment, where they share a double bed. This enables the mother to make sure that the daughter never touches herself improperly. Her greatest fear is that Erika should fall in love with a man who would then in turn take her away from her mother and destroy her mother's plans for her. She therefore makes sure Erika hardly ever goes anywhere without her supervision, and if she does, she will phone her at her destination to check up on her. Also, she strictly discourages, and if that does not work, actively forbids, Erika's spending time with anybody other than herself. When Erika does come home late, or does something forbidden like buying herself a new dress, mother and daughter fight, wrestling and pulling out each other's hair. All this is even more disturbing, considering that Erika's age in the novel is given as at least thirty-five years of age.

The mother has been systematically destroying her daughter's personality and has hindered any kind of healthy growth of self. But instead of focusing all her daughter's energies into her piano playing, she has unwittingly made it impossible for her daughter to thrive musically. The model into which she tries to press her daughter is bound to and even meant to be unsuccessful — really, she is destined only for failure, to satisfy the mother's longing to see her daughter fail as she had failed herself.

Together, they are united in the obsessive belief that Erika is a genius to be protected against a hostile world which is trying to distract her and destroy that genius. In turn Erika is scared at every sign of real talent from any of her students and duly suppresses it, making sure they will only ever reach mediocrity. Mother and daughter cannot bear the thought of something thriving, being healthy, because they themselves have been stifled in their growth.

Erika does not rebel openly, but resorts to more secret and furtive escape routes: she makes intricate plans like pretending to visit a concert, and then goes to see peepshows, the only female intruder into a world of cheap thrills and soiled tissues. These excursions advance to Erika spying on couples on the Prater meadows, armed with binoculars. Her new assertiveness progresses into an attempt to embark on a sado-masochistic relationship with one of her students. Unfortunately, she puts him off by handing him a list detailing suggestions of how she might best be tortured and humiliated. Having known nothing else she can only relate to pain and as she has no experience of human understanding, warmth or passion they are therefore meaningless to her.

At the same time, she is afraid of really being hurt, and therefore manages effectively to close the door on any affection the student might otherwise be prepared to give her.

After the student duly beats her up and leaves in disgust, she resigns herself to the failure of her social experiment and retreats to her mother.

Although it sometimes feels like Jelinek is merely caricaturing human relationships so that her characters become rather hard to believe in on the whole her observations are original and sharp, and often quite funny. Maren M

'Mother grabs a light-blue angora jacket that she crocheted herself and drapes it over Erika's shoulders. The lubricant mustn't suddenly freeze in these joints, raising the frictional resistance. The little jacket is like a cozy over a teapot. Sometimes useful things like toilet-paper rollers have such homemade caskets on them, with colourful pom-poms. They decorate the rear-windows of cars. Right in the centre. Erika's pom-pom is her head, which looms proudly. She trips along on her high heels across the smooth ice of the inlaid floor (areas subject to great stress are protected today by cheap runners). Erika heads toward an older colleague in order to receive congratulations from expert lips. Mother gently pushes her forward. Mother has a hand on Erika's back, on her right shoulder blade, on the angora jacket.' p68-69

## Wonderful, Wonderful Times [Die Ausgesperrten]

One of the most famous women writers in German, Jelinek said in 1980 'Austria is a criminal nation', referring to the largely unacknowledged Austrian participation in the crimes of the Third Reich, as a province of Greater Germany after 1938. From the very first page where she alludes to 'innocent perpetrators... with their wartime memories' she begins to beat her fellow countrymen with the stick of their enthusiastic participation on all fronts in the Nazi war against humanity.

Because this is a novel — and a good one — rather than a speech at the Nuremberg War Crimes Tribunal, the story of Austria's dirty war and the subsequent failure to come to terms with it is told through specific individuals. In particular there is an all-round monster of a man, who served with the SS on the Eastern Front 'up to... the ankles of our riding-boots in blood in Polish villages' and who is now trying to recapture the thrill of humiliating others by bullying his wife into posing for porno photos in the kitchen. His son, Rainer, is a kind of twisted boy genius sprung from the thin intellectual soil of the impoverished petty-bourgeoisie and full of bitterness and frustration. With his sister and two other youngsters he forms a little gang of nihilists who, from a mixture of personal motives and hang-ups, plot and carry out acts of random violence. Part of Jelinek's genius is to make this deeply unsympathetic quartet of adolescents sympathetic. Their world is one where the rapidly developing consumer prosperity of the 1960s of American youth fashions and music coexists with an older generation made up of 'war invalids ...thinking of the time when they were still somebody, on enemy territory in a foreign land, somebody they no longer were...'. She is writing of the time in which she herself grew up and brings a lovely detail of texture to her novel, felicitously translated by Michael Hulse.

What makes the book indispensable is its insistent air of reality, of honesty about things, for instance the limits of some peoples' lives — 'If you don't have the cash you get your sunshine from things you don't really need. Or else the daily grind...' — while others coast by sleazily on their borrowed grace 'Sophie's mother materialises, from out of a huge inherited fortune, in front of the huge iron gateway'.

A well-written assembly of characters that beautifully encapsulate the major strands of postwar Austrian everyday life, not so different from England — 'Sunday outings with Mother surface, trains smelling of damp socks, crammed with pathetic grey crowds of people of the kind a long war produces and cannot disperse right away' — but with the great difference that instead of having fought with sacrifice a just war this small nation is up to its gills in the blood of others. R K

'Father often thinks of the dark skeletons of people he killed. The white and immaculate snow of Poland turned bloody and maculate. But snow goes on falling, again and again, and by now it bears no trace of those who disappeared there.' p32

# JÜNGER
## Ernst

## Aladdin's Problem [Aladins Problem]

Written at the age of eighty-five, *Aladdin's Problem* shows the influence of the eighteenth-century mystic Emmanuel Swedenborg's philosophy on Jünger. It is clear that he became obsessed with the materialising of matter in the modern world and the problems that stem from it. In a first-person narrative he traces the life of Friedrich Baroh as he talks about his youth, marriage, subsequent divorce and his desertion from the Polish People's Army for the material wealth of the West. Very badly off, he manages to finish a degree in media and statistics (a curious coalescence of images and finance) and finally secures an entry-level position in his uncle's funeral parlor, *Pietas*. He continually improves on his position and, as the funeral home becomes more and more successful, so too does Baroh who uses his background in media for the commercial advancement of the business. Eventually, Pietas is bought out by a bigger company which plans something akin to a 'Disneyland for the Dead' known as *Terrestra*. Located in Turkey, the place is to be the final resting place for thousands, to the great financial enjoyment of the investors.

Though symbols and mythology generally abound in Jünger's work, in a way, the growth of the funeral business is reminiscent of the great Norwegian writer Knut Hamsun's *Growth of the Soil* as Baroh moves from his humble beginnings as an impoverished graduate student to wealth and respectability in the material world. However commerce and spirituality make uncomfortable partners and by the fourth section of the novel,

Baroh too finds that he has become a part of one of the more insidious forms of commercialisation which reduces the dignity and integrity of the deceased to plots of statistical size and measure that will be cost effective for the corporation. As Baroh improves economically, he regresses intellectually. The things that interested him as a young man — philosophy, literature, art — pale as he becomes financially solvent and as the metaphysical becomes undermined by the material.

In fact, the notion of some colossal social and spiritual disaster haunted Jünger all his life and writing specifically about 'the problem' he says, 'Aladdin preferred the life of a minor despot. Our lamp is made of uranium. It establishes the same problem: power streaming toward us titanically.' M R A

'The problem is invisible; man is alone. Ultimately, one cannot rely on society. Although society usually wreaks harm, indeed often havoc, it can also help, although not more than a good physician — up to the inevitable limit where his skill fails.

Above all, no melancholy. The individual can comfort himself by recognizing his situation. Earlier, the religions contributed to this. Their close link to art is no coincidence, for they are its most sublime inventions.

Now that the gods have abandoned us, we must fall back on their origin: art. We have to gain an idea of what or whom we represent. There has to be a workshop somewhere. A potter throws vases, pitchers, ordinary tableware. His material is clay. Everything emerges in the ebb and flow of tides, then crumbles into dust, and becomes new material for us.

Our social or moral position makes no difference in this regard. You may be a prince or a wage earner, a shepherd, a prostitute, a pickpocket — but usually you are like me, an ordinary person.

Everyone had his duty, his task. What was the idea when we were created, what was our mission? — anyone who gives us even an inkling of that has ennobled us.' p11-12

Jelinek

Jünger

## On the Marble Cliffs [Auf den Marmorklippen]

Jünger is as famous for who he was and what he did (and didn't)
do as for his books, of which this is the most celebrated. Unlike
most of the authors of his generation who are still read he was
not a left-winger or a liberal forced to keep a very low profile or
flee from Germany altogether in the Hitler period. Jünger was,
rather, a professed right-winger, associated with various
nationalistic and militaristic circles. He neither openly espoused
nor resisted the Nazi regime but enlisted in the *Wehrmacht* and
was part of the forces occupying Paris.

One might say that he behaved rather like some institutions
that managed to coexist fairly conveniently with Nazi barbarity,
the Catholic Church for instance, and that had it both ways; so
that after the war one could see Bishops who had shamelessly
collaborated (in Belgium for example) while there were Catholic
priests who had been supporters of the resistance in France.
Jünger willingly served as an officer in Hitler's Wehrmacht and
attended meetings of the order of the Iron Cross even as the war
was ending, while also having friends amongst the anti-Hitler
Stauffenberg plotters — although he wasn't part of that plot.

But more interesting in the end is the book, the work of art
this morally ambiguous man leaves behind him.

*On the Marble Cliffs* is undoubtedly one of the most intense
and virtuoso pieces of writing in German in the twentieth century.
It is set in a kind of Utopia, 'the Marina', a tranquil, exquisite
place of quiet libraries, jolly taverns and lovely gardens. The joys
of drinking new wine with old friends in a beautiful place are
appropriately celebrated — 'more highly than those hours which
sped in sparkling wit we treasured the quiet homeward path under
the deep waters of intoxication through garden and field.' Marina
is a permanent spring carnival, an ideal town for lovers, drinkers
and scholars. Inevitably there is a snake in this Eden — a power
struggle breaks out and rather like in Tolkien's *Lord of the Rings* a
Dark Lord gathers up all the most evil and embittered riffraff of
the countryside and launches a war that results in horrible
destruction. As the churches and libraries of Marina burn one is
chillingly reminded of the fate of Germany itself in 1944-45 as
enthusiastic bombing reduces ancient cities to rubble. The really
chilling thing though is that Jünger published this book in 1939.

It's not hard then to read *On the Marble Cliffs* as an allegory of the Hitler time and its likely (and actual) outcome. The book is a marvellous, acute account of how a dictator conserves and consolidates his power by spreading suspicion and embroiling as many as possible in his dirty deeds. It is not however an anti-war book. It can't be because it is a celebration of the warlike manly spirit. (Jünger's women, predictably enough in this scenario, are bearers of sons and bakers of cakes). Side by side with a respect for learning and reason that populates his Utopia with libraries and herbariums is a parallel worship of the dark gods generally held to be their opposite; 'Once when we were drinking with the Condottiere he looked into his wine-dewed glass as if it were a mirror that held the images of times long past, then he said pensively: "No glass of noble wine was more precious than the one they handed to us beside our machines the night we burnt Saguntum to the ground". Then we thought: "It is better to fall with him than live with those who grovel in the dust from fear."'

Hundreds of thousands of copies of *On the Marble Cliffs* were in circulation in 1939 and 1940 when the German military were 'joyously' burning down plenty of Saguntums.

Nevertheless this is a stunning book, with many grains of truths amongst the poisoned fruit. R K

'When we are happy our senses are contented with however little this world cares to offer. I had long done reverence to the kingdom of plants, and during years of travel had tracked down its wonders. I knew intimately the sensation of that moment when the heart ceases to beat and we divine in a flower's unfolding the mysteries that each grain of seed conceals... I caught the fragrance of the white-starred thorny valleys where I had drunk in the bitter springtime of Arabia Deserta, or the scent of vanilla which refreshes the wanderer in the shadeless furnace of the candelabra woods. Then there opened up like the pages of some old book memories of hours spent amidst savage profusion — of hot marshes where the Victoria Regia blooms, of tidal groves seen sweltering at noon on their pale stilts far from the palm-lined coast.' p26-27

# KAFKA
Franz

## Stories 1904-1924

Kafka is one of the defining writers of the twentieth century, perhaps the one who, more than any other writer, reflected modern man's feeling about the world. In particular, it is his articulation of the sense of being an outsider, which can be seen by different readers in personal, social, religious or psychological terms, that so many have found compelling.

The very nature of Kafka's stories means there is a multitude of opinions as to their precise significance. With their realistic style and fantastic content, they are not portrayals of individualised characters, but parables of existence. What Kafka has left out, is the truth these parables illustrate: 'The kingdom of heaven is like unto a mustard seed' Christ said; what is 'like unto' being transformed into a gigantic, verminous insect? This openness of interpretation is one reason for the power these stories have exerted over readers all over the world.

The most famous story of all, *The Metamorphosis*, begins with the hero Gregory Samsa (his surname, like those of so many of Kafka's main characters, echoes the author's) waking up to find he has been transformed into a huge verminous insect. As he tries to get up and carry on with his normal life, there is a touching and humorous contrast between his thoughts, which try to ignore the change, and his actions, which implicitly acknowledge it. There is more humour in Kafka than is often recognised.

Much of the story concerns the reactions of the family, as observed and interpreted by Gregory. His sister is the only one able to accept Gregory in his new form and she automatically takes charge of looking after him. But she is also the first to face up to the fact that for her this insect is no longer her brother, the first to call him 'it'. At the end Gregory's transformation is paralleled by his sister's positive change from an adolescent girl into a young woman.

His mother swoons at the sight of him in a bustle of underskirts, and avoids actually having to see him, thus managing to retain her image of Gregory her son. His father reacts aggressively, and also reassumes his role as family breadwinner which Gregory had taken over from him. (The same father-son relationship/conflict is the subject of another story, *The Judgement*.)

The story is in three sections. At the end of each Gregory 'breaks out' (as the family see it) of his bedroom, to be driven back by his father. In his final emergence, he is drawn by his sister's violin-playing. For some time he has found the insect-food his sister puts out as unpalatable as human food, and the music seems to be the spiritual nourishment he has been looking for. His death is peaceful, just a gradual fading away, a willing sacrifice to, or at least acquiescence in, the family's interests. The acceptance of guilt (whether real or imagined) is one of the pervading themes of Kafka's stories and novels.

Guilt, punishment and redemption are the themes of another of the longer stories, *In the Penal Colony*. A distinguished foreign traveller is visiting a penal settlement situated in some tropical colony where he witnesses a demonstration of a curious execution machine. The condemned man is strapped into the device, which then inscribes the law he has broken on his body, gradually cutting deeper and deeper until, after twelve hours, the man dies. The officer in charge of the machine is both judge and executioner, although his first role is not very onerous, since he bases his decisions on the principle that guilt is invariably beyond doubt. He believes that before they die the victims achieve insight into their crimes, and transfiguration, which is visible in the look of enlightenment that appears on their faces at the sixth hour.

The officer's demonstration of the machine develops into a harangue to persuade the traveller to speak up in support of it. It was developed by the old commandant, and the new commandant would like to see it abolished. When the traveller refuses, the officer lets the condemned man out of the machine, strips, and takes his place. The machine adjusts itself to receive him and starts of its own accord. Soon the old machine begins to disintegrate and the officer, instead of being inscribed, is merely spiked. The end is typically ambiguous. The expected look of enlightenment cannot be seen on his face, but the expression in the dead man's eyes is 'one of calm conviction'. M M

'Gregory Samsa woke from uneasy dreams one morning to find himself changed into a giant bug. He was lying on his back, which was of a shell-like hardness, and when he lifted his head a little he could see his dome-shaped brown belly, banded with what looked like reinforcing arches, on top of which his quilt, while threatening to slip off completely at any moment, still maintained a precarious hold. His many legs, pitifully thin in relation to the rest of him, threshed ineffectually before his eyes.

"What's happened to me?" he thought. This was no dream. His room, a normal human room except that it was rather too small, lay peacefully between the four familiar walls.' p91

# Kafka

## KAFKA
Franz

### The Trial [Der Prozeß]

An uncanny book, written in the early 1920s before the totalitarian bureaucracies, Communism and Fascism, that reduced everyone to frustrated impotence were fully in place, and yet capturing exactly the powerlessness of the citizen of an uncivil society.

We are given an imaginative reconstruction of a textbook case; a man is kidnapped by the state but has no redress or argument to make because his kidnappers act under orders of a higher, quite impersonal authority — 'we are humble subordinates'. The victim is the profoundly respectable, respectful K. Happy with his routine life as Chief Bank Clerk and his regular visits to his mistress he only wants to smooth out the waves created by his arrest. Predictable enough, but far less predictable and with a delicious element of truth, is the scene where he acts out with a female accomplice an eroticised version of his arrest and appearance before the elusive but powerful 'commission' that is investigating him. In the course of this private action replay we realise that the 'application of the law' sexually excites them both; we are then forced to realise that the obedient citizens of the state are, au fond, in some kind of masochistic thrall to it. Kafka is poking about into the deepest, darkest most secret links between man and man (and no doubt woman and woman) in a hierarchical system of power... He is the literary sociologist and psychoanalyst of our modern corporatist society.

As well as this *The Trial* is a metaphor for how we experience life; the self-doubt and the appeal to outside opinion for reassurance. All this is told with Kafka's unique and hard to replicate style of apparent naturalism interlarded with bizarre details — a fat old washerwoman is endlessly pursued by an infatuated young student — why? No explanation, no rationale, just the juggernaut of a reality somehow made more real by details that don't appear realistic at all.

Kafka himself had studied law and worked in a bureaucracy and flashes of sardonic wit based on close acquaintance with the real procedures of authority light up the book — the court 'is impervious to proof... but it is quite a different matter with one's efforts behind the scenes'. The tribunal that has arraigned him is always associated with rooms full of stifling never-changed air; a hallmark to this day of the machineries of justice and bureaucracy, with their sealed windows, their sealed-off environments impervious to common logic and humanity.

After K.s multiple and hopeless battles with the wily and nebulous operations of the law the book finally reaches an abrupt and terrible ending, which chillingly prefigures the operations of the law courts of the Stalinists and Nazis, whose 'judges' and officials have never, in Russia or Germany or Austria, been punished for their cruel assaults on ordinary citizens... R K

'The great privilege, then, of absolving from guilt our Judges do not possess, but they do have the right to take the burden of the charge off your shoulders. That is to say, when you are acquitted in this fashion the charge is lifted from your shoulders for the time being, but it continues to hover above you and can, as soon as an order comes from on high, be laid upon you again. As my connection with the Court is such a close one, I can also tell you how in the regulations of the Law-Court offices the distinction between definite and ostensible acquittal is made manifest. In definite acquittal the documents relating to the case are said to be completely annulled, they simply vanish from sight, not only the charge but also the records of the case and even the acquittal are destroyed, everything is destroyed. That's not the case with ostensible acquittal. The documents remain as they were, except that the affidavit is added to them and a record of the acquittal and the grounds for granting it. The whole dossier continues to circulate, as the regular official routine demands, passing on to the higher Courts, being referred to the lower ones again, and thus swinging backwards and forwards with greater or smaller oscillations, longer or shorter delays. These peregrinations are incalculable. A detached observer might sometimes fancy that the whole case had been forgotten, the documents lost and the acquittal made absolute. No one really acquainted with the Court could think such a thing. No document is ever lost, the Court never forgets anything. One day — quite unexpectedly — some Judge will take up the documents and look at them attentively, recognize that in this case the charge is still valid, and order an immediate arrest.' p177-178

# KÄSTNER
## Erich

### Fabian [Fabian]

In the English-speaking world Erich Kästner is chiefly known as the author of *Emil and the Detectives*, the first of a long series of children's books. But in German-speaking lands his reputation rests on two other genres. He is known as a poet, writing *Gebrauchslyrik* ('useful poetry'), comparable perhaps to John Betjeman in England, but dark where Betjeman is genial. The other celebrated work is his first novel, *Fabian* (1931), a satirical portrait of the last years of the Weimar Republic — the state that came into being at the end of World War One with the collapse of the Kaiser's German Empire in 1918 and that lasted until Hitler's Third Reich (that began in 1933).

The central character is Jakob Fabian, thirty-two, well-educated but pretty hopeless, and working in Berlin as an advertising copywriter. He wanders like a latter-day Candide (the naïve protagonist of Jean-Jacques Rousseau's book of the same name) through the 'telephone bars' with their easy pickups, the fairgrounds where working people compete to win a stick of salami, and (when he loses his job) the unemployment exchanges whose every applicant inevitably lands up in the wrong place. He comments on events but cannot influence them. He loses his girlfriend to the cinema and sees his best friend commit suicide. Finally, he returns to his home town, but there the peace is of the grave.

Such a summary makes *Fabian* sound despairing, and so it is, but the book is redeemed by strong humour, the vividness of its many cameo-like scenes, and the accuracy and insight it consistently shows about both people and society. Fabian is a partially-developed character, and the rest are flat, so the novel is poised between satire and semi-autobiographical realism, which may weaken it artistically, but sometimes strengthens its interest. The scenes which show Fabian's attachment to his mother for instance increase the book's emotional depth, and hint at another novel, never written.

*Fabian* has always been a controversial book. On publication, it was attacked by the German right as sexually explicit and hostile to tradition. Nowadays it is more likely to be viewed as sexist in its view of women, particularly lesbians. At the Nazi book-burning of 1933, Kästner was the only author present to see his book burned. This unflinching observer can still touch us today. C H

'There was a mirror on one side of the lift. Fabian took out his handkerchief and rubbed the red blotches from his face. His tie was askew. His temple was burning; and the pale blonde was looking down at him. "Do you know what a megaera is?" he asked. She put her arms around him. "Yes, but I'm prettier."'
p11

## Infanta [Infanta]

In an imaginary ('Don't get lost on the way home. Bear right and keep heading for the silence.') but well-detailed — including plant-names and climatic nuances — tropical outpost called Infanta, located somewhere between Guatemala and the Philippines, a mysterious stranger, Kurt Lucas, arrives and ends up staying at a charming run-down Catholic mission. The missionhouse is inhabited by five elderly priests, greedy for jam, cake and the distraction a stranger brings. There is also, need we say, a beautiful woman — Mayla — very young but with a past.

*Infanta* seems to be the classic tropical scenario, the Englishman Somerset Maugham's Singapore or the Uruguayan Juan Carlos Onetti's Santamaria, with the difference that somewhere slightly offstage an enormous political struggle is going on, similar to the one that overthrew the Philippine dictator Marcos in the name of 'Peoples' Power'.

Directly on-stage however is the love-affair of the handsome but vacuous Lucas (he's a male model!) and the tropical thunderstorm of a woman, Mayla. There's also a *simpatico* defrocked priest who runs a shop that hires out paperback romances by the hour, a nightclub singer with the voice of the century and a police chief who is, naturally, in charge of all smuggling operations.

As in the Maugham tradition figures from nearer home — Lucas the model with his *Milano* jetset life-style or his erstwhile agent, the power-lunching Elisabeth Ruggieri — are examined against an exotic backdrop (and found wanting).

Along the way there is a rather good evocation of a certain kind of third world locale, all written with knowingness and good humour — which make it seem an extraordinarily unGerman book, if a slightly overlong one. R K

'Flanking the main street were Infanta's few solidly-constructed buildings; town hall and school, mayor's office and church, police headquarters and post office. A little way off the road, cobbled together with planks, was the cockfighting arena. The rest of the town consisted of shacks, shanties and diminutive shops resembling abandoned puppet theatres. Many sold nothing but bananas suspended on lengths of thin string, no more than six or seven at a time. Others exuded an aroma of rubber goods and liquorice or rented out serialised books, which also dangled from strings.' p25

# The Gunner Asch Trilogy [Die 08/15 Trilogie]:

# The Revolt of Gunner Asch [08/15 in der Kaserne]

# Gunner Asch Goes to War [08/15 im Krieg]

# The Return of Gunner Asch [08/15 bis zum Ende]

These novels present a picture of the German army in what was perhaps the most crucial period of Germany's modern history. The reader is taken from prewar 1938 in a small barracks town (*The Revolt of Gunner Asch*) to the Russian front and the home front (*Gunner Asch Goes to War*), and on to Germany in defeat and the arrival of the American occupation forces with the task of denazifying the German population (*The Return of Gunner Asch*).

The first novel introduces the main characters, most of whom appear in the later books, and concerns itself with the senseless rules and physical and mental cruelty used by the army to break down individual thought and, with it, individual free will. Herbert Asch, however, refuses to allow his individuality to be compromised. Throughout the novel, Asch is presented as a smooth operator who manages to use the system to his personal advantage, but the point comes when he decides to openly take a stand against absurd regulation. There are no procedures for dealing with flagrant insubordination, except to declare him psychologically disturbed, and the irony is that he ends up being promoted, making his campaign of defiance something of a failure.

Kirst does not confine himself to a simple evocation of prewar army life, but attempts to explain the support for the Hitler regime among the army and the German people itself. We are invited throughout the novel to laugh at the less sympathetic characters, with the interior monologue as a favourite device.

By the time we see Asch actually involved in war, his character has hardly developed. He continues to use the system for himself and the protection of his fellow soldiers. In *Gunner Asch Goes to War*, the German and Russian armies are in a stalemate, staring at each other across no man's land, with the ordinary soldiers on both sides sensing their common situation. With the advent of spring, though, the soldiers anticipate more action. Lieutenant Wedelmann, a loyal (but sympathetic!) Hitler supporter, commands the unit until he is replaced by Witterer, who has seen no active service, but says he intends to show the 'Russkies' what's what. Women are not entirely absent from the action — we have the mysterious Natasha, the Russian patriot whom Wedelmann falls for, and a young concert-party singer who, with Asch's help, fights off Witterer's advances. Much of the comedy in the novel emerges from the scenes back at the home barracks where the trivial concerns of the characters here stand in marked contrast to conditions in Russia.

Although the final novel in the trilogy shows how the various characters from the previous two novels (and some we had not yet met) cope with impending defeat, it also tells the story of how Asch pursues a certain Colonel Hauk and his murderous henchman, Greifer, opportunists who have sacrificed ordinary soldiers' lives to break through an American-held crossroads in order to retrieve their caches of black-market goods. Asch is determined to bring them to justice. This novel is the least comic of the three and deals in most depth with what motivated German soldiers and civilians to support the Nazi regime. The American Counter Intelligence Corps is hard at work looking for Nazi sympathizers and Kirst presents various shades of grey — in one case, there is a distinction drawn between being a member of the National Socialist party, and being a 'Nazi', a view which many would regard with some suspicion.

These novels do not have to be read in sequence, although it is interesting to see one view of the German army and civilian population developing through the years of the Third Reich. All three are entertaining in their own right, and all concern themselves with some of the serious issues arising out of Germany's involvement in the Second World War. M B S

"'You know as well as I do what you think of Witterer. He's a candidate for a bullet in the back if ever I saw one. Look, Lieutenant: Colonel Luschke is fighting this war for his Fatherland. His trouble is he doesn't know just where to find his Fatherland at the moment. You are fighting it because you believe in your Führer and Fatherland and you want to keep it a clean war. But this man Witterer is a very different proposition. He's fighting the war for its own sake. He enjoys it. He enjoys the idea of killing men and walking about with a chest full of medals. And I haven't got any use for a creature like that. Nor have ninety per cent of the troop.'" *Gunner Asch Goes to War* p135-136

## The Night of the Generals [Die Nacht der Generäle]

*The Night of the Generals*, like most of Kirst's novels, has the German army as its backdrop. It is a detective novel, but not in the conventional sense, since its setting (Warsaw 1942; Paris 1944; East and West Berlin 1956) also provides the opportunity to discuss serious issues such as the question of personal responsibility for Germany's involvement in the Second World War among the higher ranks of the army.

The novel opens with the discovery of a Polish prostitute's brutal murder in German-occupied Warsaw in 1942. There is only one clue to the murderer's identity: a witness has seen someone in the building wearing a German general's uniform. Major Grau, the maverick head of counter-espionage, is determined to identify the murderer, high-ranking officer or not. There are three possible suspects, all generals of one sort or another and all of whom may have had motive and opportunity. By the time we reach the Paris of 1944 it is obvious who has committed the original murder and a further carbon-copy, and the focus switches from solving the crime to catching the villain. By this time, Grau has been cleverly disposed of because he is getting too close to the truth and it is now up to Prévert, Grau's contact in Paris, to bring the murderous general to justice. Although the 'whodunit and how is he caught' part of the novel drives the plot, the real meat is the development of the main characters' personalities, peculiarities, relationships with each other and attitude to the war.

One entertaining subplot involves Wilhelmine von Seydlitz-Gabler (the General in command's wife) and her attempts to marry off her wayward daughter to General Tanz. Regarded by many as the epitome of the German warrior, his various obsessions (he even checks whether his car engine is clean with a white handkerchief) arouse our suspicions. Many of the comic elements of the novel emerge through such subplots, but there is also an atmosphere of biting irony as we see various characters trying to justify their part in the events of the war as they happen and again fifteen years later. This is probably most clearly seen in the evocation of the Stauffenberg plot which was an assassination attempt on Hitler on 20 July 1944 by high-ranking officers in the armed forces. In the course of the book, one of the generals tries to persuade von Seydlitz-Gabler to support the planned coup, but he refuses to commit himself and, despite his later claims to have acted honourably, it is obvious that he is never willing to take personal responsibility for anything until the outcome is clear and his personal safety is assured.

The concluding part of the novel which takes place in Berlin fourteen years after the Warsaw murder is orchestrated by Prévert. He brings together all the main characters in order to catch the murderer and it is here in particular that some of the characters rewrite their own histories.

The structure of the novel is episodic and because each scene is relatively short and imbued with suspense the pace is sustained. Each chapter is interspersed with an 'interim report' consisting of retrospective personal statements, extracts from official reports and diary excerpts by the characters involved in the events. This additional detail often guides the reader on the trustworthiness or otherwise of some of the characters and contributes to the ironic tone.

This novel is certainly worth reading for its entertainment value, but also because it deals with the issue of German officers' personal responsibility for the war, a subject which continues to exercise the minds of many today. M B S

'Frau Wilhelmine slept the sleep of the watchdog. Ulrike dozed uneasily, either because her conscience pricked her or because the thick duvet on her bed was too hot for her. General von Seydlitz-Gabler sweated profusely and dribbled into his pillow. Kahlenberge tossed and turned, dreaming of labyrinthine intrigues. Grau lay curled up like a worm. Prévert stared wearily into the darkness. General Tanz lay supine, deathly still and smiling faintly like a marble effigy on some medieval tomb.' p207.

KOEPPEN
Wolfgang

## Death in Rome [Der Tod in Rom]

According to an impelling and artfully concise introduction by the book's translator Michael Hoffman *Death in Rome* is the work of a brilliant German novelist caught between two eras; the bestial time of the Nazis and the idiot time of 1945-1960, the 'blank slate' when Germans preferred to pretend one could just start from the 'Year Zero' of 1945 and lay aside the memory of the preceding period.

From the first few pages it is clear what an exceptionally

fine (if under-recognised) writer Koeppen is as the reader is taken up and swirled along in an exciting rush of perfectly-chosen and placed words. Here is the rhythm of a passionate and powerful thought-stream, something like Thomas Bernhard but with a wider scope than the Austrian locales that that author restricted himself to. To illustrate the skill of Koeppen (and his exceptional translator, a successful poet) a barracks scene; 'There had always been a picture of that twitchy and repressed type, the Führer, with his Charlie Chaplin moustache, looking benevolently down on his herd of sacrificial lambs' or an old woman feeding members of that tribe of cats that inhabit Italy's ancient monuments; 'Severed heads of sea-creatures, dull eyes, discoloured gills, opalescent scales, tumble among the yowling moggy mob' or, irresistibly, about a cabman's horse 'The horse had a fly-net over its head and ears. It looked down on the paving-stones with the empty disappointed expression of an old moral theologian.'

There is more here though than descriptive fireworks as the participants for the first postwar reunion of a powerful German family meet in Rome in the early 1950s. The lynch-pin of this family gathering is a monstrous old brute called Judejahn, former SS-man and now working as a superior officer for an Arab country's army. He, it emerges, is an utterly brutal and brutalised man, an intimidated little boy inside but one clothed in the black uniform of power. He seems to represent the German soul itself, feeling weak and fearful inside but corrupted by a stifling and vainglorious militarism and nationalism already a hundred years old when Hitler cashed in on it. This state of affairs led in this German author's view inevitably to the gigantic national disgrace of the Third Reich.

*Death in Rome* in fact, through the various characters of a German family tells the chilling story of the aftermath of Nazism. An aftermath which, rather than an attempt to atone for recent crimes was the recreation of German arrogance in a society of petty ambitions and fat bellies, portrayed here as already cautiously sniffing around for future 'glory'. It is also an affectionate portrait of a fabulous city, Rome. R K

'I love the Via Veneto, the cafés of Vanity Fair, with their funny chairs and colourful awnings, I love the leggy, slim-hipped models, their dyed hair the colour of flame, their pale faces, their great staring eyes, fire that I can't touch, I love the happy, stupid athletic gigolos in attendance, traded by the wealthy corseted ladies... I love the old mouldering bathing-ship anchored in front of the Castle of the Angels on the turbid Tiber, and its naked red light-bulbs in the night, I love the small, secret, incense-steeped, art- and ornament-crammed churches... I love the priests in their robes of black, red, violet and white, the Latin Mass, the seminarians with fear in their faces, the old prebendaries in stained soutanes and beautiful greasy Monsignor hats... I love the little shop-keeper in the Street of the Workers, cutting great slices of Mortadella like leaves, I love the little markets, the fruit-sellers' stalls all green red orange, the tubs of the fishmongers full of obscure sea-creatures and all the cats of Rome prowling along the walls.' p51-2

KUBIN
Alfred

## The Other Side [Die andere Seite]

Kubin was an artist whose primary medium was pen and ink. He was one of the best-known and most influential book illustrators of the first half of this century. His works record a fascination with the grotesque, with decay and horror, and dark sexual fantasies; the writer for whom he illustrated the greatest number of books was Edgar Allan Poe. Among his contemporaries he is probably closest in feeling to Mervyn Peake, illustrator and author of the wonderful *Gormenghast* trilogy.

He was originally commissioned to illustrate Gustav Meyrink's *The Golem* (see review here), the author supplying him with the text chapter by chapter, as it was written. When Meyrink's inspiration dried up, Kubin used the illustrations he had done as the starting point for a fantastic novel of his own, *The Other Side*, the only novel he wrote.

The story is told by a graphic artist living in Munich who is visited one afternoon by an emissary of an old school-friend, Claus Patera, who has inherited fabulous riches. He has used his wealth to found an empire of his own, the Dream Kingdom, cut off from the rest of the world by an immense wall somewhere in central Asia. Patera rejects the modern world of science and technology and has built and furnished his realm by buying up old objects — everything from small utensils to whole buildings — in Europe and transporting them to Asia. Nothing later than the 1860s is allowed in the Dream Kingdom.

The narrator accepts Patera's invitation, and he and his wife travel — via Samarkand — to Perle, the capital of the kingdom, being forced at the frontier to jettison any possessions the officials consider too modern.

Perle turns out to be a murky, twilit world, full of dilapidation and decay, where the logic of everyday existence appears not to apply. The Dream Kingdom gradually takes on the atmosphere of a nightmare. A visit to the dairy behind their flat, for example, turns into a descent through a labyrinth of dripping passages; a runaway horse, so emaciated it is no more than a living skeleton, suddenly charges past; when the narrator emerges the door leads into the coffee house where the customers and waiters are just recovering from the 'Brainstorm' which visits all the inhabitants whenever the inhabitants' resistance to their fate grows too strong.

Patera remains inaccessible to his old school friend, ensconced in a huge palace and guarded by an impenetrable bureaucracy that anticipates Franz Kafka's *The Castle*. Under the strain of the grotesque irrationality of this world, the narrator's wife falls ill and dies. The narrator himself, after his initial resistance, succumbs to the all-pervading atmosphere, allowing himself to be drawn into the twilight world of Patera's kingdom and experiencing a series of surrealistic dreams. He also produces his best work as an artist.

Into this lethargic community bursts a dynamic figure: Hercules Bell, an American multimillionaire who is the exact opposite of all that Patera represents. The two, Patera and Bell, gradually swell into gigantic figures and the conflict between them assumes apocalyptic proportions, the final battle that destroys Patera and his kingdom turning into a cosmic cataclysm.

The narrator survives to tell the tale, which reads like an allegory of a journey into the unconscious, to the dream world which is an essential part of creation. But only one part. The world, the final paragraphs seem to say, is a hybrid of the dark forces of death and the bright sunlight of life. M M

'As I started across the river, I sensed that the miller was standing behind me. "I murdered him," he growled, and tried to push me into the water. Then, to my astonishment, my left leg grew to enormous length so that I could step efforlessly across into the motley crowd on the opposite bank. And then I heard about me a multifarious ticking, and became aware of a great number of flat clocks of almost every size, from church clocks and kitchen clocks down to the smallest pocket-watches. They had short stubby legs and were creeping about in the meadow like turtles to the accompaniment of an excited ticking. A man dressed in soft green leather with a cap that looked like a white sausage was sitting in a leafless tree and catching fishes out of the air...' p150

## The Lovely Years [Die wunderbaren Jahre]

Christa Wolf, the most celebrated East German writer and privileged member of the GDR's (German Democratic Republic, the official name of Communist-ruled East Germany) licensed cultural elite shouldn't become the only literary witness to that peculiar ex-country. Reiner Kunze who experienced life there both as a part of that elite — a university teacher who resigned his post in disgust — and then as an industrial worker tells a very different story.

In forty-nine little episodes, *The Lovely Years* provides flashlight portraits of telling incidents in the lives of young GDR citizens, from schoolchildren learning their Leninist ABC to teenagers arrested for trying to escape the socialist paradise. The tone is generally pretty scathing as an atmosphere of crippling pettiness combined with terribly efficient surveillance in the streets, railway stations and schools is described.

The period is the late 1960s and early 1970s and there is something fascinating about seeing the preoccupations of those times; anti-war movement, spirituality, rock music — the prevalent youth culture in fact but from the perspective of East German youth. While anti-war goes down well enough in the GDR as long as you don't try to get out of serving in the Peoples' Army it's perilously easy to be branded an 'unreliable element' and from there things can only go downhill. However a good deal of the petty cruelty of policemen and teachers towards rebellious, perhaps longhaired, youth is extremely reminiscent of Britain in the same period, where dissidence against a dying Victorian morality and petty-bourgeois rectitude was not widely welcomed.

There are things here that would be funny if they weren't so sad; the East German troops drafted in to help 'liberate' liberal-communist Czechoslovakia in 1968 are kept in the Bohemian woods completely cut off from the outside world but treated to two to four hours 'political instruction' every day. Similarly the little kid asked who the 'good guy' Lenin is replies, after some thought 'The Captain'. There's a lack of irony or other sophistication here that stops it becoming outstanding writing but it's a very readable, concise document of a particular time and place of European history, a history lived by millions of people. R K

'The girls and the boys who were sitting on the corner bench in the empty railway station had come from a pop concert. Their conversation soon dried up. One after the other they rested their heads on the shoulder of the person next to them. The first train didn't go until 4.46 a.m.

Two railway policemen, with an Alsatian on a leash, peered round the doorway, walked over to the bench and tugged the sleepers' sleeves. "Either you sit up straight or you leave the station. We must have order here!"

"How do you mean, order?" one of the boys, having straightened up, asked. "Can't you see we've each got our head on our own shoulders again?"

"Any more lip from you and we run you in, understood?" The policemen continued their round.

The youngsters leaned the other way.

Ten minutes later the patrol returned and turned them out of the railway station. A fine drizzle was falling. The hand of the big clock flicked to the figure one like a rubber truncheon.' p3

LASKER-SCHÜLER
Else

## Concert [Konzert]

The famous Viennese critic, Karl Kraus, called German-Jewish Else Lasker-Schüler 'the strongest and most impenetrable lyrical force in Germany' but this collection of charming and tender short prose pieces — reminiscent of the American avant-garde writer Djuna Barnes at her best — is highly 'penetrable', in fact enjoyable and often lighthearted. In pieces with titles like *The Sea*, *The Ginger Cat* and *The Inca Butterfly* an unusual and winning talent produces an elliptical but emotional vision of life.

Lasker-Schüler is generally seen as part of the Berlin Expressionist group of poets and painters. Her particular obsession was the attempt to leave the 'exile of everyday life' via the transfiguration of reality through art. Exile from the consciousness imposed by everyday routine became real physical exile from Germany after Hitler's ascent to power and her move to Palestine.

As one can divine from the famous photograph of Lasker-Schüler dressed up as 'Prince Jussuf', on which the Babel Guide's illustration is based, the writer was fascinated by Middle Eastern themes, part of a reaching out from the secular rationalism of her German background towards the Jewish roots she saw as suffused with mysticism and exotic knowledge. Perhaps more in tune with current preoccupations is her mixing — again like Djuna

Barnes or the Brazilian writer Ana Cristina César — of her real self and her literary self in her pieces, delighting in creating a seamless fabric of I, not-I and fantasy persona that perhaps mirrors more accurately than the fixed positions of narrator/author/character the actual way of human consciousness.

In the end though this is simply the unique voice of a brilliant and unusual woman and a very enjoyable book; a translation that is a fine tribute to a person who represents so well the synthesizing and hopeful directions that Weimar culture of the 1920s and 1930s was taking in literature, drama, painting, film and music. It was a great cultural renaissance for a land previously laid low by Prussianism but one that was soon to be dismantled and destroyed by the provincial nationalistic beasts that took the country over in 1933 and forced the likes of the gentle and sensitive Else Lasker-Schüler into exile. C C & R K

'When I ride back to Berlin from my lecture tours, I look out the train window, and my eyes leaf through the living picture-book of the world, and on my last trip home, it happened that the setting sun actually spoke with me. I was crying a little, but I was like a child, with a tear still hanging from its lashes. It was seen by the white sun, which I at first thought was the moon; it was already past twilight, and I was tired and sleepy from looking at the striped fields and the meadows' delight in flowers, and the trees marching along; the fir trees and poplars run with giant strides out of the way of the rushing train. I think they hate the sprinter, it frightens the birch brides and the harmony of growth, its breath makes the silver grasses in the fields dusty and their heavenly ally is happy to rain on the flag of grey and black sparks that blows from the train. I gazed into the pale white moon, into the little tent of peace. "It's the sun," said a fellow passenger. She understood the geography of heaven and earth better than I, because even before the train stopped, she knew where we would stop; she was familiar with even the smallest village. However, I asked the faithful, white-filled circle again: "Are you the sun? So light up my belief in this world in which I have to live, year after year, hour after hour with its sixty minutes; have to stay awake, subject of the most everyday chamberlain. And I would like to sleep a thousand times, if that were possible in a miracle minute." A frightened rabbit ran across the path, and for the first time I saw a deer in its natural habitat, with yellowy-brown branches on his head. He wasn't frightened either by the tempestuous insistence of my heart or by the speed of our machine, and I smiled questioningly at the white sun, which suddenly, in response to a magic word from God, turned into a glowing red ball and — fell into my lap.' p138-139

**Laske-Schüler**

## The Monument [Völkerschlachtdenkmal]

As an idealistic young journalist and writer in the East Germany of the 1950s, Erich Loest fell foul of the authorities and was sentenced to seven years in prison. After his release he resumed his career as a writer. A novel chronicling the lives of ordinary people in the Communist state was published, but led to further difficulties with officialdom, so that Loest eventually moved to West Germany in 1981. Since then he has achieved both critical acclaim and a wide readership for novels which tell stories of ordinary people, at the same time reflecting wider issues of recent history and politics.

*The Monument* is the only novel of Loest's to have been published in the UK so far. The monument of the title is the tower dominating Leipzig built in 1913 to celebrate the hundredth anniversary of the Battle of the Nations, in which various the Allied Powers defeated Napoleon, bringing about the end of his domination of central Europe. The theme of the novel is German history from the Napoleonic period to the present, seen from an unusual perspective, that of the perpetual underdogs and losers, the Saxons, whose capital Leipzig is: they remained loyal to Napoleon in 1813, and they fought on the Austrian side when Prussia defeated them in 1866; in 1871 they were mere adjuncts to the Prussian victory over France; their moment of glory in 1913, when the building of the monument put Leipzig in the forefront of German nationalist sentiment, was soon eclipsed by the war, inflation and then Hitler.

After the founding of the GDR, Leipzig bathed in the limelight for a few years as Ulbricht's (Walther Ulbricht 1893-1973, Leipzig-born, was a dominant figure in the GDR 1951-1971) Communist state seemed to be dominated by Saxons. With Honecker's (Erich Honecker 1912-1994 a miner's son, ruled the GDR 1973-1989) accession, however, the traditional domination reverted to 'Prussia': even though many of the Berlin elite came from other parts of Germany, they are felt to have absorbed the 'Prussian' ethos, which the German Communist seems to embody.

Loest tells his story through a very imaginative flashback technique that gives it a lively tone, at the same time constantly relating the events of the past to the present. The narrator is

Alfred Linden, a demolition expert, who is being interrogated by the security service after being caught entering the monument with the intention of blowing it up. Although for many years a loyal citizen and a member of the local establishment, Linden is dismayed by the plans to complete the obliteration of Leipzig's identity by demolishing the central church and the university (the local beer has already been 'rationalised'), and he decides to blow up the monument in protest. That, however, is not what leads to the lengthy interrogation. It is the result of what Linden stumbled on when he broke in: the cellars, which the SS had used as a hidey-hole at the end of the war, have been turned into the control centre of a nuclear power complex, which the Communist government has secretly leased to a West German power company.

Through his researches into the past, Linden has come to identify with several figures associated with the battle and the monument. The attachment is so close that at times during his interrogation he speaks with the voices of these other personas. The figures include a simple Saxon soldier, who tried to defect when Napoleon's defeat was obvious, but who was killed by marauding Prussians; a member of the local gentry who collects skulls from the battlefield which he plans to erect into a monument; a Polish-German worker who was employed as a mason on the monument; and his own father, who worked in the quarry that supplied the stone. A future perspective is provided by Linden's son, who has moved to Berlin — joining the 'Prussians' — and made his career in the Communist Party.

Loest handles the complex interweaving of voices and time-scales with great confidence and skill. The lively, amusing narrative articulates the experience of ordinary people, and is particularly good at creating a sense of what life was like for working men and women behind the façade of battles and monuments and party propaganda. M M

'I had to clean soil and grass off a metal ring in the slab in front of the Pussenkomm family stone — this would be a week ago now — before I could pull the covering of the vault to one side. I found the SS-men's escape tunnel intact, droplets of water glistening on the beams. For about twenty metres in, it was shored up with short-barrelled Carbine 98s, of which there was an abundance lying around the end of the war. As I moved forwards on hands and knees, I held my torch between my teeth. I recognised one niche; tins of dripping and beef had been piled up in there. And Scho-Ka-Kola — a chocolate confection whose name has become a historical byword. At the first main pillar there was a bend in the passageway, I looked up and saw the initials VM: Voiciech Machulski had immortalised himself in the pressed concrete. Under them lay my five ack-ack shells. I can tell you, my mouth went dry. The shells lay there wrapped up like papooses. I unpicked the knots in the string and undid the wrappings; the leaf-patterning on the tarpaulin was still discernible, it was well known that the Waffen-SS used a particular design. The grease broke open with a crackle, under it the metal lay shiny and dry, the detonators were in perfect condition. I caressed the shells, lifted one and carried it to the foot of the buttress I intended to blow up. That was when I came across the unexpected door and stepped into the brightly lit room. And at that moment the men in the yellow overalls rushed me.' p30-31

MANN
Thomas

## Buddenbrooks. The decline of a family [Buddenbrooks. Verfall einer Familie]

*Buddenbrooks* is based on the story of Thomas Mann's own family, a North German merchant dynasty. Originally it was planned as a brief work but expanded to become the massive epic that made Thomas Mann's name.

It is a chronicle of the half-century from 1835 to the 1885 covering the vicissitudes of four generations of a Lübeck merchant family, through the four firstborn sons Johann senior, Johann-Jean junior, Thomas and finally Hanno. At the same time as we learn of the fate of the Buddenbrooks we follow the fortunes of the North German bourgeois class in general and of the historic port city of Lübeck in particular.

Within the solid, confident structure of the novel the slow decline of a family unfolds. While Johann senior incarnates the perfect bourgeois citizen who is perfectly in accord with his surroundings and follows the norms without even having to think about them, his son Jean is already, if only occasionally, questioning them, thereby initiating the process towards decay. With Thomas, one of the major protagonists of the novel, the crisis shows itself. Despite the success that seems to follow him and his sticking to a rigid self-discipline that maintains him in the groove of family tradition, Thomas is anxious, unsettled and becomes ever more doubtful and impotent.

Thomas is the one to introduce the artistic strain that Mann sees as so irreconcilable with solid bourgeois pragmatism into the family line. This comes about through his marriage to the fascinating and exotic Gerda, who plays the violin. Their son, the delicate and weak-willed young Hanno, is very far from being a model bourgeois with his hypersensitive aesthetic nature and succumbs to a premature death. His sister, Tony, goes on to become custodian of the dynasty's ashes and is one of the most moving characters of the book in her fierce attachment to memories of the family's glorious past and her ingenuous conviction that this glory will eternally survive. C C

The contradiction or conflict between the solid and self-confident (and no doubt rather insensitive) bourgeois character and the artistic soul was a great theme with Mann, returned to in much of his most celebrated work and something that emerged very clearly from his own background. However one responds to this theme — and today perhaps the dichotomies of human types have shifted ground a little — Mann's brilliant use of language and the superb architecture of his books continue to make him essential reading and a bridge into a wise and human world. R K

'One day, some three quarters of an hour before dinner, Hanno had gone down alone to the first storey. He had practised for a long time on the piano, and now was idling about in the living-room. He half lay, half sat, on the chaise-longue, tying and untying his sailor's knot, and his eyes, roving aimlessly about, caught sight of an open portfolio on his mother's nut-wood writing-table. It was the leather case with the family papers. He rested his elbow on the sofa-cushion, and his chin in his hand, and looked at the things for a while from a distance. Papa must have had them out after second breakfast, and left them there because he was not finished with them. Some of the papers were sticking in the portfolio, some loose sheets lying outside were weighted with a metal ruler, and the large gilt-edged notebook with the motley paper lay there open.

Hanno slipped idly down from the sofa and went to the writing-table. The book was open at the Buddenbrook family tree, set forth in the hand of his various forbears, including his father; complete, with rubrics, parentheses, and plainly marked dates. Kneeling with one knee on the desk-chair, leaning his head with its soft waves of brown hair on the palm of his hand, Hanno looked at the manuscript sidewise, carelessly critical, a little contemptuous, and supremely indifferent, letting his free hand toy with Mamma's gold-and-ebony pen. His eyes roved all over these names, masculine and feminine, some of them in queer old-fashioned writing with great flourishes, written in faded yellow or thick black ink, to which little grains of sand were sticking. At the very bottom, in Papa's small, neat handwriting that ran so fast over the page, he read his own name, under that of his parents: Justus, Johann, Kasper, born April 15, 1861. He liked looking at it. He straightened up a little, and took the ruler and pen, still rather idly; let his eye travel once more over the whole genealogical host; then, with absent care, mechanically and dreamily, he made with the gold pen a beautiful, clean double line diagonally across the entire page, the upper one heavier than the lower, just as he had been taught to embellish the page of his arithmetic book. He looked at his work with his head on one side, and then moved away.

After dinner the Senator called him up and surveyed him with his eyebrows drawn together.

"What is this? Where did it come from? Did you do it?"

Hanno had to think a minute, whether he really had done it; and then he answered "Yes."

"What for? What is the matter with you? Answer me! What possessed you, to do such a mischievous thing?" cried the Senator, and struck Hanno's cheek lightly with the rolled-up notebook. And little Johann stammered, retreating, with his hand to his cheek, "I thought — I thought — there was nothing else coming.'" p424-425

MANN
Thomas

## Death in Venice [Der Tod in Venedig]

*Death in Venice* is currently the single most celebrated work by Thomas Mann, even though in fact it is extremely short and, narratively speaking, simple. A successful German composer takes a holiday in Venice, becomes infatuated with a beautiful young boy staying at the same hotel, nothing happens and he dies. And so much happens, and so much is said; about the fatal link of passion and obsession (Stendhal said 'a man without obsessions has not lived'), about the vulnerability of the cultivated soul, the aesthete, to the raw and wayward force of sexual attraction...

The fate of the composer, Aschenbach, a figure reminiscent of the real composer Gustav Mahler, in Venice, portrayed here as a heavenly, corrupt and voluptuous maze, has been read as a literary statement about the decline of the self-confident European civilization of the turn of the century. A civilization shortly to fatally disenchant itself in the blood and mire of trench warfare. But most striking is the portrayal of a finely-tuned, detached and solitary personality unwittingly (but at the same time somehow willingly, greedily) led into a hell of unrealisable passion.

Aschenbach is neurotic, artistic, alone and consequently the rebellion of his inner, repressed nature that topples him is devastating and unforgettable. In awesomely limpid prose Mann uncovers the contradictory construction that every human soul must in some degree be as he unravels the specific mystery of an artist's nature, that combustible mix of discipline (for the sake of artistic practice) and licence (for the sake of artistic sensibility). One of the small group of genuinely unmissable twentieth-century works... R K

'Afterwards he mounted again in the lift, and a group of young folk, Tadzio among them, pressed with him into the little compartment. It was the first time Aschenbach had seen him close at hand, not merely in perspective, and could see and take account of the details of his humanity. Someone spoke to the lad, and he, answering, with indescribable lovely smile, stepped out again, as they had come to the first floor, backwards, with his eyes cast down. "Beauty makes people self-conscious," Aschenbach thought and considered within himself imperatively why this should be. He had noted, further, that Tadzio's teeth were imperfect, rather jagged and bluish, without a healthy glaze, and of that peculiar brittle transparency which the teeth of chlorotic people often show. "He is delicate, he is sickly," Aschenbach thought. "He will most likely not live to grow old." He did not try to account for the pleasure the idea gave him.' p33-34

MANN
Thomas

## A Man and his Dog [Herr und Hund]

If Bertolt Brecht was the giant of German-language theatre in this century then Thomas Mann is the fiction equivalent. Some of his most famous works like *Buddenbrooks* or *The Magic Mountain* though are forbiddingly large. Mann however also wrote brilliantly-fashioned, profound novellas like *Death in Venice* which are perhaps better places to start with this unmissable writer.

Extreme sceptics who imagine German literature must be as heavy, if nourishing, as German bread could start with this beautiful, happy and lighthearted piece (usually collected with other novellas by Mann) about exactly what its title promises, a man (Thomas Mann) and his dog (called Bashan).

*A Man and his Dog* demonstrates a gentle understanding of a fellow-creature in a close relationship that develops from puppyhood on. A close relationship that was especially important for a man of difficult and cool temper like Mann. Bashan and Thomas' exploits on their walks around the neighbourhood and along the riverbank, encountering hares that Bashan can never quite catch, are pure delight. Bashan is a dog of character and independence of mind who instinctively hates and barks at 'policemen, monks and chimney-sweeps'. The details of dogness are beautifully observed and captured; Bashan is heard 'coughing in the odd, one-syllabled way that dogs have' and there is here that crucial realisation of how an animal's companionship can release us from the mad self-importance of the merely human world.

Mann was a clever writer but — and this seems a German strength — not a cerebral one, and here as in his other work he celebrates the physical, felt, simple world. A world that blesses us if we let it. R K

(A chased hare runs in desperation to Mann, *ed.*)

'Was it beside itself with fright? Anyhow, it jumped straight at me, like a dog, ran up my overcoat with its forepaws and snuggled its head into me, me whom it should most fear, the master of the chase! I stood bent back with my arms raised, I looked down at the hare and it looked up at me. It was only a second, perhaps only part of a second, that this lasted. I saw the hare with such extraordinary distinctness, its long ears, one of which stood up, the other hung down; its large, bright , short-sighted, prominent eyes, its cleft lip and the long hairs of its moustache, the white on its breast and little paws; I felt or thought I felt the throbbing of its hunted heart. And it was strange to see it so clearly and have it so close to me, the little genius of the place, the inmost beating heart of our whole region, this little being which I had never seen but for brief moments in our meadows and bottoms, frantically and drolly getting out of the way — and now, in its hour of need, not knowing where to turn, it came to me, it clasped as it were my knees, a human being's knees: not the knees, so it seemed to me, of Bashan's master, but the knees of a man who felt himself master of hares and this hare's master as well as Bashan's. It was, I say, only for the smallest second. Then the hare had dropped off, taken again to its uneven legs, and bounded up the slope on my left....' p278

## MANN
Thomas

### Tonio Kröger [Tonio Kröger]

*Tonio Kröger* is an early work by Mann, published when he was only twenty-seven, a short sweet novella of schooldays and adolescence that he still considered a favourite work at the end of a long writing career. In fact *Tonio Kröger* is dazzling; perfectly concise and well-observed throughout.

This tenderly autobiographic piece is the story of young Tonio, born into an important merchant family of the stately old port town of Lübeck in North Germany. Tonio possesses, unlike his stolid German classmates, an exotic and different woman, a Brazilian, for a mother and feels himself a sensitive 'poetic' outsider... This differentness becomes a central focus of his existence and eventually takes on a slightly farcical colouring when he becomes infatuated, in an admiring schoolboy way, with his classmate Hans Hansen. Tonio — like most of us? — finds himself loving the 'wrong people'; he is fascinated by opposites; while he is a serious, reflective youth he is fascinated by lighthearted superficial types. He is completely enchanted by the handsome blue-eyed Hans and his 'perfect life' and hopes for spiritual communion with this very down-to-earth boy.

Obviously no joy can come of this, or of a subsequent passion for a conventional blonde girl, and the book ends somewhat histrionically with young Tonio partaking in solitary, reflective travelling, brooding by lonely northern shores on the sea-coast of Sweden.

There are some enjoyable Victorian touches in this book, somewhat reminiscent of Conrad, perhaps particularly in the classic Lowe-Porter translation; 'he addressed himself constantly to the whisky-bottle, which stood at his place at luncheon and dinner, and breakfast as well'. How rarely whisky bottles are 'addressed' these days!

At the core of the book though is the true story of the emergence of an artistic sensibility, a creative personality (Mann himself) of enormous importance and gifts. The inescapable tensions between the desire to belong to our human herd, to wallow securely in common humanity and the simultaneous sharp but lonesome vision of the artist-outsider have never been more carefully or sympathetically evoked. A stunning and wise book in English or German. R K

'Tonio Kröger stood wrapped in wind and tumult, sunk in the continual dull, drowsy uproar that he loved. When he turned away it seemed suddenly warm and silent all about him. But he was never unconscious of the sea at his back; it called, it lured, it beckoned him. And he smiled.

He went landward, by lonely meadow-paths, and was swallowed up in the beech-groves that clothed the rolling landscape near and far. Here he sat down on the moss, against a tree, and gazed at the strip of water he could see between the trunks. Sometimes the sound of surf came on the wind — a noise like boards collapsing at a distance. And from the treetops over his head a cawing — hoarse, desolate, forlorn. He held a book on his knee, but did not read a line. He enjoyed profound forgetfulness, hovered disembodied above space and time; only now and again his heart would contract with a fugitive pain, a stab of longing and regret, into whose origin he was too lazy to inquire.' p121

## Silent Close No.6 [Stille Zeile Sechs]

This 'Silent Close' is a pleasant tree-lined street where members of the East German Communist party elite live and the book is an unsympathetic inside view of that elite. It probes the psychohistory of many of the 'power-hungry children of the proletariat who had worked their way to the top... their fear of everything they didn't understand, which is why they banned so much.'

The young woman protagonist, Rosalind — separated, disillusioned, sympathetic — is herself from a Communist family and has certainly had it with the German partyocracy, even though she has to study Communist Party history in the 'Barabas Research Institute' (where she has 'learnt not to think for money') until the day comes when she realises that "every day I took my one and only life to the Barabas research institute the way I threw kitchen garbage into the rubbish bin".

Her search for an alternative source of income leads her to encounter an ageing member of the party elite, Beerenbaum, who hires her to record his memoirs. Gradually, she builds up to confronting him personally with his and the party's dark deeds both in wartime exile in Stalin's Moscow (when many German Communists were executed by the secret police) and during the early years of 'building socialism' when Beerenbaum was a heavy-handed political official at a university. This confrontation between the founders of the Communist state and its children — those born and brought up under its strictures — is the novel's centrepiece, going to the heart of the tragic story of East Germany. When it was founded, amidst the ruins of Nazism, it absorbed the genuine idealism of many good men and women but ended up as worth no more than a bunch of hard-currency bananas to most of its citizens by 1989.

Although written with a certain doomy North German depressingness, *Silent Close No.6* has some interesting detail of GDR existence, such as the role of what were referred to apparently as 'the soldiers on the invisible front' — the famous *Stasi*, (for *Staatssicherheit* or State Security) the efficient and innumerable secret police, and seemingly, German Communism's 'greatest achievement'. R K

'Rosalind bent forward, her arms resting on the typewriter keys. With every syllable she jerked her head in the air like a barking dog. "Confiscating brains. You confiscated grey matter because you had too little of it yourselves... You liberators of mankind had enough body, but you lacked brains. Did you know Latin? You do not know Latin, therefore you forbade others to learn Latin. Those who did were thrown in jail so everyone would forget such a thing as Latin existed. Everything had to be forgotten in order that people didn't find out anything you didn't know."

'Supported by his healthy hand, Beerenbaum tried again to sit up straight in his chair. His voice was compressed, breathless with pain or rage. "We have forgotten nothing. Never. We always knew what hunger and cold were, damp apartments, rickets, unemployment, war. Our university was class struggle. Our Latin was Marx and Lenin. Go forward and do not forget. You have forgotten. What do you really know?"

"Nothing. We know nothing," Rosalind cried, her face so twisted she could barely recognize herself. "Nothing, because we were not allowed to live. Your own life was not enough for you, it was too mean, so you used up our life, too. You are cannibals, slave owners with an army of torturers."' p173-4

MEYRINK
Gustav

## The Angel of the West Window [Der Engel vom westlichen Fester]

*The Angel of the West Window* is based on the life of the Elizabethan scholar and sorcerer, John Dee, using much of Dee's own writings. An imagined twentieth-century descendant inherits Dee's notebooks and, with the help of drugs and a mysterious ghostly Russian, is transported back into the past and into the mind and body of his ancestor.

The theme of the novel is alchemy, which John Dee pursues as a path to spiritual knowledge, while for his associate, the rascally Edward Kelley, it is merely a means to fame and fortune. The two main settings of the story are Elizabeth's England and the Prague of Emperor Rudolf II, who was keenly interested in alchemy and occult knowledge.

More powerfully realised than Dee are the servants of the predatory goddess, Black Isais, who seek to entangle Dee and his modern cousin and drag them down to spiritual death. The most vivid is Bartlett Greene, a larger-than-life figure who embodies a kind of negative spiritual energy in some scenes — for example the *Taghairm*, the sacrifice of fifty cats, or his burning at the stake — which make the reader's flesh creep. M M

'Bartlett Greene had set his huge body swaying from the iron chains, as if he were dancing. As the first light of a may morning filtered into the cell, the crucified outlaw swung higher and higher, and with a lithe gracefulness, as if he were enjoying the motion of a hammock slung between two silver birches. And all the while his joints and sinews crunched and cracked as if he were stretched on the rack.

And then Bartlett Greene began to sing! At first his voice was almost melodious, but it soon took on the screech of bagpipes, as he ground out a hoarse hymn to earthly pleasures:

> heave ho! All night Tom plays on his fiddle
>
> After the moult of May.
>
> heave ho!
>
> While Kitty sings hey diddle diddle
>
> To the moon and Black Isaye
>
> Heave ho!' p61

MEYRINK
Gustav

## The Golem [Der Golem]

*The Golem* was Meyrink's most successful novel — it sold 150,000 copies within two years of its publication — and the one for which he is still remembered. It is *not* the book of the famous Expressionist film of the same name, the first version of which was made in 1914, just after Meyrink's novel was serialized in a magazine. The legend of the Golem, the artificial creature made from clay by the sixteenth-century Rabbi Löw of Prague, which is the subject of the film, appears only indirectly in the novel, as a mysterious presence symbolizing the spirit of the old Jewish ghetto, and as a ghostly *Doppelgänger* of the hero, Athanasius Pernath.

The main story is set in the old Jewish quarter of Prague, whose dark alleyways and labyrinthine houses had, since the ghetto had been formally abolished in 1852, become an attractive resort for thieves and prostitutes. Until it was largely pulled down in the decade following 1895, the old Jewish quarter had the exotic attraction of a district of ill repute, and this is the setting for *The Golem*, the brooding atmosphere of which Meyrink evokes with the vivid intensity of Dickens' London.

The story revolves around the search of the central character, Athanasius Pernath, for identity and self-knowledge in a sequence of mysterious and mystifying events, many relating to the harelipped Jewish junk-dealer, Wassertrum, who lives opposite. The half-crazed student, Charousek, is plotting Wassertrum's murder; Wassertrum is Charousek's father , but he sold Charousek's mother into prostitution after seducing her; Wassertrum wishes to destroy Dr.Savioli, whom he believes drove his son to suicide, and attempts to blackmail Savioli's lover, Angelina, whom Pernath feels he knew before he lost his memory after an unhappy love-affair; the wanton Rosina, who lives with Wassertrum — is he her father? — is the mistress of Loisa, who commits murder to get money for her; Wassertrum plants the victim's watch on Pernath, who is arrested for the murder; in prison he meets Laponder, a sex murderer; he is a medium, and through his dreams Pernath makes contact with his spiritual love, Mirjam — but it is hinted that she was Laponder's victim, as it is also hinted that Charousek and Laponder are other identities of the hero, Pernath.

The narrative thread is tangled, precise relations and outcomes often being left unclear. But this adds to the powerful suggestiveness of the novel, which charts the spiritual progress of Pernath from confusion to transfiguration. This is reflected in his relations with women: after a crude sexual experience with Rosina and a romantic interlude with Angelina, Pernath is united with his spiritual love Mirjam, in a consummation in some realm 'on the other side.'

*The Golem* teems with mystery, dreams, crime and the supernatural. It also contains a search for occult truth and mystical enlightenment, largely represented by Mirjam's father, the archivist Hillel, whose teaching combines the mysticism of the Jewish Cabbala and the symbolism of the Tarot pack.

In the brooding sense of *angst* with which the ghetto is suffused, the novel comes close in feeling to Expressionist films such as *The Cabinet of Dr.Caligari*, and this, combined with the occult and mystical elements, produces a dreamlike novel of haunting power. M M

'And again and again, that smudge of white... that smudge of white! "It's a card, a miserable, stupid little playing card!" I sent the scream echoing round my skull, but in vain... now it was... was taking on human form... the Juggler... and was squatting in the corner and staring at me with vacant eyes out of *my own face!*

For hour after hour I sat there without moving, huddled up in my corner, a frozen skeleton in mouldy clothes that belonged to another. And across the room he sat, he... I... myself.

　　　　Mute and motionless, we stared into each other's eyes, the one a hideous mirror-image of the other. Can he see the moonbeam too, as it sucks its way across the floor as sluggishly as a snail, and crawls up the infinite spaces of the wall like the hand of some invisible clock, growing paler and paler as it rises?' p110-111

MEYRINK
Gustav

## The Opal and other stories

Meyrink's short stories contain the elements of the grotesque, horror, the supernatural, and the interest in the occult that are found in his novels. Many also have a strong satirical element directed at the sacred cows of imperial society (both the German and Austrian versions), and not a few have a touch of the absurd.

His most stinging mockery is reserved for the military (*The Black Ball, Wetherglobin* and incidental digs in many others), followed by doctors (*Blamol, The Ardent Soldier*) and academics (*The Automobile*).

Many stories seem to meander from one mode to another, from horror to satire, to eroticism or humour and back again. In *The Ring of Saturn* for example, a science-fiction story is hijacked halfway through to satirize the church; *Bal macabre* is the disjointed result of eating magic mushrooms; in *What is the Use of White Dog Shit?* we follow the narrator's unsuccessful attempts to discover why army veterans collect the strange substance mentioned in the title.

While some attack targets belonging to the past, *Petroleum, Petroleum,* in which a disgruntled scientist threatens to avenge himself by covering the seas in crude oil, becomes more and more relevant with every shipwrecked oil-tanker.

The tales of the macabre, especially those involving the gruesome preparation of human organs, are probably the most powerful and most disturbing. The masterpiece of this genre is undoubtedly *Dr. Cinderella's Plants.* M M

'Everywhere the same wooden trellis-work and, as I could now clearly see, overgrown with veins, evidently all patched together, in which blood was coursing.

　　　　In amongst them countless eyeballs glistened horribly, sprouting alternately with hideous warty nodules like blackberries, and following me slowly with their gaze as I passed. Eyes of all sizes and colours, from brightly shining irises to the light blue tone of the eye of a dead horse...' p109

## Punishment [Die Züchtigung]

Written in 1985 *Punishment* was Anna Mitgutsch's debut novel which won two literary prizes: the *Brüder Grimm Preis* and *Die Goldene Claassen Rose*. With its roots in autobiography Mitgutsch's book confronts the ambiguous and complex relationship of mother and daughter via the sad and traumatic life story of three generations of daughters in rural Upper Austria from the 1920s to the present day.

The novel is a chronicle of the repeated mistakes of each mother, the mistreatment of each daughter, the cruel and callous physical and mental torture passed down from one woman to the next. The narrator is a contemporary mother, Vera, who has resolved not to beat her daughter, but with whom even so she fails to have a happy relationship. The book comes out of her analysis of her own upbringing and of her mother's life in an attempt to find reasons for this absence of happiness and the repeated transference of hatred.

For the daughter initial analysis of the mother merges into self-analysis — a common trait of many contemporary autobiographical, quasi-autobiographical or confessional novels by women, where the daughter has to undertake a psychological journey in order to achieve separation from her mother and break free from dependence. The uneasy process of writing is often indicative of self-therapy and self-affirmation. Even though the mother of the narrator has been dead for sixteen years, she continues to influence her daughter. The mother-daughter bond is so inextricably linked that the daughter suggests that she belonged to her mother because she created her identity, so that when her mother died, she also died. Their interdependence was such that the daughter could not imagine surviving without her mother.

Motherhood itself brings her back to her own mother. When she becomes pregnant herself she starts to think about her — with her own screaming baby the adult daughter wishes that she was being nurtured once more. She doesn't want to face the responsibility of motherhood, the reality of another mother-daughter relationship taking shape, and the fear she has of being her mother all over again. Scarred by her mother's sado-masochism, Vera risks expressing feelings of guilt in sado-masochistic behaviour towards her child. She becomes so obsessed with being a 'good mother', so concerned about not making the same mistakes as her mother, that she does not see how this continuous self-analysis adversely affects her own daughter.

In Mitgutsch's novel beatings, according to Vera's mother, are equivalent to God's wrath and fulfil the Old Testament proverb 'He who spares the rod hates his son, but he who loves him is careful to discipline him' (Proverbs 13:24). The 'perfect' mother is, therefore, the punishing mother. The daughter is brought up to believe that love and torture are one and the same. In this way the portrayal of these monstrous mothers illustrates how the mother in traditional, Austrian society is able to rule the home, whilst the daughter takes on the role of servant. P M B

'For sixteen years I buried her over and over, but she always rose and followed me. She caught up with me long ago. She looks at me with the eyes of my child; she observes me from the mirror when I think I'm unobserved; I meet her in my lovers, and I run off with her own arguments. Then she punishes me with loneliness, and I try to win her back through achievement, brilliant achievement, the epitome of achievement. I never please her....

She has transformed herself into me; she created me and slipped inside me; when I died sixteen years ago, when she beat me to death thirty years ago, she took my body, appropriated my ideas, usurped my feelings.

She rules and I serve her, and when I gather all my courage and offer resistance she always wins, in the name of obedience, reason, and fear.' p215-216

MUSIL
Robert

## The Man without Qualities [Der Mann ohne Eigenschaften]

*The Man without Qualities* is one of the defining works of twentieth-century fiction, a novel which aims to reflect the intellectual, cultural, social and scientific state of Europe in the early 1900s. Set in the years immediately preceding World War One, it dissects in an elegant and ironic style the society of the Habsburg Empire, which, in the range of ideas and attitudes analysed, is seen as representative of Western European society.

Musil calls the Habsburg Empire *Kakanien* (Kakania), from the initials k. u. k. — *kaiserlich und königlich*, imperial and royal — which preceded the titles of most public institutions; it also contains a deliberate echo of the word *Kacke* — crap.

The satirical depiction of a society in terminal decline is contained mostly in the long second part of the first volume entitled 'The like of it now happens'. This part deals with the activities of the 'Collatoral Campaign', a committee, of which the hero, Ulrich, is the secretary, set up to organise a celebration for the eightieth jubilee of Emperor Franz Josef's rule, due in 1918. It is called the *Collatoral* Campaign because the Germans are planning grand celebrations for the thirtieth anniversary of Kaiser Wilhelm's accession, which also falls in 1918. The workings of the committee, which display good intentions, overblown rhetoric, and stupidity in almost equal proportions, reveal a society so hidebound, so ossified that nothing can divert if from its course to disaster: with the advantage of hindsight, the reader knows that the Emperor of Peace the committee hope to celebrate became the warlord of 1914, and that 1918 saw not a national celebration of Habsburg rule, but the collapse of the Empire and its dismemberment into eight separate 'successor states'.

The main character, Ulrich, is an exemplar of modern man. He has tried to become a man of significance, to make a career for himself as a soldier, then an engineer, and finally a mathematician (this mirrors Musil's own early development). This attempt to define himself in a way which will give him both an identity and status in the world fails. Ulrich comes to realise that the idea of a fixed, stable personality is restrictive, limiting, rigid. The individual is characterised by fluidity and a fixed, defined personality is nothing more than a façade, just as the glittering outward appearance of imperial society is a façade.

Actuality is seen as only one *possibility* among many equally possible states. This is why Ulrich is 'the man without qualities': he rejects the idea that he is a fixed psyche defined by certain qualities which are 'characteristic' of him. He is nothing more than a transient nexus where various ideas, thoughts, sensations and emotions crystallise momentarily before dissolving again. (This reflects the influence of the Austrian physicist and philosopher, Ernst Mach, under whom Musil wrote a doctorate. For Mach the self was only a *relatively* stable complex of memories, moods, feelings'.)

Ulrich is an extreme rationalist. With his scientific and mathematical training, he believes in precision, and rejects what he sees as metaphysical effusions, exemplified in the figure of Clarissa, for example. But he also believes in the spirit (and proposed to his committee the establishment of a secretariat for 'precision and the spirit'). In the second volume, entitled 'Towards the millennium', he pursues an increasingly mystical path, though it is a mysticism which goes beyond reason, rather than denying it. He withdraws into an incestuous relationship with his sister Agathe, a relationship which is more spiritual than physical. With his sister, he approaches a state of mystical ecstasy called the 'other condition', in which his longing for wholeness and unity would be fulfilled. But this is never actually realised: does Ulrich's life lead to consummation or failure? The book is unfinished (unfinishable?), and ends with 'A sort of an ending', which perhaps reflects Musil's intention anyway. He once said he would like his novel to stop in the middle of a sentence, with a comma. M M

'It is always wrong to explain the phenomena of a country by the character of its inhabitants. For the inhabitant of a country has at least nine characters: a professional one, a civic one, a class one, a geographical one, a sex one, a conscious, an unconscious and perhaps even too a private one; he combines them all in himself, but they dissolve him, and he is really nothing but a little channel washed out by all these trickling streams, which flow into it and drain out of it again in order to join other little streams filling another channel. Hence every dweller on earth also has a tenth character which is nothing more or less than the passive illusion of space unfilled; it permits a man everything, with one exception: he may not take seriously what his at least nine other characters do and what happens to them, in other words the very thing that ought to be the filling of him. This interior space... is of a different shade and shape in Italy from what it is in England... In so far as this can at all become apparent to every eye, it had done so in Kakania, and in this Kakania was, without the world's knowing it, the most progressive state of all.' p34 (Book One)

MUSIL
Robert

## Posthumous Papers of a Living Author [Nachlass zu Lebzeiten]

Musil is especially celebrated for his long major work *The Man without Qualities*, reviewed above. This book is rather the opposite, being made up of short pieces collected by the author — despite its title he was actually still alive but getting a jump on any future editors — basically early pieces and pieces written while he was occupied with his masterwork.

These are 'pieces' rather than short stories; extended

thoughts, reflections on objects, little situations (like the ghastly experience of flies on flypaper!) and a good deal else. The writing is, to say the least, extremely accomplished while Musil's speciality here is to view familiar things from a radically original perspective. Perhaps the most startling and delicious examples are *Sheep as seen in Another Light* ('they had the long faces and the delicate skulls of martyrs. Their black stockings and hoods against the white fur reminded of morbid monks and fanatics') and *Maidens and Heroes* (which is an extraordinary piece about dogs). Throughout the book, one encounters the pleasure of perfect 'poetically correct' prose; 'How lovely are you servant girls with your peasant legs', where one single sentence contains a whole rushing world.

Another marvellous piece is *Boardinghouse Nevermore* which is a kind of Teutonic mini-*Room with a View* (E.M.Forster) about the inhabitants (and proprietress) of a splendid German Pension in Rome in which 'everything was so impeccable there you wanted to cry'. It has less romance than *Room with a View* but even wackier boardinghouse characters; the Swiss Pastor staying in Rome 'to represent the interests of a Protestant sect not much larger than himself' and the Englishwoman of a certain age, Miss Frazier, who sits bolt upright in the lounge, doing her crochet, her 'daily lesson' and then 'with quick fingers played two rounds of solitaire' before going to bed and is always ultra-careful not to exchange a single word with her fellow-guests...

Also to especially note is *Slovenian Village Funeral* a lovely, dignified word-picture... part of a book made up of marvellous writing exercises and pocket masterpieces, unique and unmissable, particularly the early and middle sections... R K

'Somewhere to the rear of the Pincio, or already in Villa Borghese, two sarcophagus covers of a common sort of stone lie out in the open between the bushes. They constitute no rare treasure, they're just lying around. Stretched out on top of them, the couple who once as a final memento had themselves copied in stone, are at rest... as though on a picnic, the figures stretched themselves out, and seem to have awakened from a little sleep that lasted two thousand years.

They've propped themselves up on their elbows and are eyeing each other. All that's missing between them is the basket of cheese, fruit and wine.

The woman wears a hairdo of little curls — any minute now she'll arrange them according to the latest fashion from the time before she fell asleep. And they're smiling at each other; a long, a very long smile. You look away: And they still they go on smiling.

This faithful, proper, middle class, beloved look has lasted centuries; it was sent forth in ancient Rome and crosses your glance today.

Don't be surprised that even in front of you it endures, that they don't look away or lower their eyes: this doesn't make them stone-like, but rather all the more human'. p23-24

MUSIL
Robert

## Young Törless [Die Verwirrungen des Zöglings Törless]

Musil's short, first novel (which appeared in 1906, his first work to be published), focuses on the problems of adolescence. Set in an exclusive military academy in Austria, it deals with the confusions (the German title is literally 'the confusions of Törless'), of awakening sexuality.

The main plot centres on two pupils, Beineberg and Reiting, who have discovered that a third, Basini, has been stealing from his fellow students. This knowledge gives them power over him, and they use it to see how far they can go, subjecting him to brutal floggings and compelling him to take part in homosexual activities. What interests Musil is not the sex and violence as such, but the reactions of the fourth member of the group, Törless. Although he is present when the two torment Basini, and although he has his own homosexual encounters with him, he is more an observer than a participant. He insistently questions Basini as to what he feels at various moments, just as he observes and questions his own reactions and emotions. He is aware of a great gulf between the polite, disciplined surface of society and the turbulence of feeling inside him and, he assumes, others. The adult world, as represented by his teachers and parents, fails to provide him with the assistance he needs to come to terms with the two sides of human nature, and he is abandoned to a cynical detachment which seems the only solution.

The combination of the realistic description of the milieu of the military academy (which is clearly the one at Weisskirchen which Musil, and, some years earlier, Rainer Maria Rilke, the great poet, attended), and the intense potrayal of Törless' almost obsessive inner life make this one of the most absorbing works from the age and ambience of Freud. M M

'Törless was not in control of his actions. For a moment he sat still, staring into the sleeper's face. Through his brain there jerked those short, ragged thoughts which do no more, it seems, than record what a situation is, those flashes of thought one has when losing one's balance, or falling from a height... and without knowing what he was doing, he gripped Basini by the shoulder and shook him out of his sleep.

Basini stretched indolently a few times. Then he started up and gazed at Törless with sleepy, stupefied eyes.

A shock went through Törless. He was utterly confused; now all at once he realized what he had done, and he did not know what he was to do next. He was frightfully ashamed... without having uttered a word, Törless withdrew his arm, now he slid off the bed and was about to creep soundlessly back to his own bed — and at this moment Basini seemed to grasp the situation and sat bolt upright.

Törless stopped irresolutely at the foot of the bed. Basini glanced at him once more, questioningly, searchingly, and then got out of bed, slipped into coat and slippers and went padding off towards the door. And in a flash Törless became sure of what he had long suspected: that this had happened to Basini many times before.

In passing his bed, Törless took the key to the cubbyhole, which he had been keeping under his pillow.' p130-1

# NOLL
## Ingrid

### Hell Hath No Fury [Der Hahn is tot]

*Hell Hath No Fury* is the unoriginal title of what translates as *The Cock Is Dead*. It tells the story of how a nice, gentle woman suddenly finds herself in a position where, unfortunately, she has to kill her best friend and a couple of other people.

Rosemarie Hirte is respectable, in her early fifties and works in an insurance company, she wears impeccable suits and does not particularly mind coming home to an empty, though very tidy, flat. That is, until she sets eyes on Rainer Witold Engstern, a teacher in the local secondary school who has published a small monograph on painting in the fourteenth century. Rosemarie, who had long since embraced a future as a respectable spinster, suddenly finds herself spying on Witold (as she affectionately chooses to call him), trying to meet him by chance in the street and becoming a phone pest. Not having had great success with relationships earlier in her life, she reckons it would only be fair if at least once she got what she really wanted, even more so as she feels this might well be her last chance. She proceeds to make a pact with God promising to forsake whatever happiness he might have in store for her, if only she could have Witold, please. God, who had not been consulted before, moves in mysterious ways, and has to be helped along. Rosemarie is happy to take the initiative, but finds that she gets more than she had bargained for.

What makes this novel enjoyable is that it is told from the perspective of a very proper, likeable woman, respectable, sympathetic and a little old-fashioned. When she recounts her murderous schemes you hear the all-too-reasonable voice of a confident, dignified and mature lady, ever so slightly tinted with frustration and restraint.

If you ever had murderous thoughts, you will feel strangely at home with this intensely readable book and its humour that seems to stem from a distinctly female point of view. Maren M

'In the evenings, I now had a fixed routine: in the twilight, I would set out with Dieskau to try to meet my dream-man. In the darkness, I would creep around in his garden — without the dog, of course, and only in dark slacks; like a burglar, I had adopted a kind of working outfit. In addition, I would occasionally dial his number, not, I might add, from my own phone (there had been so much talk of phone-tapping, I was too scared), but from a phone-box. I would hear him give his name, sometimes brightly, sometimes sounding weary, and then hang up again at once, knowing that he was at home, maybe sitting at his desk. A second time, I almost collided with his bicycle, this time quite intentionally. He smiled again, just like the first time, and said, in his breath-stopping voice, "Good evening. Still lost in thought, eh?"

I returned the smile, but was unable to come back with anything clever or quick-witted.' p24

PAUSEWANG
Gudrun

## Fallout [Die Wolke]

Gudrun Pausewang's story of a nuclear explosion at a power station appeared in 1987, a year after the real nuclear disaster at Chernobyl in the Ukraine. *Fallout* was intended for teenagers and won an important prize as a work of literature for young people. How much it is a young person's book is questionable, although the central figure, Janna-Berta, is a schoolgirl in her early teens, left in sole charge of her younger brother while her parents are away close to the centre of the power station explosion which kills them. Although not a first-person narrative, there is a circular effect to the novel, which concludes with Janna-Berta relating her experiences (that is, the substance of the book) to her blinkered grandparents, who have been out of the country, but who always asserted that the Green Party were an uncultivated lot and that such a disaster could not happen, and if it did, the authorities would soon be in control. In fact when the nuclear power station explodes and a wide area has to be evacuated, chaos soon breaks out. Janna-Berta heads away with her bewildered little brother, who is soon killed on a busy road, and she goes on alone in the mass of people desperately trying to save themselves. The veneer of civilisation is very thin indeed. Caught in the contaminated rain, she is even turned away in fear when she asks for a drink of water. We also hear of the possibility that the police turned guns on those caught in the immediate area to prevent them leaving. Later, in a radiation hospital, after a Turkish friend Ayse has died, Janna-Berta expresses her (impotent) rage at those who sanctioned the nuclear policy by hurling a stone figurine at the door behind a visiting politician. Unhappy with an aunt in Hamburg who seems to want to suppress it all (Janna-Berta even refuses to wear a wig), she leaves and joins another aunt, Almut, in a kind of commune for the contaminated Hibakushi (the name they take from the survivors of Hiroshima), now separated from a terrified society-at-large. Eventually she returns to the field where her brother's body still lies and buries him, then goes back to the family home to explain it all to an incredulous grandmother.

The novel has flaws: the style is sometimes heavy-handed, and those who are not actively against nuclear power are somehow linked with the Nazis. The child's-eye-view of events cuts out any political responsibility, and the worst-case scenario is presented without consideration of any alternatives (to the situation or indeed to nuclear power itself). But it is a moving and passionate book, reacting to Chernobyl and Three-Mile-Island, not only indicating the dangers inherent in nuclear power, but also showing us quite clearly (the narrative pulls no punches) that in extreme circumstances the whole social fabric can crumble and break down very easily indeed. The book is a warning. B M

"'And — they say that anyone who tried to escape was shot. With machine guns."

Janna thought of what Aissa had once told her.

"Do you think it's true?" Janna asked.

"Yes," said Almut. "They tried to keep it secret, but that kind of thing can't be kept secret."

"And why —"

"They say that the people in restricted zone one were so contaminated that they were a danger to others. And they say they had no chance of survival anyway. They would have died slowly and in agony."

After a long pause Janna asked: "But the police and soldiers, how could they —?"

"Human beings are capable of anything," said Almut'

PERUTZ
Leo

## The Master of the Day of Judgement [Der Meister des Jüngsten Tags]

Leo Perutz was an immensely popular writer of the 1920s and 30s who was largely forgotten after his enforced emigration (he was Jewish) to Palestine after the *Anschluß* (the union of Austria with Nazi Germany in 1938). In the 1970s and 80s he was republished, and many new translations have recently appeared.

In its combination of murder mystery, supernatural horror, and historical background, *The Master of the Day of Judgement* contains the elements which are present, in varying mixtures, in most of Perutz's novels (for example *The Swedish Cavalier, The Marquis of Bolibar, St. Peter's Snow* or *Leonardo's Judas*). A critic of the day described Perutz as the offspring of an illicit liaison between Franz Kafka and Agatha Christie. The crimes and mysteries in his novels are not resolved with Hercule Poirot-like neatness; the uncertainties of the characters themselves often leave other possibilities open, besides the 'official' solution. (The computation of possibilities was Perutz's profession: he worked as a mathematician in insurance, for, by a strange coincidence, the company with which Franz Kafka began his career, both starting in the same month in 1907, Kafka in Prague and Perutz in Trieste.)

*The Master of the Day of Judgement* revolves around the deaths in Vienna of a number of artists (painters and an actor): were they murders or suicides? None left a suicide note, but there is no evidence of the presence of another person; the death with which the book starts is a variant of the locked-door mystery. The narrator is a wealthy — and somewhat unsympathetic — cavalry officer, Baron Yosch, who is accused by the victim's brother-in-law of causing one of the deaths. After the death, he is in an unusually lethargic and somewhat confused state, and at times actually accepts his guilt. (He has had an affair with the victim's wife, and is still in love with her.) His participation in the rather amateurish attempts at detection results more from a spirit of competition with the man pursuing them, whom he dislikes, than from a desire to clear his name. The solution, which almost leads to the death of the narrator, is connected with a sixteenth-century Florentine painter known as the 'Master of the Day of Judgement'.

Appended to Yosch's narrative is a note from the person who caused the manuscript, which was found in Yosch's pocket after his death in World War One, to be published. The 'editor' maintains that Yosch's account of the investigation and discovery of the cause of the deaths is a fabrication, a work of art, perhaps, but also a means of concealing his guilt from his own eyes. He recommends we read it as a fiction — which is what we do, with enjoyment, anyway. M M

'So the family refused to believe it was suicide, and the elder brother came to Vienna determined to do everything possible to throw light on the matter.

He had a fixed plan which he carried out doggedly. He lived in his brother's flat, assumed his daily habits and daily routine, and sought out and made the acquaintance of everyone with whom his brother associated or came into contact, and he avoided opportunities of meeting anyone else. He became a pupil at the Academy, he drew and he painted and spent a few hours every day at the café where his brother had been a regular customer, and he even went so far as to wear his dead brother's clothes and join an elementary Italian class that his brother had attended; and he never missed a lesson, though as a naval officer his command of Italian was complete. He did all this in the belief that in this way he was bound eventually to stumble on the cause of his brother's puzzling death, and nothing would divert him from his purpose.

"He led this life, which was not really his but someone else's, for two whole months, and I can't say whether it brought him any nearer his objective. But one day he came back to his lodgings very late. His landlady, who took up his dinner, noticed this because it was in striking contrast to his usual habits, which were marked by meticulous punctuality. He was not actually in a bad mood, though he made some irritable remarks about the food, which had got cold. He told he landlady he wanted to go to the opera that evening and hoped he would still be able to get tickets, and ordered a cold supper in his room for eleven o'clock.

"A quarter of an hour later the cook took up his black coffee. The door was locked, but she could hear the young officer striding up and down the room. She knocked at the door and called out: "Your coffee, sir," and left the cup on a chair outside the door. Some time later she went up again to fetch the empty cup, but it was still outside the door and had not been touched. She knocked, but there was no answer, she listened, but nothing stirred, and suddenly she heard voices and brief cries in a language she did not understand, and soon afterwards there was a loud cry.

"She shook the door, called out, raised the alarm, the landlady arrived, the two of them forced the door — and the room was empty. But the windows were open, there was a noise down in the street, and they realised what had happened. Down below a crowd had gathered around a body. Half a minute before, the young officer had flung himself from the window — his cigarette was still glowing on his desk.' p13-14

PERUTZ
Leo

## By Night under the Stone Bridge

After his enforced emigration from Vienna in 1938, nothing by Perutz appeared until *By Night under the Stone Bridge* in 1953. Subtitled 'A novel from old Prague', it is rather different in structure from his other works. It consists of fourteen chapters, each of which is a novella complete in itself, using stories and legends of the Prague of Emperor Rudolf II (reign: 1576—1612). From the various novellas a story emerges, involving the most famous characters of sixteenth-century Prague: Emperor Rudolf himself, who was more interested in alchemy and art than in ruling, Rabbi Loew, with whom the legend of the golem is associated (see review of Meyrink's *The Golem* in this book), and Mordechai Meisl, the fabulously wealthy Jew who financed Rudolf's art collection. But the real subject of the novel is Prague, especially the Prague ghetto, the destruction of which in the name of urban renewal the young Perutz observed as a schoolboy.

The linking story is the love of the Emperor for Esther, the beautiful wife of Mordechai Meisl, whom he saw when riding through the Jewish quarter. He calls Rabbi Loew and describes the woman, whose image will not leave him in peace. When the Rabbi replies that she is the wife of a Jew and cannot be his, Rudolf threatens to expel the Jews from all his lands. To protect the Jews, the Rabbi uses magic to fulfil the Emperor's desire: he plants a rose and a rosemary bush on the banks of the Moldau, under the great stone bridge, and says a magic formula over them. The two plants intertwine, and every night the Emperor dreams he is in Esther's arms. But, although only fulfilled in dreams, their love is still sinful, and the Lord sends the plague to the Jewish ghetto, until Rabbi Loew pulls up the rosemary bush and throws it into the Moldau.

Around this love story, which he weaves from a few delicate threads, Perutz has painted a lively picture of the Bohemian capital at the beginning of the seventeenth century, just before the religious wars were to deprive it of much of its glory. The ghetto, palaces, streets and squares are thronged with soldiers, beggars, minstrels, clowns, alchemists, nobles, among whom historical figures such as the astronomer Kepler and the young Wallenstein (a famous General in the Thirty Year's War) appear. It adds up to a portrait of a civilisation at its vigorous peak, with, behind it, constant reminders that the tragic end of Rudolf was the harbinger of the disasters and destruction of the Thirty Year's War. M M

'Young Waldstein (Wallenstein, ed.) smiled, his gloom had vanished, and he couldn't help thinking of Johannes Kepler, who had told him that not Mars but Venus was going to preside over his adventure.

"As the loveliest of all women has been pleased to choose me as her lover," he began, taking her hand...

"Don't misunderstand me," the loveliest of all women interrupted. "For one night," she said, freeing her hand and starting to fumble with her dark violet dress. "For one night only, captain, please note. Because I want to be free to do what I choose with myself. But that one night will be worth a hundred to you."

"If," said young Waldstein, without showing much disappointment, "if you have decided to make me your lover for tonight why will you not show me your face, so that I may caress it?"

"Because," said the lady, still fumbling with her dress, "I am more concerned than you think with my reputation... You can ask anything of me tonight, but the mask stays on."

She threw back her head, dropped her arms, and the dark velvet dress slipped to the floor.' p101

PIRINÇCI
Akif

## Felidae [Felidae]

Literary detectives can be unusual — oddballs like Agatha Christie's Hercule Poirot or elderly ladies like her Miss Marple — or they may come from a different age altogether, ancient Egypt, classical Rome or medieval Shrewsbury. As the title hints, *Felidae*, a detective story in German by a writer of Turkish origin, has an even less usual detective, who is also the first-person narrator: a cat named Francis, who solves crimes — a series of murders, of course — in a feline world. Francis lives with an overweight, and from Francis's point of view not terribly bright, human called Gustav, a writer with a penchant for Egyptology. Humans in general are referred to as 'tin-openers' and much of the incidental attraction of the novel is the cat's-eye-view of our own world (from which, incidentally, he has to run away, temporarily, in the sequel *Felidae on the Road*, when a certain familiar operation looks imminent). At the same time, the cat world mirrors that in the human detective novel, with a wide range of characters including feline gangsters, religious zealots and a computer-operating professorial type called Pascal. There are scenes of sex (involving a seductress, all nicely observed and with a footnote on feline copulation) and plenty of violence, while the cats demonstrate their superiority by using such human things as they like or need, including books and computers.

On arrival in a new neighbourhood, Francis comes upon a series of murders, which he begins to investigate, together with a somewhat battered sidekick called Bluebeard. Francis, the gifted amateur and crime-solver goes through the stages so familiar to the human detective: he works out that the murdered cats were all unneutered killed when about to mate, but then a female is killed (though of course this is because she knows too much). He encounters a dangerous feline cult, worshipping a deity called *Claudandus*, and eventually unmasks the villain, uncovering a plot the he and his henchcats have masterminded and carried out for a selective breeding-programme of a race of pure-bred supercats. Thanks to Francis, all the records (and the cat behind the killings, a kind of embodiment of evil) are destroyed in a fire. The parody element is not only of the detective story, which is more of the intellectual and donnish variety than Raymond Chandler (though Francis does at one point 'adopt a Humphrey Bogart look'), but also of master-race theories. The closed genre of the detective story (now almost always self-parodying to some extent), requires strikingly original features if it is to be memorable, and *Felidae* is highly effective in this respect. B M

"'I have an idea," I said. "Tell the computer to find out the breeds of the murder victims."

"Not a bad idea," agreed Pascal with pleasure. Now he was in his element. The joy of having found an equally enthusiastic game partner was written prominently on his face, although he must already have known the answers because he himself had entered the data. His paws whooshed with blinding speed over the keyboard.' p79

## The Last World [Die letzte Welt]

The starting point for Ransmayr's powerful and poetic novel is the Roman poet Ovid's exile in distant Tomi on the Black Sea, where he spent the last nine years of his life. When a rumour of Ovid's death reaches Rome, one of his admirers, Cotta, sets out for the Black Sea with the hope of bringing back definite news of the poet and copies of any works Ovid, who burnt his manuscripts on banishment, might have written in his exile, in particular his *Metamorphoses*. Cotta does not find Ovid, nor his books, but uncovers more and more traces of his presence: in the stories told by Echo, in the quotations Pythagoras writes on scraps of cloth, and in the landscape itself.

Tomi is a town of iron-founders, recalling Ovid's description, at the beginning of his *Metamorphoses*, of the fourth age of mankind, the age of 'hard iron' in which 'all manner of crime broke out; modesty, truth and loyalty fled', all of which, of course, provides ample material for the storyteller. Hideous crimes certainly abound in the iron-town, which is a derelict habitation for a degraded humanity. It is permeated with the rust of decay, and its inhabitants all come from elsewhere and have ended up there like so much flotsam and jetsam on the shores of time. They are morose and unresponsive, until they briefly erupt in the grotesque orgy of carnival.

All the people Cotta meets or hears about in this town 'at the end of the world' are variants of figures from the myths and legends Ovid used in his book: the village prostitute, who has been so brutalised she simply repeats the words of those talking to her, is called Echo; Arachne is a deaf-mute weaver; Tereus, the butcher, has raped his sister-in-law; Fama is a gossip who runs the local store. (At the end of the book is a repertory of characters, reminding the reader of Ovid's version of the legends.) Their stories are interwoven and told by different voices, by Cotta, by Echo, by Fama; and everywhere is change, in the landscape, in the climate, in the people, 'nothing retains its own shape': *The Last World* is a metamorphosis of the *Metamorphoses*.

Ransmayr's 'last world' is a hauntingly strange amalgam of legend, Roman history, and our modern world: in Tomi people change into stones and animals, and Ovid is banished by Augustus from Rome for a speech delivered through a microphone. *The*

*Last World* is not a retelling of classical legends, nor a historical reconstruction of Ovid's exile, nor a modernised version of either; the two are combined, with a few modest anachronisms, to create a timeless poetic world through which Ransmayr deals with themes of universal and contemporary interest, in particular the mind-set produced by an absolute dictatorship, and the threat of ecological disaster.

The power of the book resides in Ransmayr's power of description, especially in his vision of the decrepit, decaying town with inhabitants that are at the same time ordinary and yet strange. Equally vivid is the evocation of the shifting landscape, the instability of which contributes to the sense of a disintegrating world. At the end, growth and luxuriance overwhelm the world of man and even the narrator seems about to metamorphose into a plant. Finally literature is overtaken by reality; Ovid is perpetuated not in his works, but in the new mountain which now rises majestically above the town: Olympus. M M

'Wolves, Cotta said, turning now to the woman in black. Who are you? And getting no answer, asked Lycaon, Who is she?

Now the kneeling woman laid a hand flat to her mouth, as if to try to stop herself from speaking. Flakes of skin fell like snow over her chest. She stared at Cotta and repeated, *Who are you?* then stretched her hand toward the ropemaker and asked him in Cotta's tone of voice, *Who is she?*

Confused and embarrassed, feeling he was the victim of a word game these two were playing for the hundredth time, Cotta fled into helpless chatter. Does she work for you? he asked Lycaon, who did not look at him. What's her name? And then he introduced himself to the woman as he would to a simpleton, pointing to his chest and saying, Cotta.

*Cotta*, the woman in black repeated, refusing to take her eyes from him, *does she work for you? What's her name?*

Echo, the ropemaker said at last, her name is Echo. She cleans my house.

*House*, Echo whispered, bending deep over the pattern of tracks again, *my house.*' p58-59

RANSMAYR
Christoph

## The Terrors of Ice and Darkness [Schrecken des Eises und der Finsternis]

Ransmayr's novel is based on a real event, the Austro-Hungarian expedition to the North Pole in 1872—74 that charted the land beyond Spitzbergen and Novaya Zemlya, and discovered Franz

Joseph Land, naming it after the Austrian emperor. Their ship, the Tegetthoff, became locked in the pack ice and the expedition had to over-winter in the Arctic, eventually abandoning the Tegetthoff and making their way back in a desperate journey in the lifeboats. They reached the Norwegian coast after over two years on the Arctic ice.

Ransmayr makes use of existing documents, reports, diaries, letters and memoirs by members of the expedition. Much of the story of the journey is told in the words of the men who took part in it. The book also includes illustrations, engravings taken from the leader's report.

Interwoven with this reconstruction of a real expedition is the fictional account of a young man who becomes obsessed with the story of the polar journey and eventually sets off to retrace its steps. The fictional figure is a young Italian laborer called Mazzini who lives in Vienna; Ransmayr presumably chose that nationality because the ordinary seamen on the Tegetthoff came from Italy. While the expedition eventually returned, Mazzini disappears without trace in the Arctic wasteland.

The skilfully interwoven narratives build up into a compelling picture of the inhospitable polar region. The strength and courage of the men who confront it are portrayed, but deglamorised in what becomes a desperate struggle simply to survive. Their arrival in the safety of Novaya Zemlya is not the glorious homecoming of a band of heroes, but the last gasp of an exhausted and disenchanted crew for whom survival had become no longer a hope, but a mere continuation of mechanical movements.

The physical and emotional deprivations of the journey contrast with the ecstatic reception the members of the expedition received on their way home across Germany to Vienna. The armchair explorers could still bathe in the national glory and adventure which Ransmayr's chronicle reveals as an illusion. M M

'Since most of Novaya Zemlya's coast is unapproachable, we were forced to continue our journey without stopping, although our arms were stiff and swollen with the constant exertion of rowing... We rowed on mechanically through the endless flood, towards the secret of how all this would end. (Julius Payer)

On 24 August 1874, at seven in the evening, with only a breeze from the southwest, crews on the Russian whalers Vasily and Nikolai anchored in Duna Bay off Novaya Zemlya see four boats approaching but hear no sounds of jubilation, only the slap of the oars. They recognize the flags and realize that these are the missing men who are the talk of the Arctic harbour towns. Some of these foreigners cannot climb the gangway of the Nikolai on their own and have to be helped. Without a word Weyprecht hands Captain Feodor Voronin the safe-conduct letter issued by the tsar in St. Petersburg. Into the silence Voronin haltingly reads aloud that Tsar Alexander II commands the Austro-Hungarian North Pole Expedition to the care of his subjects, and the Russian sailors bare their heads and sink to their knees before these emaciated strangers whose faces are disfigured by ulcers and frostbite.' p185

REICHART
Elisabeth

## February Shadows [Februarschatten]

Relatively few Austrian authors have delved into Austria's Nazi legacy and even fewer women writers have addressed the theme. In her debut novel *February Shadows*, for which she was awarded the Austrian prize for literature in 1993, Elisabeth Reichart makes her own distinctive contribution to the literature of 'Vergangenheitsbewältigung' ('coming to terms with the past') by focusing on the way in which women too bear responsibility for having supported Nazism through their complicity and silence.

In this very moving story the daughter-figure, a writer with a strong political conscience, attempts a reconciliation with her mother through her book project, thereby confronting taboos and overcoming the estrangement between them. By writing her mother's life story this daughter wants to make up for her previous neglect and pay tribute to her mother. Good intentions, however, turn sour, for the mother begins to resent the fact she is being used as an object of critical interest. She does not welcome the intrusions into her personal recollections and the uncovering of certain well-kept secrets.

The title *February Shadows* refers firstly to the bloody manhunt of the 2nd of February 1945 when the rural population of the area around the Austrian concentration camp Mauthausen brutally killed hundreds of fugitive Russian officers; secondly, the mother, Hilde, is haunted by dark shadows because she cannot forgive herself for betraying her brother, Hannes, who hid one of the fugitives but — once his action had been discovered — hung himself. The shadows, then, symbolise Hilde's guilt-ridden conscience.

Reichart cleverly interweaves history and fiction, the political and the personal, past and present by depicting a mother-daughter relationship fraught with problems and tensions. Not only does she draw attention to the personal guilt as experienced by the mother as well as the collective guilt of Austrian society, which the daughter recognises, but she also highlights the conflict between two generations in their differing attitudes towards moral responsibility and civil courage. Reichart does not point an accusatory finger but, via the mother's weak character, reveals the price of voluntary amnesia, so that when the mother does, eventually, share her burden, she passes on to her daughter both the guilt and sense of shame. The reader is left to speculate about how the daughter will cope with the revelation. P M B

'Why should I think about my childhood? I learned after all from the time I was little the only way to survive is to forget...

Forget Hannes. Forget the cold February.

At first because of the command of the adults. Forget what you have heard. What you have seen. Forget it! But soon it was no longer necessary to shout this command into her. Soon this command of all the other people became her own. Soon she would pass on this command to others.' p31

REMARQUE
Erich Maria

## All Quiet on the Western Front [Im Westen nichts Neues]

Remarque's most famous work is one of the bestselling German books of all time and one of the best-known anti-war novels ever. Written in 1928, it provides an impression of World War One from the point of view of the ordinary soldier. The author drew on some of his own experiences, but the work is by no means autobiographical.

The book is (mostly) a first-person narrative by the twenty-year-old Paul Bäumer, who joins up with all his grammar-school class, bullied emotionally into doing so by their teacher. Bäumer's immediate group includes some schoolfellows, some ordinary workers, and Katczinsky, an older man, whose skills at 'requisitioning' are much valued. The group goes through basic training under a martinet postman-turned-drill-sergeant (whom they eventually ambush and beat up), and then they go to the front.

The style varies as we see military action through Bäumer's eyes, hear the different soldiers speaking and become aware of the narrator's private thoughts as he tries to cope with it all. There is violent death and horror as the men come under heavy shelling in a recently dug military cemetery (even the dead cannot sleep for long); we hear the scream of horses and the cry of a wounded man who cannot be found in no-man's-land; just as unbearable are the hours of waiting in the trenches for the fury to begin.

Bäumer goes through a whole range of situations, such as a visit to some French girls where the soldiers buy a night's love in exchange for food. At home on leave, he realises that the war has changed him completely, and guarding Russian prisoners makes him aware of their humanity. When he returns to the front he stabs a French soldier who lands in the same shell-hole. After a brief respite guarding food supplies, he is wounded and sent to a military hospital.

The war is lost, not because Bäumer and the others were bad soldiers, but because the allies could bring in fresh supplies and American troops. Back at the front in late 1918, with all his friends dead, Bäumer comes to terms with the fact that he just has to carry on, but he is killed a week or so before the armistice. A new voice at the end tells us that on the day he was killed the despatches said there was 'nothing new to report'.

The war experiences of the ordinary soldier are in the foreground, and we hear these (mostly young) men trying and failing to understand what is going on, resorting to meaningless clichés like 'war is war'. The book starts in 1917 after a battle (other things are seen in flashback), in which half of Bäumer's company has been killed, and next time only thirty-two men come back. Gradually all the group are killed. But although Bäumer comes near to despair, the spark of life in him is inextinguishable, and his death is ironic.

The book spoke to the 'Lost Generation' — the young and uncomprehending majority of all soldiers — but it also makes clear that the much-vaunted camaraderie was also a superficial solidarity of the condemned. There is action, but no heroics or exciting exploits; the men are victims of a machine that rolls over them like tanks, and the message is that war is the real enemy. B M

'There are rumours of an offensive. We go up to the front two days earlier than usual. On the way we pass a shelled schoolhouse. Stacked up against its longer side is a high double wall of yellow, unpolished, brand-new coffins. They still smell of resin, and pine, and the forest. There are at least a hundred.

"That's a good preparation for the offensive, says Müller astonished.

"They're for us," growls Detering.

"Don't talk rot," says Kat to him angrily.

"You'll be thankful if you get so much as a coffin," grins Tjaden, "they'll slip you

a waterproof sheet for your old Aunt Sally of a carcase."
The others jest too, unpleasant jests, but what else can a man do? — The coffins are really for us. The organisation surpasses itself in that kind of thing [...]

The front is a cage in which we must await fearfully whatever may happen. We lie under the network of arching shells and live in a suspense of uncertainty. Over us Chance hovers. If a shot comes, we can duck, that is all; we neither know nor can determine where it will fall.

It is this Chance that makes us indifferent, A few months ago I was sitting in a dug-out playing skat; after a while I stood up and went to visit some friends in another dug-out. On my return nothing more was to be seen of the first one, it had been blown to pieces by a direct hit. I went back to the second and arrived just in time to lend a hand digging it out. In the interval it had been buried.

It is just as much a matter of chance that I am still alive as that I might have been hit. In a bomb-proof dug-out I may be smashed to atoms and in the open may survive ten hour's bombardment unscathed. No soldier outlives a thousand chances. But every soldier believes in Chance and trusts his luck.' p69-67 (from new translation by Brian Murdoch, Vintage)

RINSER
Luise

## Jan Lobel from Warsaw [Jan Lobel aus Warschau]

*Jan Lobel from Warsaw,* first published in 1948, is a plaintive little novella about the emotional deprivations of war. In the portrait of the title figure it was one of the first post-war works that attempted, in a very quiet, unemphatic way, to encourage the Germans to face up to what had happened under Hitler. Rinser, who was imprisoned during the Third Reich for defeatist talk, does not preach, but concentrates on the delicate evocation of mood and atmosphere. She does not need to tell the reader that Jews are human beings just as much as Germans, it is there in the reactions of the family that hides Jan Lobel.

The story is set in a market garden in Brandenburg, the province at the heart of Prussia. The husband is away in the army, and it is run by his wife, Frau Olenski, with her grown-up daughter, Julia. Frau Olenski's twelve-year-old son, Thomas, and her elderly mother-in-law also live in the house.

One night in the spring of 1945 a group of prisoners is being taken past when there is the sound of shots. Later, when all is silent, Frau Olenski goes out and brings in Jan Lobel, a Polish Jew, whom she hides. The spring is followed by a magical summer, as the emotions of all four members of the household focus on this frail figure. He becomes, it is suggested in a very understated manner, the lover of Frau Olenski and then of Julia; he becomes the companion and model the son lacks; surprisingly, he even becomes a kind of surrogate son to Frau Olenski's mother-in-law, the person one would most expect to resent him.

Olenski's return does not bring the expected clash. He accepts Jan Lobel's presence, it is almost as if he expected it. Eventually, though, Jan Lobel leaves, quietly, secretly, without telling the daughter and the son, who both want to go with him. The market garden returns to a stable but rather drab, utilitarian normality (they give up growing flowers and concentrate solely on vegetables).

Jan Lobel goes because he feels he does not belong in this place, with these people. This sense of not belonging is partly, but only partly connected with the fact that he is a Jew (he is eventually drowned trying to stow away on a boat to Palestine). There is a rootlessness about him which is personal as well. He is an exotic bird of passage, and that is part of his attraction, which would be lost in the routine of everyday life. 'People like that come and go', the mother-in-law comments.

It is the strength of Rinser's novella that the focal figure is *also* a Jew, rather than his Jewishness being the whole *raison d'être* for the story. M M

"'Come inside,' repeated Frau Olenski. He shook his head. "You needn't be afraid," he said. "It's turned how I've been expecting it to. You were always waiting for something like this, Anna." There was no bitterness in his voice, and nearly no expression at all. Then he looked across at Jan: "Is it true that he's a Yid?"

"Yes," said Julia loudly. "It's true. And Polish. He was in a camp for six years, Father. They killed his wife." She looked at her father with passionate defiance. He waved his hand dismissively. "I don't need to know.' p55-56

ROSENDORFER
Herbert

## The Architect of Ruins [Der Ruinenbaumeister]

Rosendorfer's first and perhaps best novel is a Chinese box of a work. An amusingly intricate construction of twenty stories within stories within stories inside a narrative that is a descent into ever more distant levels of reality, until, with an elegant twist of his Möbius strip, Rosendorfer returns his hero to the point from which he started.

The narrator sets out in a train in which six hundred nuns are going to Lourdes, and on which he meets a petty criminal who, before he escapes from the police, gives him a scrap of paper with a pattern of dots on it. Falling into a dream, or memory (or a previous existence?), he meets Weckenbarth, the 'architect of ruins', who has constructed a huge armageddon shelter called, from its shape, the 'cigar'. Its main protection is not ferroconcrete — warfare has developed from the nuclear, through the biological to the spiritual — but the dislocation of reality, which means that time, in particular, has gone haywire. The narrator's dream within the 'cigar' is the longest section of the book, a kind of *heptameron* (from Greek for 'seven days') in which the seven nieces of a retired castrato each tell a story on a different day of the week. At the end all the figures from the various levels of reality appear together, before the hero wakes up on the train full of nuns again. The mystery of the pattern of dots is resolved, but only to lead to a further mystery: they represent the Latin word square 'sator arepo tenet opera rotas', an inscription on a monument created by Weckenbarth as a ruin, and on which the inscription never appeared, only the holes for the letters.

The characteristic that distinguishes *Architect of Ruins*, and distinguishes it from the rather po-faced tradition of much postwar German fiction, is its playfulness, its witty style, its delicate interweaving of stories and narrative, its juggling with time, and its wealth of allusions, some more obvious, some concealed.

For example, Don Juan meets Leporello at an inn 'close to the walls of Seville'; one of the central figures, Don Emanuele da Ceneda has a similar biography to Mozart's librettist, da Ponte, who was born in the Italian village of Ceneda. (Many of the stories woven into the narrative have a musical element.)

A further elaboration amongst all the genial elaborations of *Architect of Ruins* is the reflection on the nature of fiction and the relationship between fiction and reality that some of the storytellers within the novel indulge in, as well as reflections on the nature of reality, which themselves are reflected in the structure of the novel. Everything is interwoven, interrelated, yet at no point do the readers feel firm ground under their feet; everything is relative to something else. (It is not purely by chance that the petty criminal the hero meets on the train is called Einstein.) Behind all its playfulness, the novel has a serious point to make, namely that the world is not as straightforward as devotees of the 'false prophet *technology*' would have us believe. But Rosendorfer's point is not an earnestly propounded message, it is a feeling which hovers over the novel, which can be read simply to be enjoyed. M M

"'So I was right" I whispered.

"It's not what you think, really; I'm not a criminal. I was in prison because a few times I had spent the night, not completely sober, I must confess, on building sites or in ruined houses. Once I made the mistake of choosing the garage of a police station. In the middle of the night a policeman peed all over me — not on purpose, I wouldn't dream of accusing the police of a thing like that — I' sure it wasn't on purpose. I shouted... But all that's beside the point. — Anyway, the prison was full of creepy-crawlies and it was those bugs which gave me the idea of the automatic cleaning device. If — this was my idea — if you were to attach tiny india rubbers to the feet of the bugs and then let them loose in the room, they would crawl all over the place and rub away the dirt. Bugs are very light in weight, I grant you, so they could not exert much pressure on the rubbers, but they are very determined and crawl around a lot, often in the same area, the frequency was the key. So I drew up plans for a bug attachment to fit the rubbers to their feet.'" p19-20

## ROSENDORFER
### Herbert

### German Suite [Deutsche Suite]

Rosendorfer's second novel was a romp through recent German history in which real historical figures, Hitler, Adenauer, the Cardinal Archbishop of Munich, rub shoulders with fictional characters, and satire shares the pages with grotesque fantasy.

The story assumes the Wittelsbachs, the Bavarian royal family, (Rosendorfer has lived most of his life in the Bavarian capital, Munich) survived the revolution after World War One and continued to rule, unlike all other German royal houses. Its two main representatives in the years of the *Bundesrepublik* after World War Two are the king, Otto II, who cannot stop growing and is, by the end of the novel eight-and-a half feet tall, and the Socialist mayor of Munich, Dr. Hermanfried Schneemoser, who is the result of an indiscretion of one of the royal princesses with a gorilla, and who therefore needs daily attention from his personal barber.

The book is imbued with a cynicism about politics and especially politicians of all stripes, who are merely concerned with themselves and their own interests. The *éminence grise* pulling the strings behind the scenes is the wealthy banker, Baron von Speckh, who survives the change from Third Reich to Federal

Republic with nonchalance, and finances both the right-wing NPD (neo-nazi party important in the 1960s) and the left-wing Federation of Socialist Students, both on behalf of the communist rulers of East Germany. The precursors of the student movement of 1968 (the novel ends in 1963) are portrayed as clowns, the more serious satire being focused on the representative of mainstream conservative Bavarian politics, Josef Kofler. Kofler, a minor Nazi official, is one of the 'cautious Nazis and myopic members of the former Centre Party' who founded the Bavarian CSU (Christian Social Union — the right-of-centre Catholic majority party in South Germany) after the war. In his mixture of self-seeking, religious posturing and covert fascism, Kofler embodies the shady side of conservative Catholic German politics, which dominated Germany in the fifties and sixties. All this is done in an amusing and sharply satirical manner. M M

'Gicki was no beauty: perhaps she was not even good-looking. She was tall, had long dark hair, a slight double chin and the inturned nostrils of so many sexually athletic women. Gicki, it was said, made quantitative rather than qualitative demands of her lovers. She was, as many could have told you, not difficult to satisfy, provided it happened often enough. Quite a few of her partners confessed contritely that after their initial delight they had rushed out of her studio in Clements-Strasse, in fear of their lives. One who was able to give a particularly dramatic account of his encounter with Gicki was Iwan Hungertobler, later renowned as a painter of horses. Iwan, a Swiss despite his Christian name, had cast all the warnings of his friends to the wind, and, worse still, had grossly overestimated his staying powers. Although he came from a good family in Winterthur, Iwan had had no moral or aesthetic objections to Gicki's erotic demands. However, after two or three hours, he was suddenly alarmed by the terrifying thought that Gicki's frenzy might assume bestial proportions, that once fully satisfied she might bite off his head in the manner of certain locusts. Saying that he had a sudden call of nature he jumped out of Gicki's bed at about 2 a. m. and took to his heels, even though Gicki, obviously forewarned by experience, had previously taken the precaution of hiding his shoes. When Gicki realized that despite the season (it all happened in March), Iwan had decamped in his bare feet, she ran after him, as was her wont. At the corner of Clements-Strasse and Viktoria-Strasse, Iwan chanced upon a policeman, who looked properly embarrassed when the fugitive asked to be protected from his relentless pursuer. The policemen could only turn helplessly to Gicki and ask: "Have you any means of identification?" Iwan, who at once took advantage of this official interlude to seek safety in darkest Victoria-Strasse, was still able to hear Gicki reply with great dignity: "Don't be an ass. I am the Princess Judith"' p3-4

## The Night of the Amazons [Die Nacht der Amazonen]

*The Night of the Amazons* is the blackest of black satires on Nazi Germany. It charts the rise of Christian Weber, one-time groom and pub bouncer, who exploits his status as one of the 'Grand Old Soldiers' of the 'Movement' (i.e. the Nazi Party), and certain compromising facts he knows about Hitler, to a position of power and influence and an immense fortune. Weber's breathtakingly complete lack of any moral sense gives him total self-assurance and he proceeds to gratify his appetites in episodes of self-indulgence which are both chilling and grotesquely comic.

The absolute control the Nazis exerted gave figures like Weber the means to act out their own private fantasies at public expense and, often, in public, presenting them as concerns of 'national importance'. In Weber's career this culminates in the 'Nights of the Amazons', grotesque Wagnerian pageants financed by the City of Munich, in which well-developed members of the Bund Deutsche Madeln (the Nazi girls' squad) parade naked, apart from cardboard helmets and the odd sash, on horseback before an audience of tens of thousands.

Christian Weber, Munich city councillor and President of the Upper Bavarian Regional Council was a historical figure, not a creation of Rosendorfer's fertile imagination. (Many documents are quoted, especially legal ones, revealing Rosendorfer's own professional expertise as a trial judge). As a historical figure he was very minor, meriting little more than a footnote in the history of the Third Reich. Is it not, then, to do him too much posthumous honour to make him the hero of a novel? That is a question *The Night of the Amazons* itself asks, and the answer is that the scum that rises to the top of the fascist ferment reveals the utter emptiness of all its ideology, all its nationalist bombast and patriotic posturing. The patriotic sham is summed up in the picture of the corpulent Weber, at the end of the war, still driving his own private car round a bomb-ravaged city, while the Luftwaffe can do nothing to repulse the Allied bombers because of fuel shortages.

Weber's biography is interspersed with short conversations between a pair of 'respectable' citizens which reveal the attitudes of the population at large which, with the pusillanimous acceptance of those in power, coupled with a denial of real knowledge and a rejection of responsibility, show an attitude which it is made clear continues into the postwar period.

There is a scene in the novel in which Hitler, a great Chaplin fan, watches, with growing rage, the comedian's demolition of him in *The Great Dictator*. One response, and perhaps the most appropriate one, to a figure like Hitler and a movement like National Socialism is not serious discussion of their ideas, but satire, satire of a savagery that leaves all their pretensions in tatters and reveals the brute flesh beneath. It is a satire that *The Night of the Amazons* provides in rich measure. M M

'The compromising details about the Nazi bosses that were known to Esser ran the gamut of all aspects of life, one might say from the purse to the penis. If he had blown the gaff, the Nazi government would have disintegrated like the piece of rotten fruit it in fact was. A rotten apple that was held together only by the hands of the Old Comrades. All for one, one for all. If one of them had taken his hand away, then the filth would immediately have gushed over the hands, arms and bodies of the rest.' p123

ROSENDORFER
Herbert

## Stephanie [Stephanie]

*Stephanie* is another of Rosendorfer's experiments with time. The story concerns what the subtitle calls the 'previous existence' of the heroine, Stephanie, a very ordinary German housewife who finds that what first appear to be dreams are in fact trips back in time. She 'wakes up' in eighteenth-century Spain as a duchess who, she discovers, has just murdered her husband. When she learns how to control these trips back in time — the key is a ring her husband has given her — she eventually stays in eighteenth-century Spain, only returning after she has been arrested for the murder of her husband. She arrives back in the twentieth century mortally ill, and the story of her time in the past is told through a diary she has written and hidden at a spot which she knew from her visit to the palace in the twentieth century would not have been built on or otherwise disturbed.

In her conscious mind Stephanie remains the twentieth-century German, but her emotions become deeply involved with those of the Spanish duchess who is wed to an insensitive and violent boor, and who has fallen in love with another man. It is not just that she can understand what drove her to murder, she is, in some way, that woman herself. In returning to eighteenth-century Spain, she accepts the guilt of the Spanish duchess, as she accepts her love for another man as her own.

As with most of Rosendorfer's novels, *Stephanie* is an intriguing story intriguingly told which, with the lightest possible touch, raises profound questions of individual identity and existence. For all the fantasy of the time-travel mechanism, the story is told with a psychological realism which renders Stephanie's situation convincing and compelling. At the same time it provides a vivid portrait, told from the inside, so to speak, of the sights, sounds smells, especially the smells, and attitudes of a past age. M M

'So I visited the 'National Museum of Spanish-Musulman Art' and the 'Museum of Fine Arts'. [...] On the Sunday I hired a small car and drove out to the wild and stony Sierra del Aquila, going up to the pass they call the 'Puerto del Suspiro del Moro' and looking for the spot where the unfortunate Mohammed Boabdil, the last Moorish king in Spain, had turned around for the last time, because from there one has a final glimpse of the Alhambra glinting in the sun before the stony road to the south rapidly drops down towards the coast. The verses from Heine's ballad about Boabdil's departure kept running through my head,

On the pass where, looking northwards,

All the valley of the Duero

And the towers of Granada

Spread out in a farewell vista,

There the exiled king dismounted

And looked back to see his city

Gleaming in the evening sunlight

As if decked in gold and purple...

but it was too hazy, or perhaps it wasn't quite the right place, anyway. I couldn't see a thing.

On both the evenings, though, I could think of nothing better to do than to go to the cinema. On the first evening there was a Spanish film. As the audience laughed, I assume it was a comedy. There is , of course, the possibility that it was seriously meant but unintentionally funny, but in such cases it is rare for everyone to laugh. In the Spanish film comedy I saw, everyone laughed, myself included, though with a delay of half a second. (Why are we so unwilling to admit that we don't understand something ? Is lack of knowledge of a foreign language something shameful? Even when one can speak other foreign languages but not the one in question?) It was naturally annoying always to be the last one to laugh, so once I laughed first, but on that occasion the happenings on the screen were obviously not a joke. No one else laughed and everyone stared at me.' p72-73

## The Radetzky March [Radetzkymarsch]

*'To all my peoples'* — were the words the Austrian Emperor used to proclaim the outbreak of World War One to his subjects. This war signalled the start of the last act of the Austro-Hungarian Empire. The sunset of the Hapsburg Empire and the consequent decline of a whole world is the theme of both *The Radetzky March* and its sequel *The Emperor's Tomb* (also reviewed here).

In this earlier novel Roth follows events in the terrain under the rule of the double-headed Hapsburg eagle over three generations of the Trotta family. The Trottas emerge from social obscurity because of the heroic act of a Slovene lieutenant — the first notable Trotta — who saves the Emperor's life on the battlefield.

Aided by his sovereign's gratitude, Franz, the son of the battlefield hero, becomes a faithful Habsburg official, Captain of a district of Moravia. However his nephew, Karl Josef, dissipates his bungler's existence — incarnation of the moribund Empire — in a hated military career, first in the Dragoons and then in an infantry regiment on the Eastern marches of the state, only to die ingloriously on the day after the outbreak of war.

In *The Radetzky March* the Trotta family legend of the hero of Solferino is linked with that of Franz Josef who, because of the battle in which he had shown an almost suicidal military valour, starts the legend; but in this way the Emperor ends up being deluded by both his own myth and that of the immutability of Austrian rule.

Roth's masterpiece is an elegiac work, but one written in a measured and unsentimental style. It mourns the loss of a past age, recreating its glamour and its atmosphere at the same time as producing a lucid chronicle of its crumbling and sterile reality. C C

'Straining greatly, Herr von Trotta managed to ask, "I don't understand. How can you say the monarchy no longer exists?"

"Naturally!", replied Chojnicki. "In literal terms, it still exists. We still have an army — the count pointed at the lieutenant — "and officials" — the count pointed at the district captain — "but the monarchy is disintegrating while still alive; it is doomed! An old man, with one foot in the grave, endangered whenever his nose runs, keeps the old throne through the sheer miracle that he can still sit on it. How much longer, how much longer? This era no longer wants us! This era wants to create independent nation-states! People no longer believe in God. The new religion is nationalism. Nations no longer go to church. They go to national associations. Monarchy, our monarchy, is founded on piety, on the faith that God chose the Hapsburgs to rule over so and so many Christian nations. Our Kaiser is a secular brother of the Pope, he is His Imperial and Royal Apostolic Majesty; no other is as apostolic, no other majesty in Europe is as dependent on the grace of God and on the faith of the nations in the grace of God. The German Kaiser still rules even when God abandons him; perhaps by the grace of the nation. The Emperor of Austria-Hungary must not be abandoned by God. But God has abandoned him!'" p161-162

ROTH
Joseph

## The Emperor's Tomb [Die Kapuzinergruft]

*'I'm not a child of my time, in fact it's hard for me not to think of myself as its enemy'*
The voice is that of Franz Ferdinand Trotta — the narrator of the book — the last in line of a branch of the family of a famous soldier who saved the Austrian Emperor's life at the battle of Solferino. The reader of Roth's *The Radetzky march*, will already be familiar with him. Five years on, Roth devised this second novel, *The Emperor's Tomb*, around the theme of *Finis Austriae* (the decline and collapse of the Austro-Hungarian Empire that covered a large area of Central and Eastern Europe until 1918). From the standpoint of his East Galician Jewish origin he explored the historical causes of the dispersal of the vibrant central European community after the collapse of the Austro-Hungarian monarchy. Roth is one of the great literary witnesses to this empire which is seen today, in the light of the subsequent unhappy history of the region, from Sarajevo 1914 to Sarajevo 1994 one might say, in as much a favourable way as a negative one. Both its strength and its weakness lay in its multi-ethnic character, uniting Germans, Jews, Czechs, Slovaks, Ukrainians, Poles, Rom (Gypsies) Hungarians, Italians, Romanians and South Slavs under one roof and thereby fermenting all kinds of marvellous cultural synthesis and interaction but also becoming a bear-pit for the conflicting state nationalisms that eventually dismembered it, with difficult consequences for most of the minority populations in the successor states.

In *The Emperor's Tomb*, on the eve of World War One, and in keeping with the customs of his generation of elegant and graciously blasé Viennese aristocrats Trotta leads a frivolous and charmed lifestyle which he renounces to take part in the war.

Moved by a new and profound feeling of affinity with the 'Hapsburg spirit', he 'betrays' his own battalion, the twenty-first Regiment, choosing instead to serve in the thirty-fifth, which also numbers Joseph Branco, Trotta's Slovenian cousin, and the Jewish cabdriver Manes Reisiger (from Eastern Poland) among its ranks. Both of these charming, somewhat folkloric, characters are fundamental to Roth's effective portrayal of the individual human types in the Austro-Hungarian empire of Kaiser Franz Josef.

Returning to Vienna three years later, after fighting in the battle of Krasne-Busk and being held prisoner in Siberia, Trotta's postwar years are spent as an outcast, an outsider among the living, unable to adapt to and understand the world around him; 'We had all lost position, rank and name, home and money and esteem, past, present and future. Every morning as we woke up, every night as we lay down to sleep, we cursed Death who had vainly beckoned us to his mighty banquet. And each of us envied the dead.'

The novel ends just before the Nazis enter Vienna, with all their sinister symbols already dotted about the city. Trotta, more than ever a symbol of a lost and already distant world, goes down into the crypt where the mortal remains of the Hapsburgs are conserved, paying homage once again to his sovereign and avowing his psychological and ideological detachment from the present.

In the end Roth is a surprise both because of his passion for Austria-Hungary, which we tend to think of as a Ruritanian backwater of big moustaches and everlasting waltzing, and for the freshness and preciseness of his style. Definitely a writer to get to know. C C

'I used to go to Sacher's then, to see my friend Sternberg. He would be sitting in a *loge*, always the same one, and he was always the last guest. I would take him away. We ought to have gone home together, but we were young and the night was young (although far advanced) and the street girls were young, particularly the older ones, and the lanterns were young, too...

So we moved through the youthful night and our own youth. The houses in which we lived seemed to us to be crypts or, at best, refuges. The police on night duty used to salute us. Count Sternberg gave them cigarettes. We would often join the watch patrolling the middle of the pale and empty streets, and sometimes one of those dear creatures would walk with us and her gait would be quite different from the one she used on her regular beat. In those days the lanterns were fewer and also more discreet, but because they were young they shone more brightly and many swung cheerfully in the wind...

Later, since I had come back from the war, not only older but grey-haired, Vienna's nights had become faded and wrinkled, like dark old women, and evening no longer slipped into night as it used to do, but withdrew from it, paled and disappeared, even before night had approached, These swift, almost timid evenings had, so to speak, to be grasped before they were ready to disappear and I preferred to catch them in the Parks, in the Volksgarten or the Prater, and then to savour their last and sweetest moments in some café into which the light would filter as gently and delicately as their scent.' p153

SANDER
Helke

## The Three Women K [Geschichten der drei Damen K]

*The Three Women K* is the first work of fiction by Helke Sander, who is otherwise a film director.

Three Women, united by the initial of their surname as well as the fact that they have been let down by the men in their lives, spend the time between Christmas and New Year together. They pass the time by telling each other stories, which 'had to be essentially true and should also have a funny side, those were the sole conditions'. Unsurprisingly, the stories centre around men and the various ways in which the three Ms K. have been disappointed by them. Even so, the stories are sharp and witty, and the clause about the funny side saves them from self-pity, if sometimes only just about.

There is the Ms K who is so grateful to her boyfriend for sorting out the paragraphs of her pension scheme that she nominates him as her heir in case she should unexpectedly die. Only years later she realises how the provisions are made out in the by now ex-boyfriend's favour, leaving no money for herself until she reaches the age of eighty-five.

Another Ms K skilfully manages to avoid sleeping with her boss without offending him, but still finds herself being sacked, much later, for no apparent reason.

It is not always clear which story belongs to which Ms K, most could have been told by any of the three. This is because they mirror the experiences of many women, and indeed most of the stories have an unsettlingly familiar feel to them. It is easy to recognise bits of yourself in the stories, and comforting to know that many of our most painful experiences are shared. Maren M.

'One day he informed her kindly, albeit without a convincing reason, that he would not be forwarding her proposal. It was a waste of money to go on subsidizing the project any longer. It had no future. The whole approach was wrong, a dead-end. She defended herself, of course, and insisted that he specify the reasons. But he was in a position not to have to give reasons... In theory she had been prepared for this blow for a long time but it still hurt when it came. She had to begin again from scratch. She wondered what it was that made her go on being polite and why on earth she had to start crying on top of everything else. It was embarrassing for him. He fetched her a fresh cup of coffee ad a schnapps. He handed her a handkerchief. Dr K cordially shook hands with this rotten little arsehole, this wanker, who had even had the gall to keep her up to date on his digestive problems and tell her all about his next holiday plans before rejecting her proposal.' p24-25

SCHNITZLER
Arthur

## Casanova's Homecoming [Casanovas Heimkehr]

*Casanova's Homecoming* was written in 1918 during the carnage of the first World War. Its publication was met with some controversy since Schnitzler's motives were questioned, given the appalling state of things in Europe then. Why, some asked, would Schnitzler be interested in writing a novel such as at a time of such universal privation? The answer lies not so much in the reputation of Casanova as a hedonistic scoundrel as it did in Casanova's human condition since the novel is a purely fictional account of Casanova, not in the figure of erotomaniac, but as a middle-aged poseur, a fiftyish nobleman who must recognize and relinquish his passing youth and accept the inevitability of ageing.

Though the novel is not without its erotic elements (in fact, Casanova sneaks into the young Marcolina's bedroom in the guise of her young lover Lieutenant Lorenzi, whom Casanova eventually kills) they are shown in contradistinction to the pathos and tragedy of ageing and its psychological effects, an approach to which Schnitzler was very much interested as seen in his collection of stories, *Vienna 1900*. But what truly stands out about the novel is its exceptionally modern tone. Given the nature of the novel as a product of the early nineteenth century, *Casanova's Homecoming* has many of the distinguishing features of mid to late 20th century Modernism and Postmodernism not only in its contemporary approach to understanding the psychology of certain characters, but in its postmodern fictional historicising of Casanova, his ribald antics and, ultimately, his acquiescence to the inevitability of old age. M R A

'Did he regret what he had lost through his perpetual seeking and never or ever finding, through this earthly and superearthly flitting from craving to pleasure and from pleasure back to craving once more? No, he had no regrets. He had lived such a life as none other before him; and could he not still live it after his own fashion? Everywhere there remained women upon his path, even though they might no longer be quite so crazy about him as of old'. p74-75

STRAUSS
Botho

## Tumult [Rumor]

Bekker is a man in his forties who works for a mediocre, semi-academic company that deals in information, known as 'The Institute'. He keeps trying to escape this place, but never quite makes it to a permanent position in academia proper and has to return each time to ask for his old job back.

This time round though, Bekker, morbidly drawn to the Institute and at the same time dreading his return there, resolves to spend some time with Grit, his grown-up daughter he had lost touch with during most of her upbringing.

At first, Grit, the long lost daughter, does not come over as much of a character, in fact, she is pure cliché: young and beautiful, she trained as a language secretary and now runs a little travel agency, inhabits a nice flat, possesses the female sentimentality of wanting to repeat a childhood holiday, and comes complete with a green Peugeot.

The holiday is doomed from the beginning. The place is the scene of the last, nasty arguments of Bekker's marriage that turned sour. While at least it was summer then, it is the middle of November now, they are the only guests in the pension, it is altogether the wrong place. The attempts of father and daughter to enjoy their time together come to an abrupt halt when Grit develops an infection of the spine and has to have an operation.

After the operation Bekker, having moved in with his daughter, fusses over her, following her around with unwanted attentions, and becomes generally overbearing. Feeling misunderstood, Bekker turns to drink and degenerates more and more, still not making the decision to return to the Institute. Finally, he gets himself arrested in a bizarre incident involving a group of illegal immigrants who he first befriends and then betrays to the police. That is the point from which on he completely lets go of himself. He neglects his personal hygiene as well as the conventions of civilisation, until, towards the end of the novel, he can be found masturbating in front of the television, next to his daughter. Grid eventually throws him out, reasoning with herself that this is probably for the best of both of them.

*Tumult* deals with the inherent difficulty of interpersonal communication — with Bekker as an especially hopeless case. Botho Strauss, a noted playwright and a controversial figure in German intellectual life, has created an intense evocation of the isolation and progressive alienation of a disaffected individual in an over-ordered world. He sees around him a society with no place for dark, messy emotions, and where 'sanity' is more likely be found in the mediocrity of a travel agency.

Maren M

'Her father gets up from the armchair and stands at the window. He looks out and entwines his hands firmly behind his coccyx. "Only hatred unites. Hatred, hatred, always be up front, always be the first."

Grit opens all the brochures on Tunisia once again. She says softly, as she reads: "That is absolutely evil."

This was spoken so matter-of-factly and her voice was so devoid of purpose that her father continues to hear her for a long time. The little simple sentence has so much space to it that he loses himself in it for a long time, just as at times you can hear deep down into a person through a certain hollowness in speech.' p30-31

SÜSKIND
Patrick

## The Pigeon [Die Taube]

This slim novella tells the story of Jonathan Noel. Somewhere along the path of growing up, Jonathan has lost any adventurousness he might ever have possessed. He moves to Paris, and when he finds a job as a bank guard, which requires him to stand on the marble steps of the entrance during opening hours, he decides that this is as good as life is going to get for him.

Jonathan has been in this job for twenty years before he suffers the existential crisis described here. He has, by his own calculations, spent fifty-five thousand hours standing on the very same spot, and he has never been able to find fault with his employment situation. He even wishes to consolidate his life so far by actually buying the tiny room in the hostel where he has been staying since his arrival in Paris, conveniently located only five minutes' walk from work.

It is the confrontation with a common pigeon standing in the corridor outside his room that throws him completely off balance. The thought of this pigeon watching him, fouling the corridor and putting his home under siege oppresses him so that he takes fright and resolves to escape to a hotel for the time being.

When, to his surprise, he survives the following night, dramatically heightened by a thunderstorm, he finds that he is able to confront the challenges of life just ever so slightly better than he had thought.

*The Pigeon* lacks the grand scale of Süskind's earlier and more famous novel *Perfume*, and little happens in the way of action, at least from a normal point of view. However in this very introspective novella, little things assume immensurable proportions and prove themselves too big for Jonathan's frightened, little soul. Unlike *Perfume*, which recounts the story of a murderer bizarrely obsessed with smells and blessed as well as cursed with a superhumanly developed olfactory sense, *The Pigeon* is concerned not so much with the outwardly extreme but with exploring the terrors that lie hidden behind an all-too-normal existence as well as the human tragedy of an unloved life. Maren M

'Now he saw the pigeon. It was sitting to his right at a distance of about five feet, at the very end of the hall, crouched in one corner. So little light fell on the spot, and Jonathan cast such a brief glance in that direction, that he could not discern whether its eye was open or closed. He did not want to know either. He would have preferred not to have seen it at all. In his book in tropical fauna he had once read that certain animals, above all orangutans, pounced on you only if you looked them in the eye; if you ignored them, then they left you alone. Perhaps this was true of pigeons as well.' p19

TRAVEN
B

## Government [Regierung]

'A job in government is far and away the best. A man has only to keep his eyes open and pounce as soon as the prey shows its nose.' And that's how the worldly-wise and mysterious author of the famous *Treasure of the Sierra Madre* (made into a Hollywood film with Humphrey Bogart) saw and exposed the workings of political power in the Third World and elsewhere.

Traven was a German radical who went to live in Mexico after revolutionary activity at home towards the end of World

War One. His dissection of Mexican political corruption in *Government* and the savage exploitation of the poor, especially of the Indian population is brilliant and terrifying; particularly as, judging from the popularity of SubCommandante Marcos and the recent revolt in Chiapas state, things don't seem to have changed much in the countryside since the turn-of-the-century conditions Traven describes.

Mexico at that time was a run-for-profit dictatorship under Porfirio Diaz and what Traven convincingly and wittily shows is how a big dictator operates through a system of little dictators, each taking their slice out of the person beneath them in the hierarchy of greed. Traven lived in Mexico and *Government* is part of a whole cycle of novels about the origins and progression of the Mexican revolution of 1910–12. What this means is that, rather than being a superficial drop-in exposé by a foreign journalist, *Government* comes from knowing the territory inch by inch and it is the telling details that make the book. Traven understood too a very modern point; that brutal regimes work hard to have themselves seen in a good light to keep investment flowing — exemplified here by the hilarious and tragic description of a local school for Indian children, one of the funniest set-pieces in the book.

As well as a being a striking analysis of 'the system' *Government* is full of fascinating detail of rural Mexico, of Indian culture and observances; it is a respectful and appreciative understanding by a writer of working-class origin, very different from the patronising tone we expect from Europeans writing about the Third World in this period. He ends with a nice description of the Indian system of annually elected chiefs, a wonderful contrast to the dictator Diaz's thirty-two year rule. R K

'A few weeks later don Casimiro was on an inspection tour of the district and ran across don Gabriel again. Don Gabriel reminded him of his unfortunate situation, and as don Casimiro had a good heart and could not bear to see his friends suffer, he said, "I haven't much for you. Everything's gone. And they all sit as tight as sticks. But I've got a little Indian village — Bujvilum. A bad lot there. Won't behave themselves. Kick up against everything, we send soldiers to burn their huts down time after time — but can't catch one of them. They always clear out into the jungle and you can't get 'em there. When everything's burnt and their maize fields laid flat and the soldiers are gone, out they come and build their village again as if nothing had happened. Then we leave them alone for a bit, but we can't get any taxes out of them. If you'd like to go there, I'll make you local secretary. You open a tienda, a little store. And I'll give you an exclusive permit to sell brandy. You have a lockup — prison, in fact. I needn't say more. Well, there you are — it you want to go, the job's yours. I've nothing else for you at the moment."

Don Gabriel had a good revolver and he could shoot as straight as the next man. The Indians had no revolvers and could not buy any either; they had no money and, in any case, it was strictly forbidden to sell them revolvers or rifles, apart from muzzle-loaders for game. So don Gabriel accepted the post. He would have accepted the post of watching boiling cauldrons in hell if anyone had offered it to him. He was so down on his luck that he had no choice. It was getting on to twenty years since he had sought a way out in honest work. And a job in government is far and away the best. A man has only to keep his eyes open and pounce as soon as the prey shows its nose.'
p2-3

TUCHOLSKY
Kurt

## Castle Gripsholm: A Summer Story [Schloß Gripsholm]

Kurt Tucholsky was born in 1890 and ended his life in 1935, with fascism unmistakably becoming the dominant political force in Germany. He worked mostly as a journalist, writing poems, travel articles, book reviews and polemical commentaries. Later, from his exile in Sweden, he provided text to go with the illustrations of the famous German photomontage artist John Heartfield, and together they aggressively and desperately attacked German nationalism and emerging fascism.

*Castle Gripsholm* is Tucholsky's only novel. With the description of an idyllic holiday, unaffected by a political context, it makes a strong contrast to Tucholsky's critical and politically committed journalism. It is a short novel that captures the enchantment conveyed by its subtitle *a summer story*.

Whilst he describes a five week holiday in Sweden, Tucholsky himself was living there, and, unlike the heroes of his story, he knew that he was not going to return to Germany after one summer, and most likely not at all. The novel was finally published in 1931, — two years before his books were burned and he lost his citizenship, and only four years before his suicide. He was buried in the churchyard at Mariefred, a place that he describes in the novel, and that is only a short walk from the actual Castle Gripsholm.

At the onset of summer, Kurt, a young writer, sets out with 'the Princess' to spend five weeks, their summer holiday, in

Sweden. The princess is really called Lydia and works as 'the secretary of a monstrously fat boss' who is in the soap business. They spend their days in blissful harmony, see Stockholm, go on excursions and hire a guide-cum-translator who finally leads them to the ideal place; Castle Gripsholm. Their guide arranges for them to be put up for little money in the annex of the castle and then leaves them to it: doing nothing and forgetting about Berlin, bosses, offices. For a week, they are joined by a friend, Karlchen, in their now positively bucolic idyll.

They tread lightly, avoiding all heaviness. Because they know how uncertain their future is, they make the best of what they have got. So they happily, self-sufficiently live the day, enjoy their time together and do not search for each other's shortcomings. When Billie, a friend of the Princess, arrives, the relationship turns into a threesome, but this only deepens their friendship and strangely contains either hurt or pain.

This harmonic life gets a more serious dimension when they happen upon Ada, a maltreated little girl from a children's home run by a despotic headmistress. The Princess and Kurt, supported by Billie, now make it their vocation to free the little girl from her surroundings, and, after much hassle they finally succeed in uniting little Ada with her mother.

What makes the book so touching is that it reads like a wish, a dream — that Kurt Tucholsky, like the narrator, could spend some time of carefree bliss, that he could return to Germany untroubled and continue his work, that the most threatening monster to be fought and defeated might be some scary headmistress. Kurt, the narrator, is aware that this holiday cannot be extended indefinitely, believing and accepting that happiness is only ever possible for a brief time. In much the same way Tucholsky knew that his novel was a flight from an unpleasant reality to a place full of light, love, friendship and good food. Whilst in the novel only a summer holiday comes to its end, for its writer there was more at stake. Maren M

'The long hours where nothing happened, only the wind fanning my body, the sun shining. The long hours where I gazed at the water, the leaves hissing gently, and the lake splashed against the shore; empty hours in which energy, intellect, health and strength can be replenished from the reservoir of nothingness, from that mysterious store which will one day be empty. "I'm afraid," the storeman will say, "we have nothing left..." and I suppose that's when I shall have to lie down.' p123.

## Institute Benjamenta [Jakob von Gunten]

This book — subject of a recent film by the Brothers Quay — is published in a series from Serpent's Tail, a UK publisher with a strong international list, in a series called 'Extraordinary Classics'. 'Extraordinary' is really the right description for a funny, original and downright eccentric book, written with an oddball perceptiveness, a fantastic sensitivity to the peculiarities of individuals and institutions. The cast of individuals here are the students and teachers of the Institute Benjamenta which is a school for servants; Walser, who had a taste for humility and simplicity, attended such a school in Berlin at the turn of the century and worked as a butler for a while. But the Institute Benjamenta of the book seems to exist not entirely on the normal plane of existence. It is run by an exceedingly odd couple; Herr Benjamenta the Principal, who spends his life ignoring the world hiding behind a sheath of newspapers, and his beautiful tragic daughter who seems to have some magical powers to transcend space, time and feeling...

The theme of servanthood itself is an extremely unusual and unlikely one which Walser celebrates, 'to be of service... a glimpse into divine and misty paradises', where the strain of constant decision making is subsumed into just following orders. A certain psychology of inner freedom through absence of personal will is suggested, or is Walser mocking German authoritarianism and leader-love? This is a book, a supposed diary, where nothing much is really definite except the often super-delicate and inspired writing itself; Walser is 'someone who can sense tremblings of beauty in defiance' and writes such magical sentences as 'For my fellow-pupil Fuchs I have only one single expression: Fuchs is crosswise, Fuchs is askew. He speaks like a flopped somersault and behaves like a big improbability pummeled into human shape.'

The eventual, predictable, dissolution of the Institute — bullying and pompous as it is, despite the kind Fräulein Benjamenta — has, retrospectively for a book published in 1908, echoes of the dissolution of uptight Bismarkian Imperial Germany at the end of the First World War in 1918 — or are these echoes in reality the first vibrations of Walser's cataclysmic mental illness which put him in an asylum for nearly twenty-five years? In any case, if you enjoy the truly quirky and unpredictable then check out Walser. R K

"'Of course there's progress on earth, so called, but that's only one of the many lies which the business people put out, so that they can squeeze money out of the crowd more blatantly and mercilessly. The masses are the slaves of today, and the individual is the slave of the vast mass-ideas. There's nothing beautiful and excellent left. You must dream up beauty and goodness and justice. Tell me, do you know how to dream?'" p55

## WALSER
### Robert

## The Walk and other stories [Der Spaziergang]

'Nobody should be afraid of his little bit of weirdness' said the Swiss writer Robert Walser and this wonderful, lively and deeply unusual book is a powerful argument for collecting and protecting that bit of weirdness, that singular, only-personal view of the world. Here are forty-two short pieces like paintings by Watteau or Constable; full of a beauty that has been long contemplated and deeply felt — as he insists in *A Little Ramble,* a tribute to the simple and strong attraction of nature 'we already see so much!'.

Perhaps there is a very Swiss delight with landscape here and in other pieces including the fabulous title story *The Walk* which explicates — in a lovely mock-pompous language, reminiscent of Raymond Queneau's hilarious *The Sunday of Life (Les Dimanches de la vie;* see French Babel Guide) — the joys, or the real Zen of a *walk.* A serious business, the walk, especially the extraordinary, passionate, uninhibited and freethinking walk that Walser takes in a world not yet flooded with stinking cars and raucous trucks...

Read this collection and meet a remarkable man who, if he had been more mentally stable, might be today as revered as Thomas Mann or Hermann Hesse, combining as they often do satire with contemplative wisdom and, while celebrating the eternal things an artist worships; the changing of the seasons, the glory of a face or a song, introduces us to his unique *Walseresque* cracked logic that renews the external world for us while feeding the inner one.

Perhaps unexpectedly for an-often satirical writer Walser's brilliance is accompanied by a tremendous warmth and gentle respect for human souls — 'every sensitive person carries in himself old cities enclosed by ancient walls' — which puts him on the side of the reader just as he is on the side of all his varied protagonists. He appreciates them all for their diverse humanities whether famous poet, twelve-year-old girl or Impressionist painter, and whatever narrow horizons or awkward personalities they may have. Read and be amazed and entertained. R K

'I always then look darkly at the wheels, at the car as a whole, but never at its occupants, whom I despise, and this in no way personally, but purely on principle; for I do not understand, and I never shall understand, how it can be a pleasure to hurtle past all the images and objects which our beautiful earth displays, as if one had gone mad and had to accelerate for fear of misery and despair. In fact I love repose and all that reposes. I love thrift and moderation and am in my inmost self, in God's name, unfriendly toward any agitation and haste. More than what is true I need not say. And because of these words the driving of automobiles will certainly not be discontinued, nor its evil air-polluting smell, which nobody for sure particularly loves and esteems. It would be unnatural if someone's nostrils were to love and inhale with relish that which for all correct nostrils, at times, depending perhaps on the mood one is in, outrages and evokes revulsion. Enough, and no harm meant. And now walk on. Oh, it is heavenly and good in simplicity most ancient to walk on foot, provided of course one's shoes or boots are in order.' p64 (from *The Walk*)

## WEISS
Ernst

### The Aristocrat [Der Aristokrat]

Ernst Weiss was a Jewish doctor born in Moravia, now in the Czech Republic, when it was still part of the Habsburg Empire. He lived in Prague, Vienna and Berlin and was a close friend of Franz Kafka. In 1934 he went into exile in Paris, where he died in 1940. In the 1920s he was widely regarded as one of the leading figures in modern German fiction but exile and the loss of his manuscripts during the war meant that he was largely forgotten until his novels were republished in Germany in the 1980s.

*The Aristocrat* has been described as his most optimistic work. Its brief plot, set during a few months of summer in 1913, analyses the values of aristocratic, pre-First World War society, and looks forward to a new world when an individual's function is based on his ability rather than inherited social rank.

The main character, who also narrates the story, is Botius von Orlamünde, the last scion of an impoverished aristocratic family, who is attending the exclusive school of Onderkuhle in Belgium. He has completed his schooling, which lays emphasis on the noble arts of fencing, riding, plus bearing and etiquette, rather than on academic subjects, but stays on as a boarder since he has not yet found a role in the world. Eventually he runs away to the city and finds work in a factory, earning his living by manual labour. He has renounced the role of aristocrat; but it is not a complete break with he past, more an adaptation to the present, as he wears the family signet ring which his father hands on to him before he dies.

Most of the story is set in the school, which develops character rather than the intellect. The most important figure in the hierarchy is the slightly mysterious former cavalry sergeant known as the Master of Ceremonies, not the head or the abbé who is in charge of academic studies. In order to 'prove' himself, Orlamünde constantly undertakes challenging tasks and it is on these tests that the narrative focuses with an intensity which grips the reader and takes him inside the mind of 'the aristocrat'. He is, for example, asked to break in a spirited stallion, and the process is a battle of wills between two noble beasts. Orlamünde envies animals their naturalness, their amoral joy in living and it is perhaps significant that the challenges he faces often involve helping others in ways which mean doing violence to them. When, for example, he saves his friend from drowning, he has to knock him unconscious to stop himself being dragged under by the panicking boy.

Eventually he fails one of these 'tests' when a fire breaks out in the school and he (who has already brought out one man) is told to go back to free a schoolboy who has been locked in a room (by Orlamünde) as a punishment. His response to this failure is the radical break with his world, a break which is not tragic, but forward-looking, leading, as it does, to his integration in modern society.

*The Aristocrat* won the silver medal for prose fiction at the 1928 Olympic Games, in a more idealistic phase of the Games' existence when they celebrated more in human achievement than mere meat and muscle. M M

'My first task is to remain motionless, unflinching and above all impassive in the middle of the room. The horse twists wildly. Without my intending it he has got messily tangled up in the reins as if in tethering ropes. The fine skin bulges out in swellings, whose edges, under the surface, immediately fill with pulsing blood, weals which will still be visible after months. Unavoidable. The horse cannot hold himself, he staggers, falls, he opens his mouth in astonishment. He does not whinny, however, he quickly wants to struggle up again.

The floor of the high, oval space is shaken by the dull impact of the falling horse. The white patches on the forehead gleam with the violent movement. The horse begins to roll from side to side, to hide his head in the bark, but there is too little of it, again and again the horse's eyes become visible, and the eyelashes, already sprinkled with dirt, have lost their beautiful unbroken order. Lying there on his side, he whinnies and groans. But then he explodes, he shoots up from the floor, shaking up a cloud of brown dust, violently jerking his head, mechanically, angrily, unthinkingly. But he does not free himself. The steely rings of the well arranged and cleverly concealed bonds tighten once again, and it is as if nothing had happened.' p48

WODIN
Natascha

## Once I Lived [Einmal lebte ich]

Natascha Wodin's story of an outsider in a hostile country at the end of the World War Two, was awarded the Brothers Grimm Prize on its publication in 1989.

The book tells the struggle of a foreign child to master the language, to improve her situation in the Germany of the 1950s and 60s, where there was, as now, violent intolerance of immigrants. Born in Germany to Russian parents, the child grows up in the ghetto of 'the houses' — the slum row where poor non-Germans live — rejected by her peers at school and, after the suicide of her troubled mother, at the mercy of a violent and domineering father.

Her hopes of a better life, of being accepted through marriage to a German man and of the cruel bright lights of the High Street as a forbidden paradise, are the themes of the narrative. Fearing her father's reaction to her bad school report, the girl wears her red high-heeled shoes, steals some money from a drawer and starts an independent life, yet using her house as a shelter, a place to rest and steal food when it's too cold to sleep in the cellar or in the laundry of 'the houses'. Her father accepts her way of life, throwing her the key before leaving for work, not complaining about the food missing from the cupboard, but careful to hide his pay packet.

An awkward adolescent wearing ill fitting charity clothes, the girl dreams of settling down with a nice German man in a house with white lace curtains. When she falls in love with Achim, who loves somebody else, the girl puts up with the attentions of Achim's friend to be near him.

Eventually, when all her hopes are shattered, the girl locks herself in the toilet of a train to escape her provincial hometown for the big city. But the miracle will not happen there either and she will experience even more violence.

Later in life, a journey to Moscow will grant the young woman the key to her past and reconcile her to her father now suffering from senile dementia and finally recognised as a German citizen.

Natascha Wodin writes vigorously and convincingly to provide a (rather sad) insight into contemporary German society at the blunt end. S C

'A discreet item in a German daily newspaper, entitled "Homesickness never lasts for ever. Ukrainian foreign workers remember", has this to say about it: "Some of the survivors still live among us today. Under the Nazi dictatorship during the last war, over seven million foreign workers were deported to Germany from 22 European countries. Most of them were forced to work in munitions factories while others slaved in the fields or in mines. The vast majority came from the Soviet Union. They were seen everywhere in our towns and factories, branded with the word EAST sewn onto their clothes. In Essen and its environs alone some 400 camps were erected to house this cheap labour. There is not one large company still existing today, not one factory and hardly any small firm, that did not apply to the Employment Office for "its" quota of foreign workers. By the end of 1941 some five million foreign workers had been deported to Germany and more than half had died as a result of inhumane working and living conditions. Our knowledge of this dark chapter of German history still leaves much to be desired. It was forbidden to photograph foreign workers and the death penalty threatened anyone who spoke to them. The companies concerned refuse to give information or to open their archives. Foreign workers who were unable to return home after the war are often too ashamed to speak about their experiences, or prefer to forget."

The author Reinhard Laska was lucky enough to meet Andrei and Anna Lalatsch, who once worked on a farm in the Ukraine... Cut off from their roots, they are still officially referred to as "homeless aliens". They have no passports and no legal right to claim damages for the injustice they have suffered.... I might have been reading my own family history.' p170

**Roth**

**Wolf**

## A Model Childhood [Kindheitsmuster]

Christa Wolf was East Germany's favourite writer, with her generally accessible style and within-the-limits criticisms of the regime. Criticism she managed to combine with an essential loyalty to its 'socialist mission'. A mission which can be seen as either in fact a socialist mission or the rule of a privileged elite spouting stolen slogans and backed up by a police state that minimised (generally) its use of open violence through its deadly efficiency.

It was nevertheless a dictatorship ruling in the name of a populist ideology. Which of course gives *A Model Childhood,* as a long and probing account of the Nazi years and their immediate aftermath from the double viewpoint of her remembered childhood and as a respected GDR writer in 1975 a special, probably unintended, twist. A good deal of what she says about the previous dictatorship to the one she favoured seems to apply to both.

This contradiction apart, *A Model Childhood* is a fascinating account of its period from the point of view of the small-time small-town nobodies that her family were. It is full of peculiar, frightening but enlightening details about everyday life seen from a teenage perspective. For example, one of the slogans of the *Hitler Mädeln* (Nazi Girl Scouts), which certainly bears reflecting on, was 'My will is your faith', a quotation from the Germans' famous Austrian leader himself. The inculcation of Nazi ultra-nationalism in the young is well demonstrated too by a text that hung up in the young Christa's schoolroom 'We feel as Germans, are of German mothers/ our thinking's German, has been so from birth/ First come our people, then the many others/ Our homeland first, then the entire earth.'

The details are accompanied by Christa Wolf's hindsight as she tries to bring together the hubristic Nazi past with its aftermath. She tells of witnessing as a child the destruction by arrogant Stormtroopers of her town's Synagogue in 1938 and then comments "177 burning synagogues in 1938 make for ruined cities beyond number in 1945".

It is this accounting of course that is so difficult — have the Germans in fact been punished for destroying half of Europe and 80% of its Jews? Should they be? Or has fifty years assuaged their guilt automatically? On the whole it seems they would like everyone else to think so, conveniently for them... They are thus spared the horror of remembering — a task Christa Wolf has at least attempted here — and perhaps more sadly they have missed the opportunity for seeking redemption through, for example, a sustained humanitarian contribution, rather than just trying to be the first onto the beach. R K

'Ignorance is bliss.

Their ignorance allowed them to feel lukewarm. They were also lucky. No Jewish or Communist relatives or friends, no hereditary or mental diseases in the family... no ties to any foreign country, practically no knowledge of any foreign language, absolutely no leanings towards subversive thought or, worse, toward decadent or any other form of art. Cast in ill-fitting roles, they were required only to remain nobodies. And that seems to come easily to us. Ignore, overlook, neglect, deny, unlearn, obliterate, forget.

According to recent discoveries, the changeover of experiences from short-term to long-term memory supposedly takes place at night, through dreams. You imagine a nation of sleepers, a people whose dreaming brains are complying with the given command: Cancel cancel cancel. A nation of know-nothings who will later, when called to account, assert as one man, out of millions of mouths, that they remember nothing.' p149

WOLF
Crista

## Quest for Christa T. [Nachdenken über Christa T.]

If Christa Wolf has received a lot of criticism since German reunification for her officially-sanctioned role as an East German star writer this is the text — a publishing scandal in her Communist homeland — on which the defence rests its case. It's ostensible subject is the young woman Christa T., whose entire tragically short life-history is unraveled by a former school friend. Christa T. is a wonderful person; lively, intelligent, spirited. Too much so for the new society that is born in the Eastern Zone of Germany after the war; a bleak but initially hopeful world in Christa Wolf's vision, emerging from a bleak and hopeless one; 'We crossed the empty squares where the wind was still blowing, the wind that rises out of the ruins every day in cities after the war'.

Christa is a square peg and it becomes obvious from this story that the GDR in the 1950s and 60s was a hell of a place to be a nonconformist. But not, of course, the only such place and *Quest for Christa T.* is much more than an excellent social history of East Germany 1945-1968 with its switches of party line between authoritarian liberalism, extreme 'Chinese' collectivism of communal kitchens, and the Marxism-by-numbers of the Brezhnev era. It's a tender, thoughtful tribute and lament for square pegs everywhere. It's a kind of 'tale from the Resistance' as the moral fortitude of a naturally honest person is continually battered by the truncheon of unquestioning, complacent servants of the state, like the young doctor who tells her 'the essence of health is adaptation or conformity'. Christa T., meanwhile, nurses 'her dangerous wish for a pure and terrible perfection' and in many ways her brilliant life goes to waste.

It's very clear though, despite her protagonist's possible lack of realism, where Christa Wolf stands between her woman character and the real world of 'really-existing Socialism' (as its shamefaced admirers used to call it).

*The Quest for Christa T.* is a call 'To become oneself, with all one's strength'. It's not though just a call to the victims of classic totalitarian regimes, because Christa T. is out there in every known socio-political setup when she feels 'the secret that made her life livable... relentlessly escaping from her... She saw herself melting away in an endless welter of deadly banal actions and clichés.'

Every society has a tendency to grind down the individual, to 'socialise' him or her for its own purposes and this uplifting and engrossing book shows the negative side of that process through the life of one individual, an individual of an especially original and creative type — the sort who are either destroyed or perhaps survive to be greatly celebrated. R K

'She began her walk home. In front of a flower shop in the centre of the city a dozen people were standing and waiting silently for the short midnight flowering of a rare and brightly lit orchid. Silently Christa T. joined them. Then she walked home, comforted and much divided in her mind.

Later she couldn't remember how she reached her room and got into bed. She overslept, woke up at noon, and had missed the seminar at which she was due to read a paper. She walked to the window and the snow in the yard was reduced now to a few small islands. Soon, she thought, happy for no reason, it'll be time again for this ornamental stonework to be washed. She laughed and sang, went into Frau Schmidt's kitchen and convinced her that she simply had to take a bath, though it was the middle of the week. Frau Schmidt acquiesced with a sigh but don't fill it all the way up!

Christa T., laughing still, let the water come right to the top. Then she put on clean clothes and bought, with the last of her money, the expensive bird book she's wanted for a long time. She sat in her torn leather chair and quietly looked at it. Tomorrow she'd think of all kinds of excuses; she was confident that she'd have convincing ones ready when the time came.' p58

ZWEIG
Stefan

## The Royal Game [Schachnovelle]

Stefan Zweig's last work (which he posted off from his exile in Brazil to his publisher hours before committing suicide in 1942) is a novella, a concentrated story on a single theme, but with all kinds of ramifications, a story that has almost as many possibilities as the physically equally circumscribed game of chess.

The story has several narrators, the first a detached observer travelling on a ship from Europe to South America, who hears from a friend before they leave, the tale of one of his fellow-passengers the chess grandmaster Czentovic.

Czentovic is a kind of chess-playing automaton, only semi-literate, and ignorant of practically everything else in life, but who can play chess' the only thing he can do — and which he does to earn money. On the voyage, another passenger, a rich amateur chess-player, arranges and pays for a game between Czentovic and a group of others, including the main narrator. Czentovic wins of course but a second game catches the attention of another passenger, whose advice to the rest forces a draw, but who declares himself an amateur.

His story occupies the next part of the book. He is Dr B., a highly educated Austrian refugee, conservative, a lawyer for the Habsburg royal family, fleeing from the Nazis. He tells the tale of how he had been arrested by the Gestapo and questioned repeatedly, but not tortured; instead he is kept isolated with no books and no mental stimulus for several months. Eventually he steals a book which proves to be of chess-games; he learns these and plays them in his head, which makes him an expert, but also gives him a kind of chess-poisoning; he is constantly playing against himself, and this drives him mad. By now he is of no use to the Gestapo, and they release him.

When he plays on the ship with the other passengers against the automaton Czentovic, the latter's stolid stonewalling is too much for his quick brain. He starts to play his own game in his head, and eventually breaks down, never to play again. Czentovic sums him up as 'not bad, for an amateur'.

There are all kinds of dimensions in this short tale: on the storytelling level there is genuine tension in what will happen, and there is also a symbolic tension between the rigid single-talented ignoramus and the educated, cultivated Dr B., which is almost like the brash and unpleasant new world against the civilised older one which is on the run. And again, the whole thing is played out on a ship, itself a microcosm of life. But the main image in the story is chess itself, which Zweig lets his narrator tell us about: the royal game, invented by the gods so that we can while away our time, though it can also drive us mad; a sterile art that produces nothing, yet is infinitely varied, though restricted in the number of pieces and the moves; capable of being learnt by a child and played to grand master level; and finally, like life, capable of driving you mad.

Chess is a common enough image of life (it lasts a limited time, seems real, and at the end we all end up in the box, kings and pawns alike) and an image in plenty of works of literature, from Lewis Carroll to Nabokov. Zweig's story is one of the most impressive, and it is not for nothing that he chose the restricted form of the novella to tell it in: we concentrate on the game. There is a film (called *Three Moves to Freedom*) which is loosely based on the story, and which is best avoided. B M

'I knew well enough from my own experience the mysterious attraction of "the royal game", that game among games devised by man, which rises majestically above every tyranny of chance, which grants its victor's laurels only to a great intellect, or rather, to a particular form of mental activity.

But are we not already guilty of an insulting limitation in calling chess a game? Isn't it also a science, an art, hovering between these two categories like Muhammad's coffin hovered between heaven and earth? Isn't it a unique bond between every pair of opponents, ancient and yet eternally new...Where is its beginning and where is its end'. p8

**Database of German fiction translated in the UK. Includes books by writers from Germany, Austria and Switzerland.**

This database is for anyone who wants to read writers from these countries in English. Its main goal is to let you know what's available. The reviews section of the guide generally emphasizes books that are currently in print and that you can find or order at your bookshop now but this section includes *all* the contemporary (written after 1900) fiction published in the UK and most of the those translations published in North America currently distributed in the UK, with the name of the distributor.

Please note the price and availability of books changes from day to day as publishers withdraw, re-price and reprint. This database is a handy guide but for the latest information on a particular book ask your bookseller or librarian. Remember your bookseller can order you any in-print book and that public libraries can get you any current or out-of-print title, often at no charge.

Abbreviations:
HB  = hard cover edition
PB  = paperback edition
OP  = out of print (this means your bookshop can only sell you a copy if they have one in stock already. The publisher may reprint it though, so check later.)

Record details:
AUTHOR (surname)
Author (first name)
English title
Year this edition was published in the UK
German title
Year published in the German-speaking world
Translator's name
Publisher
Pages
Hardback or paperback
Price in £
*OR*
Out of print

## ABISH
Walter
**How German Is It. A novel**
1982
*Wie Deutsch ist es?*
1980
Carcanet New Press
252
HB
4.99
**In the Future Perfect**
1984
1983
Carcanet New Press
113
PB
4.99

## AGOSTON
Gerty
**My Bed Is Not for Sleeping**
1971
*Mein Bett ist nicht zum Schlafen da*
1967
Tandem
256
PB
OP
**My Carnal Confession**
1972
1967
Tandem
251
PB
OP

## AICHINGER
Ilse
**Bound Man and other stories, The**
1955
*Der Gefesselte: Erzählungen*
1953
Mosbacher, E
Secker & Warburg
100
HB

## ANDERSCH
Alfred
**Efraim's Book**
1978, 1984
*Efraim*
Manheim, R
Penguin
297
OP
**Efraim's Book**
1972
*Efraim*
1967
Manheim, R
Cape
306
HB
OP
**Flight to afar**

1958
*Sansibar oder der letzte Grund*
1957
Bullock, M
Gollancz
192
HB
OP
**Flight to afar**
1971
*Sansibar oder der letzte Grund*
1957
Bullock, M
Cedric Chivers Ltd
192
HB
7.95
**Night of the Giraffe & other stories, The**
1965
*In der Nacht der Giraffe*
1964
Armstrong, C
Murray
179
HB
OP
**Red-head, The**
1961
*Die Rote*
1960
Bullock, M
Heinemann
238
HB
OP
**Winterspelt**
1980
*Winterspelt*
1978
Winston, R & C
Owen
480
HB
12.95

## ANDRES
Stefan
**We Are Utopia**
1954
*Wir sind Utopia*
1951
Brooks, C
Gollancz
105
HB
OP

## ANON.
**Fear-Makers, The**
1959
Coburn, O
Joseph
296
HB
OP

## ANONYMOUS

**Promiscuous Pauline; or, The memoirs of a German opera singer**
1971
*Aus den Memoiren einer Sängerin*
Krauss, R J B
Luxor Press
190
PB
OP

## ANTHOLOGY
Green, M (Ed.)
**Golden Bomb, The. Phantastic German Expressionist Stories**
1996
*n/a*
n/a
GREEN, M
POLYGON
208
PB
8.95

## ANTHOLOGY
Green, M (Ed.)
**Black Letters Unleashed. 300 years of enthused writing in German**
1989
*n/a*
n/a
Green, M et al.
Atlas
250
PB
7.99

## ANTHOLOGY
**Old Land, New People. German Short Stories.**
1960
*n/a*
n/a
Becker, J
Seven Seas (E.Berlin)
214
PB
OP

## ANTHOLOGY
Abusch, A et al
**They Lived to See It; a collection of short stories**
1963
*n/a*
n/a
Becker, J
Seven Seas (E.Berlin)
167
PB
OP

## ANTHOLOGY
Witt, H (Ed.)
**Thinking it over: 30 stories from the GDR**

1977
*n/a*
n/a
var
Seven Seas (E.Berlin)
363
PB
OP

---

ANTHOLOGY
Edited By Constantine, D
**German Short Stories 2**
1976
*Deutsche Kurzgeschichten 2*
n/a
Various
Penguin
283
PB
5.99

---

ANTHOLOGY
Edited By Lappin, E
**Jewish Voices, German Words**
1995
*n/a*
n/a
Winston, K
Catbird: dist. Turnaround
334
HB
16.95

---

ANTHOLOGY
Edited By Newnham, R
**German Short Stories 1**
*Deutsche Kurzgeschichten 1*
n/a
Various
Penguin
176
PB
5.99

---

ANTHOLOGY
Furness, Ray (Ed.)
**Dedalus Book of German Decadence**
1994
*n/a*
n/a
Dedalus
356
PB
8.99

---

ANTHOLOGY
Humann, K (Ed.)
**Night Drive: Modern German Short Stories**
1995
*n/a*
n/a
Various
Serpent's Tail
304
PB
8.99

---

ANTHOLOGY

Lukens, N & Rosenberg, D
**Daughters of Eve; Women's writing from the German Democratic Republic**
1993
*n/a*
n/a
Lukens, N & Rosenberg, D
Nebraska UP
329
HB
38

---

ANTHOLOGY
Lukens, N & Rosenberg, D
**Daughters of Eve; Women's writing from the German Democratic Republic**
1993
*n/a*
n/a
Lukens, N & Rosenberg, D
Nebraska UP
329
PB

---

ANTHOLOGY
Mackinnon,E Kalla, G & Gr
**Writings beyond the Wall; literature from the German Democratic Republic**
1979
*n/a*
n/a
Various
Artery Publications
[Distributed by Central Books]
112
PB

---

ANTHOLOGY
Mitchell, Mike (Ed.)
**Dedalus Book of Austrian Fantasy**
1992
*n/a*
n/a
Dedalus
416
PB
8.99

---

ANTHOLOGY
Rütschi, E Herrmann, Hut
**German Women Writers of the Twentieth Century**
1978
*n/a*
n/a
Various
Pergamon
148
HB

---

ANTHOLOGY

Waidson, H M (Editor)
**Modern German Stories**
1961
*n/a*
n/a
Faber
232
OP

---

APITZ
Bruno
**Naked among Wolves**
1960
*Nackt unter Wölfen*
1958
Anderson, E
Seven Seas: Collets
416
PB
OP

---

ARJOUNI
Jacob
**Happy Birthday Turk**
1994
*Happy Birthday Türke*
1987
Hollo, A
No Exit
191
PB
8.99
**More Beer: A Kayankaya mystery**
1996
*Mehr Bier*
Anselm Hollo
No Exit
191
PB
4.99
**One Man, one Murder**
1996
*Ein Mann, ein Mord*
No Exit
191
PB
4.99

---

ARTMANN
H C
**Under the Cover of a Hat, montages and sequences. Green-sealed message**
1985
*Unter der Bedeckung eines Hutes & Grünenverschlossene Botschaft*
1974
Wynard, D
Quartet
119
PB
4.95
**Quest for Dr. U**
1992
Wynand, D & Green, M
Atlas Press

PB
7.99
**Sweat and Industry**
1992
*Fleiß und Industrie*
1967
Wynand, D
Atlas Press
64
PB
5.50

AUGUSTIN
Michael
**Certain Koslowski, A**
1992
*Koslowski, Geschichten nach dem Hörensagen*
1987
Lehbert, M
Littlewood Arc
63
PB
5.95

BACHMANN
Ingeborg
**Thirtieth Year, The**
1993
*Das dreißigste Jahr*
1961
BULLOCK, MICHAEL
POLYGON
192
PB
7.95
**Thirtieth year, The**
1964
*Das dreißigste Jahr*
1961
Bullock, M
Deutsch
187
HB
OP

BALL, H, HUELSENBECK, R & SERNER, W
**Blago Bung Blago Bung Bosso Fataka: First texts of German Dada**
1995
Green, M
Atlas P
175
PB
8.99

BAUER
Wolfgang
**Feverhead, The**
1996
*Fieberkopf*
1993
Malcolm Green
Atlas
120
PB
6.50

BAUM
Vicki
**Grand Hotel**
1972
*Menschen im Hotel*
1929
Creighton, B
Joseph
315
HB
OP
**Grand Hotel**
1930
*Menschen im Hotel*
1929
Creighton, B
Bles
315
HB
OP
**Hotel Shanghai**
1986
*Hotel Shanghai*
1939
Oxford University P: Hong Kong
619
4.95
**Nanking Road**
1986
Oxford University Press
4.95
**Nanking Road**
1964
1939
Creighton, B
New English Library
558
PB
**Tale from Bali, A**
1983
*Liebe und Tod auf Bali*
1937
Oxford University Press
PB
15.95
**Tale from Bali, A**
1973
*Liebe und Tod auf Bali*
1937
Joseph
512
HB
OP

BAUMANN
Hans
**Sons of the Steppe**
1957
*Steppensöhne*
1954
Mchugh, I & F
Oxford U.P.,
273
HB
OP

BAYER
Konrad

**Head of Vitus Bering, The**
1994
*Der Kopf des Vitus Bering*
1965
Billeter, W
Atlas
64
PB
5.50
**Selected Works of Konrad Bayer**
1986
*n/a*
n/a
Green, M
Atlas
154
PB
5.5

BECHER
Johannes Robert
**Farewell**
1970
*Abschied*
Becker, J
Seven Seas (E.Berlin)
378
PB
OP

BECKER
Joan
**Old Land, New People. German short stories**
1960
*n/a*
Abbott, L
Seven Seas; Collet's
215 p
PB
OP

BECKER
Jurek
**Five Stories**
1993
Manchester U.P.
168
PB
10.99
**Jacob the Liar**
1976
*Jakob der Lügner*
1969
Vennewitz, Leila
Harcourt Brace Jovanovich
266
HB
OP
**Jacob the Liar**
1990
*Jakob der Lügner*
1969
Vennewitz, Leila
Picador
207
HB
OP
**Sleepless Days**

1989
*Schlaflose Tage*
1979
Vennewitz, L
Paladin
132
PB
3.99
**Sleepless Days**
1979
*Schlaflose Tage*
1979
Vennewitz, L
Secker and Warburg
132p
HB
OP

BEMMANN
Hans
**Broken Goddess, The**
1993
Bell, A.
Penguin
234
PB
5.99
**Stone and the Flute, The**
1986
*Stein und Flöte*
Bell, A
Viking
855
HB
10.90
**Stone and the Flute, The**
1987
*Stein und Flöte*
Bell, A
Penguin
855
PB
4.95

BENARY
Margot
**Ark, The**
1954
*Die Arche Noah*
1948
Winston, C & R
Macmillan
281
HB
OP
**Blue Mystery**
1958
*Ein blaues Wunder*
Winston, R & C
Macmillan
190
HB
OP
**Castle on the Border**
1957
*Schloss an der Grenze*
1956
Winston, R & C
Macmillan
279

HB
OP
**Dangerous Spring**
1961
*Gefährlicher Frühling*
1961
Kirkup, J
Macmillan
252
HB
OP
**Rowan Farm**
1959
*Der Ebereschenhof*
1955
Winston, R & C
Macmillan
310
HB
OP
**Time to Love, A**
1963
Emerson, J with author
Macmillan
256
HB
OP
**Under a Changing Moon**
1965
*Unter dem Sichelmond*
1965
Ockenden, R with author
Macmillan
185
HB
OP
**Wicked Enchantment, The**
1956
*Heiligenwald*
1955
Winston, C & R
Macmillan
182
HB
OP

BEN-GAVRIEL
M.Y
**Mahaschavi in Peace and War**
1958
*Frieden und Krieg des Bürgers Mahaschavi*
1952
Creighton, B
Duckworth
221
HB
OP

BERGENGRUEN
Werner
**Last Captain of Horse, The: A portrait of chivalry**
1953
*Der letzte Rittmeister*
1952
Peters, E
Thames & Hudson
304

HB
OP
**Last Captain of Horse, The: A portrait of chivalry**
1953
*Der letzte Rittmeister*
1952
Peters, E
Thames & Hudson
304
HB
OP
**Matter of Conscience, A: A novel**
1952
*Der Großtyrann und das Gericht*
1949
Cameron, N
Thames & Hudson
312
HB
OP

BERGIUS
C.C.
**Noble Forger, The. A novel**
1962
*Der falsche Mohn*
1960
Coburn, O
Barker
299
HB
OP

BERNHARD
Thomas
**Cheap-Eaters, The**
1990
*Die Billigesser*
1980
Quartet
144
PB
11.95
**Concrete**
1989
*Beton*
1982
McLintock, D
Quartet
154
PB
5.95
**Concrete**
1984
*Beton*
1982
McLintock, D
Dent
154
HB
OP
**Correction**
1991
*Korrektur*
1975
Wilkins, S
Vintage

249
PB
5.99
**Cutting Timber. An imitation**
1993
*Holzfällen*
1984
Osers, Ewald
Vintage
160
PB
5.99
**Cutting Timber. An imitation**
1988
*Holzfällen*
1984
Osers, Ewald
Quartet
148
PB
9.95
**Cutting Timber. An imitation**
1988
*Holzfällen*
1984
Osers, Ewald
Quartet
148
HB
OP
**Extinction**
1995
*Auslöschung: Ein Zerfall*
1986
McLintock, David
Quartet
148
HB
12.95
**Gargoyles**
1986
*Verstörung*
1967
University of Chicago Press
208
PB
11.95
**Lime Work, The**
1986
*Das Kalkwerk*
1970
University of Chicago Press
241
PB
6.75
**Loser, The**
1992
*Der Untergeher*
1983
Dawson, J
Quartet
189
PB
3.95
**Old Masters. A comedy**
1989

*Alte Meister*
1985
Osers, E
Quartet
156
PB
11.95
**On the Mountain**
1994
*In der Höhe*
1991
Stockman, Russell
Quartet
143
PB
5.95
**Wittgenstein's Nephew. A friendship**
1986
*Wittgensteins Neffe*
1982
Osers, E
Quartet
120
7.95
**Wittgenstein's Nephew. A friendship**
1992
*Wittgensteins Neffe*
1982
Osers, E
Vintage
5.99
**Wittgenstein's Nephew. A friendship**
1990
*Wittgensteins Neffe*
1982
McLintock, D
Univ. Chicago Press
100
PB
7.95
**Yes**
1991
*Ja*
1978
Osers, E
U. Chicago P
OP
**Yes**
1991
*Ja*
1978
Osers, E
Quartet
135
12.95

**BERSTL**
Julius
**Cross and the Eagle, The**
1954
*Paulus von Tarsus (Part One)*
1965
Graves, C
Hodder & Stoughton
319

HB
OP
**Tentmaker, The**
1951
*Paulus von Tarsus (Part Two)*
1965
Graves, C
Hodder & Stoughton
320
HB
OP

**BERTHOLD**
Will
**Brandenburg Division**
1961
*Division Brandenburg.*
1960
Neame, A
Gibbs & Phillips
222
HB
OP
**Brandenburg Division**
1973
*Division Brandenburg.*
1960
Neame, A
Mayflower
160
PB
OP
**Brotherhood of Blood**
1982
*Feldpost Nummer unbekannt*
1978
Taylor, F
Sphere
252
PB
OP
**Death's Head Brigade**
1980
*Brigade Dirlewanger*
Magnus, C
Sphere
284
PB
OP
**Eagles of the Reich**
1980
*Vom Himmel zur Hölle*
1979
Taylor, F
Sphere
281
PB
OP
**Inferno 1**
1984
*Die ersten Blitzsiege*
1982
Taylor, F
Sphere
215
PB
OP
**Inferno 1**
1985
*Die ersten Blitzsiege*
1982

Taylor, F
Severn
215
HB
OP
**Inferno II Bloody Turning Point**
1986
*Siege und Niederlage*
1983
Taylor, F
Sphere
252
PB
2.50
**Lebensborn**
1977
*Lebensborn*
1975
Sphere
208
PB
**Prinz-Albrecht-Strasse**
1981
*Prinz-Albrecht -Straße*
1978
Taylor, F
Sphere
279
PB
OP
**Siegfried's Sword**
1986
*Ein Kerl wie Samt und Seide*
1984
Taylor, F
Sphere
343
PB
2.95

**BETKE**
Lotte
**Lights by the Canal**
1979
*Lampen am Kanal*
1976
Bell, A
Macmillan
117
PB
OP

**BICHSEL**
Peter
**And really Frau Blum Would very Much Like To Meet the Milkman. 21 short stories**
1968
*Eigentlich möchte Frau Blum den Milchmann kennenlernen*
1966
Hamburger, M
Calder & Boyars
88 p
HB
11.95

**BIELER**

Manfred
**Sailor in the Bottle, The**
1965
*Bonitaz oder Der Matrose in der Flasche*
1963
Clark, J
Hodder & Stoughton
221
HB
OP
**Sailor in the Bottle, The**
1967
*Bonitaz, oder der Matrose in der Flasche*
1963
Clark, J
Panther
224
PB
OP
**Three Daughters, The**
1978
*Der Mädchenkrieg*
1977
Talbot, K
Hodder and Stoughton
352
HB
OP

**BIENEK**
Horst
**Bakunin, an invention**
1977
*Bakunin, eine Invention*
1970
Read, R R
Gollancz
119
HB
OP
**Cell, The**
1974
*Die Zelle*
1968
Mahlendorf, U
Gollancz
94
HB
OP
**First Polka, The. A novel**
1978
*Die erste Polka*
1975
Read, R R
Gollancz
293
HB
OP

**BIERMAN**
Pieke
**Violetta**
1996
*Violetta*
1990
Rieder, I & Hannum, J
Serpent's Tail Mask Noir
256

PB
8.99

**BLOEMERTZ**
Gunther
**Freedom in Love**
1959
*Dem Himmel am nächsten*
Savill, M
Kimber
159
HB
OP

**BLUM**
Lisa Marie
**Mysterious Merry-Go-Round, The**
1962
*Das geheimnisvolle Karussell*
1959
Strachan, G
Abelard-Schuman
128p
HB
OP

**BLUNCK**
Hildegard
**Marco Polo: The great adventurer**
1966
*Marco Polo: der grosse Abenteurer*
1961
McHugh, F & I
Blackie
214
HB
OP

**BOBROWSKI**
Johannes
**I Taste Bitterness**
1970
*Der Mahner + Böhlendorff und Mausefest*
1965; 1967
Linder, M
Seven Seas (E.Berlin)
163
PB
OP
**Levin's Mill**
1970 (1964)
*Levins Mühle*
1964
Cropper, J
Calder & Boyars
230
HB
14.95

**BÖLL**
Heinrich
**Absent without Leave and other stories**
1967
*n/a*
Vennewitz, L

Weidenfeld & Nicolson
393
OP

**Absent without Leave and other stories**
1983
*n/a*
Vennewitz, L
Manon Boyars
393
PB
7.95

**Acquainted with the Night**
1955
*n/a*
1953
Graves, R
Hutchinson
192
HB
OP

**Adam, where were you ?**
1955
*Wo warst du Adam?*
1951
Savill, M
Arco
176
PB
OP

**And never said a word**
1994
*Und sagte kein einziges Wort*
1953
Vennewitz, L
Northwestern UP:Illinois
195
HB
OP

**And never said a word**
1978
*Und sagte kein einziges Wort*
1953
Vennewitz, L
Secker and Warburg
195
HB
OP

**And never said a word**
1982
*Und sagte kein einziges Wort*
1953
Vennewitz, L
Penguin
151
PB
OP

**And where were you, Adam?**
1978
*Wo warst du Adam?*
1951
Vennewitz, L
Penguin
157
PB
OP

**And where were you, Adam?**

1974
*Wo warst du, Adam?*
1951
Vennewitz, L
Secker and Warburg
156
HB
OP

**Billiards at half past nine**
1961
*Billiard um halb zehn*
1959
Bowles, P
Weidenfeld & Nicolson
286
HB
OP

**Billiards at half past nine**
1965
*Billiard um halb zehn*
1959
Bowles, P
Calder
256
PB
OP

**Billiards at half past nine**
1965
*Billiard um halb zehn*
1959
Bowles, P
M.Boyars
256
PB
9.95

**Bread of Our Early Years, The**
1957
*Das Brot der frühen Jahre*
1955
Savill, M
Arco
128
OP

**Bread of those Early Years, The**
1976
*Das Brot der frühen Jahre*
1955
Vennewitz, L
Secker & Warburg
124
HB
OP

**Bread of those Early Years, The**
1982
*Das Brot der frühen Jahre*
1955
Vennewitz, L
Penguin
91
PB
OP

**Casualty, The**
1986
*Die Verwundung*
Vennewitz, L
Chatto & Windus

160
HB
9.95

**Casualty, The**
1989
*Die Verwundung*
Vennewitz, L
Hogarth
192
PB
5.95

**Children Are Civilians too**
1973
*n/a*
Vennewitz, L
Secker and Warburg
190
OP

**Children Are Civilians too**
1976
*n/a*
Vennewitz, L
Penguin
184
PB
OP

**Clown, The**
1965
*Ansichten eines Clowns*
1963
Vennewitz, L
Weidenfeld & Nicolson
247
HB
OP

**Clown, The**
1972
*Ansichten eines Clowns*
1963
Vennewitz, L
Calder and Boyars
247
PB
9.95

**End of a Mission, The**
1978(1973)
*Ende einer Diensfahrt*
1968
Vennewitz, L
Penguin
167
PB
OP

**End of a Mission, The**
1994
*Ende einer Diensfahrt*
1968
Vennewitz, L
Northwestern UP:Illinois
207
HB
OP

**End of a Mission, The**
1994
*Ende einer Diensfahrt*
1968
Vennewitz, L
Northwestern UP:Illinois
207
PB

OP
**End of a Mission, The**
1968
*Ende einer Diensfahrt*
1966
Vennewitz, L
Weidenfeld & Nicolson
207
HB
OP
**End of a Mission, The**
1968
*Ende einer Dienstfahrt*
1966
Vennewitz, L
Weidenfeld & Nicolson
207
HB
OP
**Group Portrait with Lady**
1993
*Gruppenbild mit Dame*
1971
Vennewitz, L
Minerva
416
PB
6.99
**Group Portrait with Lady**
1973
*Gruppenbild mit Dame*
1971
Vennewitz, L
Secker and Warburg
406
HB
OP
**Group Portrait with Lady**
1976
*Gruppenbild mit Dame*
1971
Vennewitz, L
Penguin
406
OP
**Irish Journal**
1994
*Irisches Tagebuch*
1957
Vennewitz, L
Northwestern UP:Illinois
127
HB
**Irish Journal**
1994
*Irisches Tagebuch*
1957
Vennewitz, L
Northwestern UP:Illinois
127
PB
**Irish Journal**
*Irisches Tagebuch*
1957
Vennewitz, L
Minerva
128
PB
6.99
**Irish Journal**

1984
*Irisches Tagebuch*
1957
Vennewitz, L
Abacus
128
PB
OP
**Irish Journal**
1983
*Irisches Tagebuch*
1957
Vennewitz, L
Secker & Warburg
128
HB
OP
**Lost Honour of Katharina Blum**
1993
*Die verlorene Ehre der Katharina Blum*
1974
Vennewitz, L
Minerva
139
PB
4.99
**Lost Honour of Katharina Blum, The or, How violence develops and where it can lead**
1978
*Die verlorene Ehre der Katharina Blum*
1974
Vennewitz, L
Penguin
116
PB
OP
**Lost Honour of Katharina Blum,The or, How violence develops and where it can lead**
1975
*Die verlorene Ehre der Katharina Blum*
1974
Vennewitz, L
Secker and Warburg
141
OP
**Lost Honour of Katharina Blum,The or, How violence develops and where it can lead**
1989
*Die verlorene Ehre der Katharina Blum*
1974
Vennewitz, L
Guild Large Print
14.95
**Safety Net, The**
1982
*Fürsorgliche Belagerung*

Vennewitz, L
Secker & Warburg
313
9.95
**Safety Net, The**
1983
*Fürsorgliche Belagerung*
Vennewitz, L
Abacus
313
PB
OP
**Silent Angel, The**
1994
*Der Engel schwieg*
1992
Mitchell, B
Deutsch
173
HB
14.99
**Soldier's Legacy, A**
1985
*Das Vermächtnis*
Vennewitz, L
Secker & Warburg
144
HB
8.85
**Stories of Heinrich Böll, The**
1986
*n/a*
n/a
Var
Secker & Warburg
HB
15.00
**Stories of Heinrich Böll, The**
1988
*n/a*
n/a
Various
Abacus
PB
5.99
**Train Was on Time, The**
1994
*Der Zug war pünktlich*
1949
Vennewitz, L
Northwestern UP:Illinois
110
HB
**Train Was on Time, The**
1994
*Der Zug war pünktlich*
1949
Vennewitz, L
Northwestern UP:Illinois
110
PB
**Train Was on Time, The**
1956
*Der Zug war pünktlich*
1949
Graves, R
Arco

142
OP
**Train Was on Time, The**
1979
*Der Zug war pünktlich*
1949
Vennewitz, L
Penguin
113
PB
**Train Was on Time, The**
1967
*Der Zug war pünktlich*
1949
Graves, R
Sphere Books
124
OP
**Train Was on Time, The**
1973
*Der Zug war pünktlich*
1949
Vennewitz, L
Secker and Warburg
110
HB
9.95
**Traveller, if You Come to Spa-;**
1956
*Wanderer kommst du nach Spa*
1950
Savill, M
Arco
199
OP
**Unguarded House, The**
1957
*Haus ohne Hüter*
1954
Savill, M
Arco
255
HB
OP
**Unguarded House, The**
1957
*Das Haus ohne Hüter*
1954
Savill, M
Arco
255
OP
**What's to Become of the Boy?, or, Something to do with books**
1985
*Was soll aus dem Jungen bloß werden?*
1984
Vennewitz, L
Secker & Warburg
82
HB
9.95
**Women in a River Landscape, a novel in dialogues and soliloquies**
1988
*Frauen vor Flußlandschaft*
1985
McLintock, D
Secker & Warburg
207
HB
10.95
**Women in a River Landscape. A novel in dialogues and soliloquies**
1988
*Frauen vor Flußlandschaft*
1985
McLintock, D
Secker & Warburg
HB
4.99

**BORCHERT**
Wolfgang
**Man Outside, The**
1996
*Draußen vor der Tür*
1947
Porter, D
Boyars
275
PB
8.95
**Sad Geraniums and other stories, The**
1974
*Die traurigen Geranien*
1962
Hamnett, K
Calder and Boyars
87
13.95

**BORN**
Nicolas
**Deception, The**
1983
*Die Fälschung*
1979
Vennewitz, L
Calder
238
PB
6.95

**BRAUN**
Hans Martin
**Flight over the Border. A novel**
1985
*Flug über die Grenze*
Marshalls
127
PB
1.75

**BRAUNBURG**
Rudolf
**Betrayed Skies. A novel**
1981
*Der verratene Himmel*

1980
Brownjohn, J M
Severn House
366
HB
OP

**BRAUNIG, W ET AL**
**Pair of Mittens and other stories, A. Stories by Braunig, W, Djacenko, B, Claudius, E, Fuhmann, F, Neutsch, E**
1961
*n/a*
n/a
Becker, J
Seven Seas (E.Berlin)
145
PB
OP

**BRECHT**
Bertolt
**Bertolt Brecht Collected Short Stories**
1992
*Kurzgeschichten 1921-1946*
n/a
Kapp, Y, Rorrison, H & Tatlow, A
Minerva
PB
5.99
**Bertolt Brecht Short Stories 1921-1946**
1983
*Kurzgeschichten 1921-1946*
n/a
Kapp, Y, Rorrison, H & Tatlow, A
Methuen
242
HB
OP
**Penny for the Poor, A**
1937
*Der Dreigroschenroman*
1934
Vesey, D & Isherwood, Ch
Hale
396
HB
OP
**Tales from the Calendar**
1961
*Kalendergeschichten*
1949
Kapp, Y & Hamburger, M
Methuen
124
HB
OP
**Threepenny Novel**
1981
*Der Dreigroschenroman*
1934
Vesey, I D &Sherwood, Ch
Granada
369
PB
OP

**Threepenny Novel**
1958
*Der Dreigroschenroman*
1934
Vesey, D & Isherwood, Ch
B. Hanison
396
HB
OP
**Threepenny Novel**
1989
*Der Dreigroschenroman*
1934
Vesey, D with Isherwood, C
Penguin
368
PB
6.99

BREISKY
Hubert Von
**Country of the Grey Gods, The**
1962
*Der Koloß*
1959
Fitzgerald, E
Putnam
423
HB
OP

BREITBACH
Joseph
**Report on Bruno**
1964
*Bericht über Bruno*
1962
Bullock, M
Cape
320
HB
OP

BREZAN
Juri
**Fallow Years, The**
1963
*Semester der verlorenen Zeit*
Becker, J, Stone, V & White, A
Seven Seas (E.Berlin)
270
PB
OP

BROCH
Hermann
**Death of Virgil, The**
1977
*Der Tod des Vergil*
1945
Untermeyer, J S
Routledge and Kegan Paul
493
HB
OP
**Guiltless, The**
1990
*Die Schuldlosen*
1950
Manheim, R

Quartet
292
PB
6.95
**Sleepwalkers, The**
1986
*Die Schlafwandler*
1930-2
Muir, W & E
Quartet
648
PB
9.90
**Spell, The**
1987
*Die Verzauberung*
1953
Broch, H F de & Rothermann
Deutsch
391
HB
11.90

BRUCKNER
Karl
**Hour of the Robots, The**
1964
*Nur zwei Roboter*
1966
Lobb, F
Burke
187
OP

BRÜCKNER
Christine
**Gabrielle**
1956
*Ehe die Spuren verwehen*
1954
Selver, P
Hale
192
HB
OP
**Katarina**
1958
*Katharina und der Zaungast*
1957
Savill, M
Hale
192
HB
OP

BRUEGEL
Friedrich
**Plotters, The**
1952
*Verschwörer*
1951
Dent, A
Gollancz
256
HB
OP

BRUNNER
Fritz
**Trouble in Brusada**
1962

*Aufruhr in Brusada*
1960
Kirkup, J
University of London P
160
HB
OP

BUBER
Martin
**Tales of Rabbi Nahman, The**
1974
*Die Geschichten des Rabbi Nahman*
1906
Friedman, M
Souvenir Press
214
HB
OP
**Tales of Rabbi Nahman, The**
1988
*Die Geschichten des Rabbi Nahman*
1906
Friedman, M
Humanities Press
232
PB
12.95

BUCH
Hans Christoph
**Wedding at Port-au-Prince, The**
1987
*Die Hochzeit von Port-au-Prince*
1984
Faber
259
HB
10.95

BUCHHEIM
Lothar Günther
**Boat, The**
1982
*Das Boot*
1973
Brownjohn, J M
Fontana
480
PB
**U-boat**
1974
*Das Boot*
1973
Brownjohn, J M
Collins
480
HB
OP

BURGBACHER
Kurt
**White Hell**
1963

*Pilot in der weißen Hölle*
1961
Humphries, S
**Methuen**
208
HB
OP

**BURK**
Michael
**Tribunal, The**
1978
*Das Tribunal*
1973
Bullock, M
**Coronet**
285
PB
OP

**CANETTI**
Elias
**Auto da Fé**
1982
*Die Blendung*
1935
Wedgwood, C V
**Cape**
464
HB
7.95
OP
**Auto da Fé**
1978
*Die Blendung*
1935
Wedgwood, C V
**Pan Books**
428
PB
OP
**Auto da Fé**
1973
*Die Blendung*
1935
Wedgwood, C V
**Penguin**
522
PB
OP
**Auto de Fé**
1965
*Die Blendung*
1935
Wedgewood, C V
**Penguin**
552
PB
OP
**Auto de Fé**
1995
*Die Blendung*
1935
Wedgewood, C V
**Vintage**
464
PB
6.99

**CANETTI**
Veza

**Yellow Street, The. A novel in five scenes**
1990
*Die gelbe Straße*
Mitchell, I
**Halban**
139
HB
OP

**CAROSSA**
Hans
**Year of Sweet Illusions, The**
1951
*Das Jahr der schönen Täuschungen*
1941
Kee, R
**Methuen**
213
HB
OP

**CESCO**
Federica De
**Prince of Mexico, The**
1968
*Prinz von Mexiko, Der*
1965
Lobb, F
**Burke**
224
HB
OP

**CONTA**
Manfred Von
**Deathbringer, The**
1971
*Der Totmacher*
1969
Figes, E
**Calder and Boyars**
224
HB
OP

**CONTE**
Manfred
**Cassia**
1965
*Cassia und der Abenteurer*
1951
Author
**Collins**
318
HB
OP

**CROSTA**
Nicolas De
**Blanche**
1958
*Bis aller Glanz erlosch*
1953
Pomerans, A
**Barrie**
381
HB
OP

**DARLTON** <aka ERNSTING, Walter>
Clark
**Escape to Venus**
1976
*Die Venusbasis*
1963
Ackermann, W
**Futura Publications**
116
PB
OP
**Challenge of the Unknown**
1978
*Aktion gegen unbekannt*
Ackermann, W
**Futura Publications**
127
PB
OP

**DE CESCO**
Federica
**Prince of Mexico, The**
1968
*Der Prinz von Mexiko*
1965
Lobb, F
**Burke**
224
HB
OP
**Wind of the Camargue, The**
1972
*Im Wind der Camargue*
1966
Humphries, S
**Burke**
191
HB
OP

**DEWOHL**
Louis
**David of Jerusalem**
1964
*König David*
1961
Abbott, E
**Gollancz**
256
OP

**DEICH**
Friedrich
**Sanity Inspector, The. A novel**
1956
*Windarzt und Apfelsinenpfarrer*
1955
Kee, R
**Putnam**
200
HB
OP

**DELBEKE**
Yvette
**Diary of an Awakening**
1986
*Tagebuch eines Erwachens*
Wilson, D H
Loxwood Stoneleigh
102
HB
5.95

**DEMETZ**
Hana
**House on Prague Street, The**
1980
*Ein Haus in Böhmen*
1970
author
Allen, W H
186
PB
OP

**DEMSKI**
Eva
**Dead Alive**
1989
*Scheintod*
1986
Heurck, I van
Methuen
304
HB
OP

**DÖBLIN**
Alfred
**Berlin Alexanderplatz. The story of Franz Biberkopf**
1978
*Berlin Alexanderplatz*
1929
Jolas, E
Penguin
478
PB
OP

**Berlin Alexanderplatz. The story of Franz Biberkopf**
1974
*Berlin Alexanderplatz*
1929
Jolas, E
Secker and Warburg
396
HB
OP

**Destiny's Journey**
1992
*Schicksalreise; Bericht und Bekentnis*
McCown, E
Paragon
338
21.99

**Journey to Poland**
1991
*Reise in Polen*

Neugroschel, J
Paragon
300
HB
29.90

**Karl And Rosa**
1983
*Karl und Rosa*
Woods, J E
Angel Books: dist Airlift
560
PB
OP

**People Betrayed, A**
*Verratenes Volk*
Woods J E
Angel Books: dist Airlift
652
HB
OP

**People Betrayed, A**
1986
*Heimkehr der Fronttruppen*
1948-50
Woods, J E
Angel Books: dist Airlift
652
PB
OP

**DODERER**
Heimito Von
**Merovingians, The**
1996
1962
Binner, V.B.
Sun and Moon USA: dist.
Passwo
420
PB
10.95

**Demons, The. (Pt 2)**
1989
*Die Dämonen*
1956
Winston, R & C
Quartet Encounters
379
PB
8.50

**Demons, The. (Pt 3)**
1989
*Die Dämonen*
1956
Winston, R & C
Quartet Encounters
484
PB
8.50

**Demons, The. (Pt 4)**
1989
*Die Dämonen*
1956
Winston, R & C
Quartet Encounters
379
PB
8.50

**DOR**

Milo
**Dead Men on Leave**
1962
*Tote auf Urlaub*
1961
Bullock, M
Barrie & Rockliff
391
HB
OP

**DÖRFLA**
Eugen
**Censored Mistletoe**
1980
*Die zensorierte Mistel*
Sail, F
S.Editions
21
PB
OP

**DORMANN**
Hans
**Soldiers and no General**
1959
*Soldaten und kein General*
1956
Cohen, R & Earney, A
Hamilton
158
PB
OP

**Soldiers and no General**
1958
*Soldaten und kein General*
1956
Coben, R & Earney, A
Angus & Robertson
175
HB
OP

**DÖRRIE**
Doris
**Love, Pain and the Whole Damn Thing. Four stories**
1991
*Liebe, Schmerz und das ganze verdammte Zeug*
1987
Woods, J E
Penguin
177
PB
5.99

**Love, Pain and the Whole Damn Thing**
1989
*Liebe, Schmerz und das ganze verdammte Zeug*
1987
Woods, J E
Viking
177
PB
11.95

**DUBINA**
Peter

**Decision in Space**
1976
*Entscheidung im Weltraum*
1973
Crampton, P
Abelard-Schuman
125
HB
OP

DUDEN
Anne
**Opening of the Mouth**
1985
*Übergang*
1982
Couling, D
Pluto
144
PB
OP

DÜRRENMATT
Friedrich
**Assignment or, On the observing of the observer of the observers, The**
1988
*Der Auftrag*
1986
Agee, J
Cape
129
HB
9.95

**Dangerous Game, A**
1960
*Die Panne*
1956
Winston, R & C
Cape
95
HB

**Execution of Justice, The**
1989
*Justiz*
1985
Wood, J E
Cape
261
HB
12.90

**Execution of Justice, The**
1990
*Justiz*
1985
Woods, J E
Picador
216
PB
4.99

**Judge and His Hangman, The**
1969
*Der Richter und sein Henker*
1951
Brooks, G
Penguin
112
PB

**Judge and His Hangman, The**
1954
*Der Richter und sein Henker*
1951
Brooks, C
Jenkins
123
HB
OP

**Judge and His Hangman, The**
1967
*Der Richter und sein Henker*
1951
Brooks, C
Cape
127
HB
OP

**Judge and His Hangman, The**
1961
*Der Richter und sein Henker*
1951
Brooks, C
Four Square
127
PB
OP

**Novels of Friedrich Dürrenmatt, The**
1985
*Der Richter und sein Henker; Der Verdacht; Grieche sucht Griechin; Die Panne; Das Versprechen*
1951-56
Pan
413
PB
OP

**Once a Greek**
1966
*Grieche sucht Griechin*
1955
Winston, R & C
Cape
180
HB
OP

**Pledge, The**
1964
*Das Versprechen*
1958
Winston, C & W
Penguin & Cape
143
PB
OP

**Pledge, The**
1959
*Das Versprechen*
1958
Winston, R & C
Cape
190
HB
OP

**Quarry, The**
1962
*Der Verdacht*
1953
Morreale, E H
Cape
162
HB
OP

EKERT-ROTHOLZ
Alice
**Marie Bonnard**
1962
*Mohn in den Bergen*
1961
Bullock, M
Cape
477
HB
OP

**Net of Gold, A**
1960
*Strafende*
1959
Winston, R & C
Cape
415
HB
OP

**Time of the Dragons, The**
1958
*Wo Tränen verboten sind*
1956
Winston, R & C
Cape
476
HB
OP

**Time of the Dragons, The**
1961
*Wo Tränen verboten sind*
1956
Winston, R & C
Pan Books
382
PB
OP

ELBOGEN
Paul
**Jealous Mistress, The**
1955
Lachenbruch, R
Redman
347
HB
OP

ELLERT
Gerhart
**Knights of St.John**
1958
*Kreuzritter*
1955
Bockett-Pugh, J
Lutterworth P
139
HB
OP

**ELSNER**
Gisela
**Giant Dwarfs, The**
1965
*Die Riesenzwerge*
1964
Carmichael, J
Weidenfeld & Nicolson
309
HB
OP
**Offside**
1985
*Abseits*
1982
Bell, A
Virago
204
HB
OP

**ERNSTING**
Walter
**Invasion from Space**
1974
Mahr, K with author
Futura Publications Ltd
187
OP
**Day the Gods Died, The**
1977
*Der Tag, an dem die Götter starben*
1976
Ackerman, W
Corgi
240
PB
OP

**ESKA**
Karl
**Five Seasons, The**
1954
*Fünf Jahreszeiten*
1952
Kee, R
Hart-Davis
331
HB
OP

**FAECKE**
Peter
**Firebugs, The**
1965
*Die Brandstifter*
1963
Pomerans, J R
Secker & Warburg
141
HB
OP

**FALKENSEE**
Margarete, Von
**Blue Angel Days**
1987
Haas, E
Allen, W H

287
2.99
**Blue Angel Days**
1987
Haas, E.
Allen, W H
287
HB
11.90
**Blue Angel Nights**
1986
Haas, E
Allen, W H
252
PB
2.95
**Blue Angel Nights**
1986
Allen, W H
252
HB
OP
**Blue Angel Secrets**
1988
Allen, W H
240
PB
2.99

**FALLADA**
Hans
**Drinker, The**
1952
*Der Trinker*
1950
Lloyd, C & A
Putnam
282
HB
OP
**Drinker, The**
1989
*Der Trinker*
1950
Lloyd, A L
Libris
282
HB
14.90
**Iron Gustav**
1969
*Der eiserne Gustav*
1938
Owens, P
H.Baker
461
HB
OP
**Little Man – What Now?**
1996
*Kleiner Mann - was nun?*
1932
Susan Bennett
Libris
325
HB
13.50
**Little Man – What Now?**
1969

*Kleiner Mann - was nun?*
1932
Sutton, E
Howard Baker Ltd
441
HB
OP
**That Rascal Fridolin**
1959
*Fridolin, der freche Dachs*
1955
Michaelis-Jena, R & Ratcliff, A
Heinemann
166
OP
**Who once Eats out of the Tin Bowl**
1969
*Wer einmal aus dem Blechnapf frißt*
1934
Sutton, E
H.Baker
568
HB
OP
**Wolf among Wolves**
1970(1938)
*Wolf unter Wölfen*
1937
Owens, P
Howard Baker
966
HB
OP

**FANGER**
Horst
**Life for a Life, A**
1956
*Wir selber sind das Rad*
1952
Winston, R & C
Hale
190
HB
OP

**FASCHINGER**
Lillian
**Magdalena the Sinner**
1996
1995
Whiteside, Shaun
Headline
276
12.99

**FEDERSPIEL**
J. F.
**Ballad of Typhoid Mary, The**
1985
*Die Ballade von der Typhoid Mary*
1983
Agee, J
Penguin
171
PB

OP
**Ballad of Typhoid Mary, The**
1984
*Die Ballade von der Typhoid Mary*
1983
Agee, J
Deutsch
171
HB
OP

---

FERNAU
Joachim
**Captain Pax**
1960
*Bericht von der Furchbarkeit und Grösse der Männer*
1954
Kee, R
Constable
134
OP

---

FEUCHTWANGER
Lion
**Jephthah and His Daughter**
1958
*Jefta und seine Tochter*
1957
Wilkins, E & Kaiser, E
Hutchinson
271
HB
OP
**Jew Süß**
1986
*Jude Süß*
1925
Muir, W. E.
Grafton
432
PB
3.95
**Racquel, the Jewess of Toledo**
1956
*Die Jüdin von Toledo*
1954
Wilkins, E & Kaiser, E
Hutchinson
415
HB
OP
**This is the Hour, A novel about Goya**
1952
*Goya*
1951
Fawcett, F & Lowe-Porete, H T
Hutchinson
480
HB
OP
**Tis Folly To Be Wise, or, Death and transfiguration of Jean-Jaques Rousseau**

**a novel**
1954
*Narrenweisheit*
1952
Fawcett, F
Hutchinson
392
HB
OP
**Ugly Duchess, The**
1972 (1927)
*Die hässliche Herzogin Margarete Maultasch*
1926
Muir, W & E
Hutchinson
335
HB
OP

---

FICHTE
Hubert
**Detlev's Imitations**
1992
*Detlevs Imitationen*
1971
Chalmers, M
Serpent's Tail
255
PB
8.99
**Orphanage, The**
1990
*Das Waisenhaus*
1965
CHALMERS, M
SERPENT'S TAIL
161
PB
6.95

---

FISCHER
Wolfgang Georg
**Lodgings in Exile. A novel**
1979
*Möblierte Zimmer*
1972
Goodwin, I & Fischer, W G
Owen
264
HB
6.95

---

FONTANE
Theodor
**Before the Storm. A Novel of the winter of 1812-13**
1985
*Vor dem Sturm*
1878
Hollingdale, J
Oxford University Press
712
PB
OP
**Beyond Recall**
1964
*Unwiederbringlich*
1891
Parme, D

Oxford U.P
299
HB
OP
**Cécile**
1992
*Cécile*
1887
Radcliffe, J
Angel
199
HB
13.95
**Cécile**
1992
*Cécile*
1887
Radcliffe, J.
Angel Bks.
200
PB
6.95
**Effi Briest**
1995
*Effi Briest*
1895
Rorrison, H & Chambers, H
Angel
245
PB
8.95
**Effi Briest**
1976 (1967)
*Effi Briest*
1895
Parme, D
Penguin
267
PB
6.99
**Entanglements: An everyday Berlin story**
1986
*Irrungen, Wirrungen*
1888
Bowman, D
Three Rivers
180
8.95
**Short novels and other writings**
1984
n/a
Continuum (New York)
352
PB
12.95
**Stechlin, The**
1995
*Der Stechlin*
1899
Radcliffe, S
Camden House, SC, USA: dist Boydell & Brewer
340
HB
33
**Suitable match, A**

1968
*Irrungen Wirrungen*
1888
Morris, S
Blackie
186
OP
**Woman Taken in Adultery, & The Poggenpuhl Family, The**
1995
*L'Adultera*
1882
Annan, G
Penguin
231
PB
6.99
**Woman Taken in Adultery, & The Poggenpuhl family**
1979
*L'Adultera*
1882
Annan, G
Chicago University Press
231
OP

**FRANCOIS**
Louise Von
**Last Von Reckenburg**
1995
*Die letzte Reckenburgerin*
1871
Laane, T
Camden Ho. USA dist
Boydell & Brewer
250
39.5

**FRANK**
Herbert
**Silent Witness, The**
1955
*Stumme, Der*
1952
Vesey, D I
Museum P.,
224
OP

**FRANK**
Leonhard
**Heart on the Left**
1954
*Links, wo das Herz ist*
1952
Brooks, C
Barker
192
HB
OP

**FRIEBERGER**
Kurt
**Simon Peter the Fisherman: A novel**
1955
*Der Fischer Simon Petrus*
1953

Lloyd, A
Heinemann
365
HB
OP

**FRIED**
Erich
**Children And Fools**
1992
*Kinder und Narren*
1965
Chalmers, M
Serpent's Tail
168
PB
8.99

**FRISCH**
Max
**Bluebeard**
1985
*Blaubart*
1983
Skelton, G
Penguin
141
PB
OP

**Bluebeard**
1983
*Blaubart*
1983
Skelton, G
Methuen
141
PB
OP

**Gantenbein. A novel**
1982
*Mein Name sei Gantenbein*
1965
Bullock, M
Methuen
304
OP

**Homo Faber**
1959
*Homo Faber*
1957
Bullock, M
Abelard-Schuman
198
HB
OP

**Homo faber. A report**
1974
*Homo Faber*
1957
Bullock, M
Penguin in association with Eyre Methuen
217
OP

**I'm not Stiller**
1958
*Stiller*
1954
Bullock, M
Abelard-Schuman

363
HB
OP
**I'm not Stiller**
1983
*Stiller*
1954
Bullock, M
Penguin
383
PB
OP

**I'm not Stiller**
1982
*Stiller*
1954
Bullock, M
Methuen
400
PB
9.95

**Man in the Holocene. A story**
1980
*Der Mensch erscheint im Holozän*
1979
Skelton, G
Methuen, E
113
HB
OP

**Novels, Plays, Essays**
1992
*n/a*
n/a
Demetz, Peter
Continuum
354
PB
14.99

**Wilderness of Mirrors, A a novel**
1965
*Mein Name sei Gantenbein*
1964
Bullock, M
Methuen
304
OP

**FRISCHLER**
Kurt
**Ayesha**
1961
*Aischa: Mohammeds Lieblingfrau*
1957
Norman, D
Barrie & Rockliff
254
OP

**FÜHMANN**
Franz
**Car with the Yellow Star, The: fourteen days out of two decades**
1968

*Das Judenauto*
Seven Seas (E.Berlin)
174
PB
OP
**Twenty-Two Days or Half a Lifetime**
1992
*Zweiundzwanzig Tage oder die Hälfte des Lebens*
1973
Vennewitz, L
Cape
258
PB
6.99
**Twenty-Two Days or Half a Lifetime**
1980
*Zweiundzwanzig Tage: oder, die Halfte des LEbens*
Vennewitz, L
Seven Seas (E.Berlin)
258
PB
OP

**FURNBERG**
Louis
**Conversations in the Night: Selected works**
1969
Becker, J
Seven Seas (E.Berlin)
257
PB
OP

**GABEL**
Wolfgang
**Breakfast together for Always**
1980
*Immer zusammen frühstücken*
1977
Bell, A
Macmillan
125
HB
OP

**GAISER**
Gerd
**Falling Leaf, The**
1956
*Die sterbende Jagd*
1953
Findlay, P
Collins
256
HB
OP
**Last Dance of the Season, The**
1960
*Schlussball. Aus dem schönen Tagen der Stadt Neu*
1958
Waldman, M

Collins
255
HB
OP
**Last Squadron, The**
1960
*Die sterbende Jagd*
1953
Findlay, P
Collins
253
HB
OP

**GEISSLER**
Christian
**Sins of the Fathers, The**
1962
*Anfrage?*
1960
Kirkup, J
Weidenfeld & Nicolson
256
HB
OP

**GERLACH**
Heinrich
**Forsaken Army, The**
1958
*Die verratene Armee*
1957
Graves, R
Weidenfeld & Nicolson
384
HB
OP
**Forsaken Army, The**
1960
*Die verratene Armee*
1957
Graves, R
Transworld
444
PB
OP

**GLAESER**
Ernst
**Shady Miracle, The**
1963
*Glanz und Elend der Deutschen*
1960
Graves, R
Secker & Warburg
287
HB
OP

**GOES**
Albrecht
**Arrow to the Heart**
1951
*Unruhige Nacht*
1950
Fitzgibbon, C
Joseph
104
HB
OP

**Burnt Offering, The**
1956
*Das Brandopfer*
1954
Hamburger, M
Gollancz
95
HB
OP

**GOLDSCHMIDT**
Georges-Arthur
**Worlds of Difference**
1993
*Absonderungen*
1991
Kirkup, J
Quartet
224
PB
12.95

**GRAB**
Hermann
**Town park and other stories, The**
1988
*Stadtpark und andere Erzählungen*
1934
Hoare, Q
Verso
250
HB
10.90

**GRASS**
Günter
**Call of the Toad**
1993
*Unkenrufe*
1982
Manheim, R
Minerva
256
PB
6.99
**Call of the Toad**
1992
*Unkenrufe*
1992
Manheim, R
Secker & Warburg
248
HB
14.90
**Cat and Mouse**
1966
*Katz und Maus*
1961
Manheim, R
Secker & Warburg & Penguin
137
PB
OP
**Cat and Mouse**
1963 (1982)
*Katz und Maus*
1961
Manheim, R

Secker & Warburg
191
HB
OP
**Dog Years**
1969
*Hundejahre*
1963
Manheim, R
Penguin
617
PB
OP
**Dog Years**
1965
*Hundejahre*
1963
Manheim, R
Secker & Warburg
570
HB
OP
**Flounder, The**
1978
*Der Butt*
1977
Manheim, R
Secker and Warburg
547
HB
OP
**Flounder, The**
1979
*Der Butt*
1977
Manheim, R
Penguin
547
PB
OP
**From the Diary of a Snail**
1974
*Aus dem Tagebuch einer Schnecke*
1972
Manheim, R
Secker and Warburg
310
HB
OP
**From the Diary of a Snail**
1976
*Aus dem Tagebuch einer Schnecke*
1972
Manheim, R
Penguin
PB
OP
**From the Diary of a Snail**
1997
*Aus dem Tagebuch einer Schnecke*
Ralph Manheim
Minerva
310
PB
7.99
**Headbirths, or, The**

**Germans are dying out**
1982
*Kopfgeburten od. die Deutschen sterben aus*
1980
Manheim, R
Secker & Warburg
136
HB
OP
**Headbirths, or, The Germans are dying out**
1984
*Kopfgeburten od. die Deutschen sterben aus*
1980
Manheim, R
Penguin
127
PB
OP
**Local Anaesthetic**
1969
*Örtlich betäubt*
1969
Manheim, R
Secker & Warburg
284
HB
OP
**Local Anaesthetic**
1973
*Örtlich betäubt*
1969
Manheim, R
Penguin
231
PB
OP
**Meeting at Telgte, The**
1981
*Das Treffen in Telgte*
1983
Mannheim, R
Secker & Warburg
224
HB
10.95
**Meeting at Telgte, The**
1983
*Das Treffen in Telgte*
1981
Mannheim, R
Penguin
152
PB
OP
**Rat, The**
1987
*Die Rättin*
1986
Manheim, R
Secker & Warburg
358
HB
12.90
**Show your Tongue**
1989
*Zunge zeigen*

1988
Wood, J
Secker and Warburg
240
HB
20.00
**Tin Drum, The**
1962
*Die Blechtrommel*
1959
Manheim, R
Secker & Warburg
591
HB
OP
**Tin Drum, The**
1993
*Die Blechtrommel*
1959
Manheim, R
Everyman
551
HB
10.99
**Tin Drum, The**
1965
*Die Blechtrommel*
1959
Manheim, R
Penguin
585
PB
OP
**Tin Drum, The**
1997
*Die Blechtrommel*
1959
Manheim, R
Minerva
592
PB
8.99
**Wide Field**
1997
Secker
HB
15.99

**GREGOR**
Manfred
**Bridge, The**
1962
*Die Brücke*
1960
Rosen, R S
Cresset
192
OP
**Bridge, The**
1963
*Die Brücke*
1960
Rosen, R S
Hamilton & Co
127
HB
OP
**Town without Pity**
1961
*Urteil, Das*

1960
Brain, R
Heinemann
245
HB
OP

## GREGOR-DELLIN
Martin
**Lamp Post, The**
1965
*Der Kandelaber*
1962
Winston, R & C
Barrie & Rockliff
OP

## GROSSER
Karlheinz
**Tamburas**
1970
*Tamburas*
1965
Szasz, K
New English Library
380
PB
OP
**Tamburas**
1967
*Tamburas*
1965
Szasz, K
Heinemann
442
HB
OP

## GUADAGNA
Ingeborg
**Proceed to Judgement**
1953
*Die Ehe der Vanna Licusu*
1950
Vesey, D I
Hale
159
HB
OP

## GUENTHER
Johannes Von
**Cagliostro, ultimate move of Freemasonry and Alchemy**
1992
*Cagliostro, Roman*
Paterson, H
Allborough Publishing
475
PB
13.50

## GUHA
Anton, Andreas
**Ende: A diary of the Third World War**
1986
*Ende: Tagebuch aus der 3. Weltkrieg*
1983

Taylor, F
Corgi
173
PB
2.95

## GÜTHERSLOH
Albert Paris
**Fraud, The**
1965
*Der Lügner unter Bürgern*
1922
Nowell, J
Owen
144
HB
OP

## HABE
Hans
**Agent of the Devil**
1959
*Im Namen des Teufels*
1956
Osers, E
Transworld
349
PB
OP
**Agent of the Devil**
1958
*Im Namen des Teufels*
1956
Osers, E
Harrap
349
OP
**Agent of the Devil**
1968
*Im Namen des Teufels*
1956
Osers, E
New English Library
400
PB
OP
**Agent of the Devil**
1973
*Im Namen des Teufels*
1956
Osers, E
White Lion Publishers
388
OP
**Black Earth**
1952
Harrap
240
OP
**Black Earth**
1968
New English Library
253
PB
OP
**Christopher and His Father**
1969
*Christoph und sein Vater*
1966

Sphere
253
PB
OP
**Christopher and His Father**
1967
*Christoph und sein Vater*
1966
Harrap
319
HB
OP
**Countess Tarnovska**
1964
*Die Tarnowska*
1962
Hutter, C
Harrap
396
OP
**Ilona**
1962
*Ilona*
1960
Bullock, M
Harrap
640
OP
**Ilona**
1964
*Ilona*
1960
Bullock, M
Hamilton & Co
478
HB
OP
**Kathrine**
1965
*Kathrin*
Hansen, H
Panther
350
PB
OP
**Mission, The**
1966
*Die Mission*
1965
Bullock, M
Harrap
316
OP
**Mission, The**
1967(1966)
*Die Mission*
1965
Bullock, M
Panther
315
PB
OP
**Off Limits. A novel of occupied Germany**
1956
*Off limits*
1955
Osers, E

Harrap
417
OP
**Palazzo. A novel**
1977
*Palazzo*
1975
Hangartner, S
W.H. Allen
343
PB
OP
**Poisoned Stream, The**
1969
Brownjohn, J M
Harrap
388
HB
OP
**Poisoned Stream, The**
1970
Brownjohn, J M
Mayflower
387
PB
OP
**Thousand Shall Fall, A**
1970
*Ob Tausend fallen*
1943
Mayflower
333
PB
OP
**Walk in Darkness**
1956
*Der Weg ins Dunkel*
1951
Hanser, R
Hamilton & Co
315
HB
OP
**Walk in Darkness**
1968
*Der Weg ins Dunkle*
1951
Hanser, R
New English Library
286
PB
OP

HABECK
Fritz
**Days of Danger**
1968
*Der Kampf um die Barbacane*
1960
Kirkup, J
Collins
256
HB
OP

HACKL
Erich
**Aurora's Motive**
1989
*Auroras Anlaß*
1987

McCown
Cape
115
HB
10.90
**Farewell Sidonia**
1992
*Abschied von Sidonie*
1987
McCown, E
Cape
135
PB
5.99

HAICH
Elisabeth
**Initiation**
1979
*Einweihung*
1960
Robertson, J P
Unwin Paperbacks
539
PB
OP
**Initiation**
1965
*Einweihung*
1960
Robertson, J P
Allen & Unwin
366
HB
OP

HANDKE
Peter
**Absence**
1991
*Abwesenheit*
1987
Manheim, Ralph
Methuen
117
12.95
**Across**
1986
*Der Chinese des Schmerzes*
1983
Manheim, R
Methuen
137
PB
3.95
**Across**
1986
*Der Chinese des Schmerzes*
1983
Manheim, R
Methuen
137
HB
9.95
**Afternoon of a Writer, The**
1989
*Nachmittag eines Schriftstellers*
1987
Manheim, R

Methuen
86
HB
11.95
**Afternoon of a Writer, The**
1991
*Nachmittag eines Schriftstellers*
1987
Manheim, R
Minerva
85
PB
3.99
**Goalie's Anxiety at the Penalty Kick, The**
1977
*Die Angst des Tormanns beim Elfmeter*
1972
Roloff, M
Eyre Methuen
92
HB
OP
**Goalie's Anxiety at the Penalty Kick, The**
1978
*Die Angst des Tormanns beim Elfmeter*
1972
Roloff, M
Quartet
91
PB
OP
**Left-Handed Woman, The**
1986
*Die linkshändige Frau*
1976
Manheim, R
Methuen
87
PB
2.95
**Left-Handed Woman, The**
1980
*Die linkshändige Frau*
1976
Manheim, R
Eyre Methuen
95
HB
OP
**Left-Handed Woman, The**
1982
*Die linkshändige Frau*
1976
Manheim, R
Abacus
89
PB
OP
**Repetition, The**
1988
*Die Wiederholung*
1983
Manheim, R
Methuen

246
HB
12.95
**Repetition, The**
1988
*Die Wiederholung*
1983
Manheim, R
Methuen Minerva
246
PB
4.99
**Short Letter, Long Farewell**
1977
*Der kurze Brief zum langen Abschied*
1972
Manheim, R
 Methuen
167
HB
OP
**Short Letter, Long Farewell**
1978
*Der kurze Brief zum langen Abschied*
1972
Manheim, R
Quartet Books
169
PB
OP
**Slow Homecoming, includes: The long way around, the lesson of Mont Sainte-Victoire, and child story**
1985
*Langsame Heimkehr, Die Lehre der Sainte-Victoire, Kindergeschichte*
1979
Mannheim, R
Methuen
278
PB
OP

HAUPTMANN
Gerhart
**Heretic of Soana, The**
1960
*Der Ketzer von Soana*
1922
Morgan, B.Q.
Calder
124
OP
**Lineman Thiel and other tales**
1989
*Bahnwärter Thiel*
1888
Radcliffe, S
Angel Books
96
HB
9.95

HAUSHOFER
Marlen
**Wall, The**
1990
*Die Wand*
1963
Whiteside, S
Quartet
244
PB
12.50

HAYNES
Sybille
**Augur's daughter, The. A story of Etruscan Life**
1987
*Die Tochter des Augurs, aus dem leben der Etrusker*
1981
Rubicon
229
CASE
14.95

HEIDGEN
Heinz
**Diamond seeker, The**
1959
*Diamentensucher in Tanganjika*
1955
McHugh, I & F
Blackie
139
OP

HEIN
Christoph
**Distant Lover, The**
1991
*Der fremde Freund*
1983
Winston, K
Picador
178
PB
4.99
**Jamie and His Friends**
1988
*Das Wildpferd unterm Kachelofen*
Bell, Anthea
Andersen
160
OP
**Tango Player, The**
1994
*Der Tangospieler*
1989
Boehm, Phillip
Northwestern UP:llinois
219
PB

HEINRICH
Willi
**Cross of Iron**
1977

*Das geduldige Fleisch*
1955
Winston, R & C
Corgi
285
PB
OP
**Crumbling Fortress, The**
1963
*Alte Häuser sterben nicht*
1960
Glenny, M
Macdonald & Co
398
HB
OP
**Crumbling Fortress, The**
1964
*Alte Häuser sterben nicht*
1960
Glenny, M
Transworld
350
PB
OP
**Devil's Bed, The**
1966
*Ferien im Jenseits*
1955
Koningsberger, H
Macdonald
313
HB
OP
**Devil's Bed, The**
1967
*Ferien im Jenseits*
1955
Koningsberger, H
Transworld
286
PB
OP
**Lonely Conqueror, The**
1964
*Gottes zweite Garnitur*
1962
Rock, S
Macdonald
352
HB
OP
**Mark of Shame**
1959
*Die Gezeichneten*
1958
Rock, S
Weidenfeld & Nicolson
316
HB
OP
**Mark of Shame**
1960
*Die Gezeichneten*
1958
Rock, S
Macdonald
284
OP
**Mark of Shame**

1974
*Die Gezeichneten*
1958
Rock, S
Corgi
277
PB
OP
**Rape of Honour**
1961
Rock, S
Weidenfeld & Nicolson
288
HB
OP
**Rape of Honour**
1974
Rock, S
Corgi
254
PB
OP
**Savage Mountain, The**
1958
*Der goldene Tisch*
1956
Coburn, O & Lehrburger, U
Weidenfeld & Nicolson
320
HB
OP
**Savage Mountain, The**
1959
*Der goldene Tisch*
1956
Coburn, O & Lehrburger, U
Transworld
319
PB
OP
**Savage Mountain, The**
1974
*Der goldene Tisch*
1956
Coburn, O with Lehrberger, U
Corgi
284
PB
OP
**Willing Flesh, The**
1957
*Das geduldige Fleisch*
1955
Winston, R & C
Transworld
368
PB
OP
**Willing Flesh, The**
1974
*Das geduldige Fleisch*
1955
Winston, R&C
Corgi
285
PB
OP
**Willing Flesh, The**
1974
*Das geduldige Fleisch*

1955
Winston, R & C
Chivers
478
HB
OP
**Willing Flesh, The**
1956
*Das geduldige Fleisch*
1955
Winston, R&C
Weidenfeld & Nicholson
478
HB
OP

**HELD**
Kurt
**Giuseppe**
1963
*Giuseppe und Maria:.Die Reise nach Neapel*
1955
Ockenden, R
Constable
184
HB
OP

**HELMS-LIESENHOFF**
Karl-Heinz
**Gretchen in Uniform**
1974
*Eine Armee Gretchen*
1956
Ross, P & B
Futura Publications Ltd
286
PB
OP

**HERBURGER**
Günter
**Monotonous Landscape, A**
1969
*Eine gleichmäßige Landschaft*
1964
Skelton,G
Calder & Boyars
184
HB
OP

**HERLIN**
Hans
**Assassin**
1987
*Grishin*
Brownjohn, J M
Hutchinson
324
HB
11.90
**Commemorations**
1975
*Friends*
1974
Mosbacher, E
Heinemann
259

HB
OP
**Last Spring in Paris, The**
1985
*Der letzte Frühling in Paris*
1983
Brownjohn, J M
Deutsch
316
HB
8.95
**Reckoning, The**
1977
*Freunde*
1974
Mosbacher, E
Pan Books
255
PB
OP
**Solo run**
1983
*Satan ist auf Gottes Seite*
1982
Brownjohn, M
Collins
281
HB
OP
**Survivor, The**
1994
*Der letzte Mann von der Doggerbank*
Brownjohn, M
Cooper
224
15.95

**HERMLIN**
Stefan
**City on a Hill: A quartet in prose**
1962
*Zeit der Gemeinsamkeit*
Becker, J
Seven Seas (E.Berlin)
158
PB
OP

**HERZL**
Theodor
**Old-New Lands**
1961
*Altneuland*
1902
Arnold, P
Deutsch
220
HB
OP

**HESSE**
Hermann
**Augustus**
1996
*Augustus*
1957
Penguin
64

PB
0.60
**Autobiographical Writings**
1985
Triad
PB
OP
**Autobiographical writings [of] Hermann Hesse**
1975
Lindley, D
Pan Books
235
PB
OP
**Demian**
1969
*Demian*
1919
Strachan, WJ
Panther
155
PB
OP
**Demian**
1995
*Demian*
1919
Strachan, WJ
Picador
184
PB
5.99
**Demian**
1989
*Demian*
1919
Strachan, W.J.
Paladin
157
PB
OP
**Demian**
1958
*Demian*
1919
Strachan, WJ
Owen
184
14.99
**Gertrude**
1955
*Gertrud*
1910
Rosner, H
Owen Vision P.,
208
HB
13.55
**Gertrude**
1973
*Gertrud*
1910
Rosner, H
Penguin
158
PB
OP
**Gertrude**

1990
*Gertrud*
1910
Rosner, H
Penguin
160
PB
5.99
**Glass Bead Game, The**
1970
*Glasperlenspiel, Das*
1943
Winston, R & C
Cape
558
HB
OP
**Glass Bead Game, The**
1987
*Glasperlenspiel*
1943
Winston, R & C
Picador
558
PB
7.99
**Glass Bead Game, The**
1972
*Das Glasperlenspiel*
1943
Winston, R & C
Penguin
519
PB
OP
**Goldmund**
1959
*Narziß und Goldmund*
1930
Dunlop, G
Owen Vision P.,
287
HB
OP
**Herman Hesse/Romain Rolland correspondence, diary entries and reflections, 1915 to 1940**
1978
*D'une rive à l'autre*
1972
Hesse, M G
Wolff [etc.]
155
HB
OP
**Hesse/Mann letters, The. The correspondence of Hermann Hesse and Thomas Mann, 1910-1955**
1976
*Der Briefwechsel Hermann Hesse-Thomas Mann*
1972
Manheim, R
Owen
196
HB
OP

**Journey to the East, The**
1956
*Die Morgenlandfahrt*
1932
Rosner, H
Owen Vision P.,
93
HB
13.95
OP
**Journey to the East, The**
1995
*Die Morgenlandfahrt*
1932
Rosner, H
Picador
93
PB
4.99
**Journey to the East, The**
1989
*Morgenlandfahrt*
1932
Rosner, H
Paladin
93
PB
OP
**Klingsor's Last Summer**
1985
*Klingsors letzter Sommer*
1920
Winston, R & C
Triad
156
PB
OP
**Klingsor's last summer**
1971
*Klingsors letzter Sommer*
1920
Winston, R & C
Cape
217
HB
OP
**Klingsor's Last Summer**
1973
*Klingsors letzter Sommer*
1920
Winston, R & C
Pan Books
156
PB
OP
**Klingsor's Last Summer**
1985
*Klingsors letzter Sommer*
1920
Winston, R & C
Granada
160
PB
2.50
**Knulp: Three tales from the life of Knulp**
1974
*Knulp*
1915
Manheim, R

Pan Books
125
PB
OP
**Knulp: Three tales from the life of Knulp**
1972
*Knulp. Drei Geschichten aus dem Leben Knulps*
1915
Manheim, R
Cape
114
PB
OP
**Knulp: Three tales from the life of Knulp**
1986
*Knulp*
1915
Manheim, R
Triad Grafton Books
125
PB
OP
**Knulp: Three tales from the life of Knulp**
1990
*Knulp*
1915
Manheim, R
Triad Paladin
125
PB
OP
**Magister Ludi (The Glass Bead Game)**
1950
*Das Glasperlenspiel*
1943
Savill, M
Aldus Publications
502
HB
OP
**Narcissus and Goldmund**
1994
*Narziß und Goldmund*
1930
Vennewitz, L
Owen
288
PB
11.95
**Narcissus and Goldmund**
1993
*Narziß und Goldmund*
1930
Vennewitz, L
P. Owen
253
HB
15.7
**Narcissus and Goldmund**
1993
*Narziß und Goldmund*
1930
Vennewitz, L
P. Owen

288
PB
11.75
**Narziss and Goldmund**
1959
*Narziß und Goldmund*
1930
Dunlop, G
Owen; Vision P
287
HB
OP
**Peter Camenzind**
1961
*Peter Camenzind*
1903
Strachan, W J
Owen; Vision P
174
HB
OP
**Peter Camenzind**
1989
*Peter Camenzind*
1903
Strachan, W J
Penguin
144
PB
6.99
**Peter Camenzind**
1970
*Peter Camenzind*
1903
Strachan, W J
Owen
174
13.95
**Pictor's Metamorphoses and other fantasies**
1991
*Pictors Verwandlungen*
1925
Lesser, R
Triad
171
PB
OP
**Pictor's Metamorphoses and other fantasies**
1982
*Pictors Verwandlungen*
1925
Lesser, R
Cape
213
HB
OP
**Pictor's Metamorphoses and other fantasies**
1984
*Pictors Verwandlungen*
1925
Lesser, R
Triad
206
PB
OP
**Prodigy, The**

1957
*Unterm Rad*
1906
Strachan, W J
Owen Vision P.,
188
HB
OP
**Prodigy, The**
1973
*Unterm Rad*
1906
Manheim, R
Penguin
160
PB
5.99
**Rosshalde**
1986
*Roßhalde*
1913
Manheim, R
Triad
153
PB
OP
**Rosshalde**
1971
*Roßhalde*
1913
Manheim, R
Cape
213
HB
OP
**Rosshalde**
1972
*Roßhalde*
1913
Manheim, R
Pan Books
154
PB
OP
**Siddharta**
1970
*Siddharta*
1924
Rosner, H
Owen
167
13.95
**Siddhartha**
1954
*Siddhartha*
1924
Rosner, H
Vision P.,
167
HB
OP
**Siddhartha**
1974
*Siddharta*
1922
Rosner, H
Pan Books
119
PB
5.99

**Six Novels, with other stories and essays.**
Includes: Life Story briefly told; The Prodigy; Wandering; Klingsor's Last Summer; Siddhartha; A Guest at the Spa; Journey to Nuremberg; Steppenwolf; Narziss and Goldmund; Journey to the East.
1980
*n/a*
n/a
Var.
Collins
987
HB
OP

**Steppenwolf**
1965
*Der Steppenwolf*
1927
Creighton, S
Penguin
253
PB
OP

**Steppenwolf**
1974
*Steppenwolf*
1927
Creighton, B
Allen Lane
253
HB
OP

**Steppenwolf**
1990
*Der Steppenwolf*
1927
Creighton, B
Penguin
256
PB
6.99

**Stories of Five Decades**
1974
*n/a*
n/a
Manheim, R
Cape
328
HB
OP

**Stories of Five Decades**
1976
*n/a*
n/a
Manheim, R
Triad Panther
333
PB
OP

**Strange News from another Star, and other stories**
1976

*Märchen*
1991
Lindley, D
Penguin
122
PB
OP

**Strange News from another Star, and other tales**
1973
*Märchen*
1919
Lindley, D
Cape
145
HB
OP

**Treatise on the Steppenwolf**
1975
*Traktat vom Steppenwolf*
1927
Creighton, B
Angus and Robertson
106
PB
OP

**HEYM**
Georg
**Thief and other stories, The**
1994
*Der Dieb*
1913
Bennett, Susan
Libris
104
HB
20

**Thief and other stories, The**
1994
*Der Dieb*
1913
Bennett, Susan
Libris
104
PB
5.95

**HEYM**
Stefan
**Collin**
1980
*Collin*
1979
Hodder and Stoughton
315
HB
OP

**Crusaders, The**
1958
*Kreuzfahrer von heute*
Seven Seas (E.Berlin)
957
PB
OP

**Five Days in June. A novel**
1977
*5 Tage im Juni*
1974
Hodder and Stoughton
352
HB
OP

**Glasenapp Case, The**
1962
*Der Fall Glasenapp*
Seven Seas (E.Berlin)
344
PB
OP

**Goldsborough**
1966
*Goldsborough*
Seven Seas (E.Berlin)
510
PB
OP

**King David Report, The**
1984
*Der König David Bericht*
1973
Abacus
254
PB
OP

**Lenz Papers, The**
1968
*Die Papiere des Andreas Lenz*
Seven Seas (E.Berlin)
550
PB
OP

**HILDESHEIMER**
Wolfgang
**Marbot. A biography**
1983
*Marbot, eine Biographie*
1981
Crampton, P
Dent
246
HB
OP

**HILSENRATH**
Edgar
**Nazi & the barber, The. A tale of vengeance.**
1975
*Der Nazi & der Friseur*
1977
White, A
W.H. Allen
302
PB
OP

**Night. A novel**
1967
*Nacht*
1964
Roloff, M
W.H. Allen

515
PB
OP
**Story of the Last Thought, The**
1990
*Märchen vom letzen Gedanken*
1989
Young, H
Scribner
455
HB
14.95

**Story of the Last Thought, The**
1991
*Märchen vom letzten Gedanken*
1989
Young, H
Abacus
471
PB
5.99

**HINRICHS**
August
**Folk of the Sea**
1954
*Das Volk am Meer*
1929
Whitmore, M M
Stockwell; Ifracombe
239
OP

**HITT**
Frisco
**Coffin Full of Dreams, A**
1975
*Ein Sarg voll Träume*
1972
Byrne, J
Souvenir Press
299
HB
OP

**Coffin Full of Dreams, A**
1976
*Ein Sarg voll Träume*
1972
Byrne, J
Corgi
341
PB
OP

**HOBERG**
Marielis
**One Summer on Majorca**
1962
*Heiner und Elsie auf Mallorca*
1955
Hollingdale, R J
Abelard-Schuman
190
HB
OP

**Voyage to Africa, The**
1964
*Heiner und Hilse fahren nach Afrika*
1955
Hollingdale, R J
Abelard-Schuman
176
HB
OP

**HOCHHUTH**
Rolf
**German Love Story, A**
1980
*Eine Liebe in Deutschland*
1978
Brownjohn, J
Weidenfeld and Nicolson
269
HB
OP

**German Love Story, A**
1981
*Eine Liebe in Deurschland*
1978
Brownjohn, J
Abacus
269
PB
OP

**HOFMANN**
Gert
**Balzac's Horse and other stories**
1989
*Gespräch über Balzacs Pferd*
1981
Middleton, C, and Hofmann, M
Secker & Warburg
285
HB
13.95

**Balzac's Horse and other stories**
1990
*Gespräch über Balzacs Pferd*
1981
Middleton, C, and Hofmann, M
Minerva
285
PB
OP

**Before the Rainy Season**
1991
*Vor der Regenzeit*
1988
McCown, E
Secker & Warburg
345
HB
14.95

**Before the Rainy Season**
1992
*Vor der Regenzeit*
1988
McCown, E
Minerva
345

PB
5.99
**Film Explainer**
1995
*Der Kinoerzähler*
1990
Hofman, M
Secker &
249
PB
9.99

**Film Explainer**
1996
*Der Kinoerzähler*
1990
Hofman, M
Minerva
256
PB
5.99

**Our Conquest**
1987
*Unsere Eroberung*
1985
Middleton, Ch
Carcanet
281
HB
OP

**Our Conquest**
1991
*Unsere Eroberung*
1985
Middleton, Ch
Minerva
288
PB
4.99

**Parable of the Blind, The**
1988
*Der Blindensturz*
1986
Middleton, Ch
Secker & Warburg
160
HB
10.95

**Parable of the Blind, The**
1989
*Der Blindensturz*
1986
Middleton, Ch
Secker & Warburg / Minerva
160
PB
OP

**Spectacle at the Tower, The**
1985
*Auf dem Turm*
Middleton, Ch
Carcanet
232
PB
4.95

**HOFMANNSTHAL**
Hugo Von
**Lord Chandos Letter, The**

1995
*Brief des Lord Chandos*
Hofman, M
Syrens
19
PB
2.99

**HOLTHUSEN**
Hans Egon
**Crossing, The**
1959
*Das Schiff. Aufzeichnungen
eines Passagiers*
1956
Kee, R. & Hughs, S
Deutsch
253
HB
OP
**Crossing, The**
1959
*Das Schiff. Aufzeichnungen
eines Passagiers*
1956
Kee, R & Hughs, S
Deutsch
253
HB
OP

**HONOLKA**
Kurt
**Magellan**
1962
*Magellan, das größte
Abenteuer der Seefahrt*
1958
McHugh, F
Blackie
200
OP

**HORBACH**
Michael
**Great Betrayal, The**
1958
*Die verratenen Söhne*
1957
Kee, R
J.Lane
240
OP
**Lioness, The**
1979
*Die Löwin*
1974
Molinaro, U & Rappolt, H
Mayflower
189
PB
OP
**Reckoning, The**
1961
*Der jüngste Tag*
1960
Denny, N
Bodley Head
222
HB

OP

**HORVÁTH**
Ödön Von
**Age of the Fish, The**
1978
*Zeitalter der Fische ( Jugend
ohne Gott + Ein Kind unserer
Zeit, 1938)*
1953
R. Wills, Thomas
Heinemann
206
HB
OP
**Age of the Fish, The**
1985
*Zeitalter der Fische ( Jugend
ohne Gott + Ein Kind unserer
Zeit, 1938)*
1953
R. Wills, Thomas
Penguin
142
PB
OP

**HUELSENBECK ET AL**
Richard
**Dada Almanac**
1994
*Dada Almanach*
1920
Green, M et al
Atlas P
180
PB
12.99

**HUG**
Hubert
**Neutra and other stories,
The**
1994
Minerva
85
PB
6.99

**IMOG**
Jo
**Demon Flower. A novel,
The**
1972
*Die Wurliblume*
1967
Hanf, C
Calder and Boyars
220
OP

**JAHNN**
Hans Henry
**Ship, The**
1970
*Das Holzschiff*
1959
Hutter, C
Owen
210

OP

**JEIER**
Thomas
**Return to Canta Lupe**
1984
*Der lange Ritt nach San
Jacinto*
1983
Wallmann, J
Hale
184
PB
OP

**JELINEK**
Elfriede
**Lust**
1992
*Lust*
1989
Hulse, M
Serpent's Tail
256
PB
8.99
**Piano Teacher,The**
1989
*Die Klavierspielerin*
1983
Neugroschel, J
Serpent's Tail
280
PB
7.95
**Women as Lovers**
1994
*Die Liebhaberinnen*
1975
Chalmers, M
Serpent's Tail
192
PB
9.99
**Wonderful, Wonderful
Times**
1990
*Die Ausgesperrten*
Hulse, M
Serpent's Tail
240
PB
8.99

**JENS**
Walter
**Blind Man, The**
1954
*Der Blinde*
1953
Bullock, M
Deutsch
119
HB
OP

**JESCHKE**
Wolfgang
**Last Day of Creation, The**
1982

*Der letzte Tag der Schöpfung*
Mander, G
Century
222
PB
OP
**Midas**
1990
New English Library
192
PB
2.90

**JOHNSON**
Uwe
**Absence, An**
1969
*Eine Reise wegwohin*
1964
Winston, R & C
Cape
61
HB
OP
**Anniversaries II from the life of Gesine Cresspahl**
1988
*Jahrestage*
1970
Vennewitz, L & Arndt, A
Deutsch
644
HB
15.90
OP
**Speculations about Jakob**
1963
*Mutmaßungen über Jakob*
1960
Molinaro, U
Cape
240
HB
OP
**Third Book about Achim, The**
1968
*Das dritte Buch über Achim*
1961
Molinaro, U
Cape
246
HB
OP
**Two Views**
1967
*Zwei Ansichten*
1965
Winston, R & C
Cape
183
HB
OP
**Two Views**
1971
*Zwei Ansichten*
1965
Johnson, U
Penguin
170

PB
OP

**JONKE**
Gert
**Geometric Regional Novel**
1994
*Geometr. Heimatroman*
1969
Vazulik, J W
Dalkey Archive: Normal, Ill.
131
OP

**JÜNGER**
Ernst
**African diversions**
1954
*Afrikanische Spiele*
1936
Hood, S
Lehmann
183
HB
OP
**Aladdin's Problem**
1993
*Aladins Problem*
1983
Neugroschel, J
Quartet
144
PB
7.95
**Eumeswil**
1995
*Eumeswil*
1977
Neugroschel, J
Quartet
300
PB
12
**On the Marble Cliffs**
1970
*Auf den Marmorklippen*
1959
Hood, S
Penguin
116
PB
OP

**KADES**
Hans
**Doctor's Temptation, The**
1962
*Ich schwöre bei Apoll*
1957
Angus & Robertson
251
OP
**Great Temptation, The**
1956
*Der Erfolgreiche*
1951
Ashton, E
Angus & Robertson
317
HB
OP

**Great Temptation, The**
1957
*Der Erfolgreiche*
1951
Ashton, E
Transworld
318
PB
OP
**House of Crystal, The**
1957
*Monte Cristallo*
1956
Selver, P
Angus & Robertson
254
HB
OP
**San Salvatore**
1959
*San Salvatore*
1946
Angus & Robertson
255
HB
OP

**KAFKA**
Franz
**America**
1992
*Amerika*
1927
Franz Kafka with an introduction by Edwin, Muir
Minerva
255
PB
5.90
**America**
1967
*Amerika*
1927
Muir, W & E
Penguin in association with Secker & Warburg
270
PB
OP
**America**
1973
*Amerika*
1927
Muir, W & E
Secker and Warburg
312
HB
OP
**Castle, The**
1992
*Das Schloß*
1926
Campbell
PB
OP
**Castle, The**
1953
*Das Schloß*
1926
Muir, W & E & Wilk, E

Secker & Warburg
451
HB
OP
**Castle, The**
1957
*Das Schloß*
1926
Muir, W & E & Wilki, E
Penguin Books in association
with Secker & Warburg
298
PB
OP
**Castle, The**
1974
*Das Schloß*
1926
Muir, W & E & Wilk, E
Penguin
298
PB
OP
**Collected Aphorisms, The**
1994
*Aphorismen aus dem Nachlaß*
1952
Pasley, M
Penguin
47
PB
2.99
**Collected Short Stories**
1988(1983)
*n/a*
1935 - 193
Glatzer, N (ed.)
Penguin
486
PB
OP
**Collected Stories**
1993
*n/a*
n/a
var.
Everyman
560
HB
10.99
**Complete Novels, The**
1992
*n/a*
n/a
Muir, W & E
Minerva
454
PB
9.99
**Complete Short Stories of
Franz Kafka, The**
1992
*n/a*
n/a
var.
Minerva
486
PB
7.99

**Description of a Struggle,
and other stories**
1979
*n/a*
1931
Muir, E & W / Stern, T & J
Penguin
152
PB
OP
**Description of a Struggle,
and The Great Wall etc.**
1960
*n/a*
1931
Muir, E & W / Stern, T & J
Secker & Warburg
345
HB
OP
**Diaries of Franz Kafka
1910-23, The**
1964
*Tagebücher, 1910 - 1923*
1948-9
Penguin
519p
PB
OP
**Diaries of Franz Kafka
1910-23, The. (ed. M.Brod)**
1992
*Tagebücher, 1910 - 1923*
1948-9
Minerva
519
PB
9.90
**Great Wall of China, The
and other short stories**
1991
*Beim Bau der chinesischen
Mauer*
1931
Pasley, M
Penguin
218
PB
5.99
**In the Penal Settlement.
Tales and short prose
works**
1973
*In der Strafkolonie*
1919
Kaiser, E & Wilkins, E
Secker and Warburg
298
HB
OP
**Man Who Disappeared,
The**
1997
Michael Hofmann
Penguin
216
PB
5.99

**Metamorphosis and other
stories**
1961
*Verwandlung, Die*
1915
Muir, E & W
Penguin
218
PB
OP
**Metamorphosis and other
stories**
1992
*Die Verwandlung*
1915
Muir, W E
Minerva
218
PB
OP
**Metamorphosis and other
stories**
1961
*Die Verwandlung*
1915
Muir, W and E
Penguin
218
PB
OP
**Metamorphosis, The**
1972
*Die Verwandlung*
1915
Corngold, S
Bantam
201
PB
OP
**Metamorphosis, The**
1993
*Die Verwandlung*
1915
Hutchinson, P & Minden, M R
Routledge
128
PB
9.99
**Metamorphosis, The**
1996
*Die Verwandlung*
1915
Stanley Corngold
Norton
218
PB
4.95
**Metamorphosis, The and
other stories**
1996
*Die Verwandlung*
1915
Appelbaum, Stanley
Dover, NY
88
PB
1.45
**Metamorphosis; The Trial;
The Castle**

1997
*Die Verwandlung; der
Process; Das Schloß*
n/a
William J. Dodd
Longman
234
HB
45

**Penguin complete novels
of Franz Kafka The trial,
The castle, America**
1983
*n/a*
Muir, E & W
Penguin
638
PB
OP

**Penguin complete short
stories of Franz Kafka,
The**
1983
*n/a*
n/a
edited by Nahum N, Glatzer
Penguin
486
PB
OP

**Penguin complete short
stories of Franz Kafka,
The**
1983
*n/a*
Allen Lane
486
HB
OP

**Stories 1904-1924**
1990
*n/a*
n/a
Underwood, J A
Cardinal
271
PB
OP

**Stories 1904-1924**
1983
*n/a*
n/a
Underwood, J A
Futura
271
PB
O/P

**Transformation and other
stories, The**
1992
*Die Verwandlung*
1915
Penguin
PB
OP

**Trial, The**
1956
*Der Prozess*

1925
Muir, E & W
  Secker & Warburg
304
HB
10.95

**Trial, The**
1992
*Der Prozeß*
1925
Muir, W E
Minerva
255
PB
5.99

**Trial, The**
1992
*Der Prozeß*
1925
Muir, W E
Everyman's Library
299
HB
8.99

**Trial, The**
1994
*Der Prozeß*
1925
Parry, I
Penguin
192
PB
4.99

**Trial, The**
1980(1974)
*Der Prozeß*
1925
Scott, D & Waller, Ch
Pan Books
254
PB
OP

**Trial, The**
1967
*Der Prozeß*
1925
Muir, E & W
Folio Society
219
HB
OP

**Trial, The**
1968(1953)
*Der Prozeß*
1925
Muir, W & E
Secker & Warburg
304
HB
OP

**Trial, The**
1974(1953)
*Der Prozeß*
1925
Muir, W E
Penguin
256
PB
OP

**Trial, The**

1994
*Der Prozeß*
1925
Muir, E & W
Compact
255
PB
5.99

**Trial, The**
1983
*Der Prozeß*
1925
Heinemann
249
HB
OP

**Trial, The**
1997
*Der Prozeß*
Idris Parry
Penguin
177
PB
5.99

**Trial, The; America; The
Castle; Metamorphosis; In
the penal settlement; The
Great Wall of China;
Investigations of a dog;
Letter to his father**
1976
*Der Prozeß, Amerika, Das
Schloß, Metamorphosen, In
der Strafkolonie, Beim Bau
der Chinesischen Mauer,
Briefe an den Vater*
1915 - 193
Secker and Warburg
Octopus
925
HB
OP

**Wedding Preparations in
the Country and other
stories**
1978
*Hochzeitsvorbereitungen auf
dem Lande und andere Prosa
aus dem Nachlaß*
1952
Penguin
190
PB
OP

**KASACK**
Hermann
**City beyond the River, The**
1953
*Die Stadt hinter dem Strom*
1949
Mendelssohn, Peter de
Longmans Green
356
HB
OP

**KÄSTNER**

Erich
**35th of May, or Conrad's ride to the South Seas, The**
1967
*Der 35. Mai*
1933
Brooks, C
New English Library
125
PB
OP

**Emil and the Detectives**
1959
*Emil und die Detektive*
1929
Cape
192
HB
5.95

**Emil and the Detectives**
1995
*Emil und die Detektive*
1929
Red Fox
176
3.50

**Emil and the Three Twins**
1994
*Emil und die drei Zwillinge*
1935
Red Fox
298
PB
3.50

**Fabian, the story of a moralist**
1990
*Fabian*
1931
Brooks, C
Libris
177
HB
14.95

**Flying Classroom**
1995
*Das fliegende Klassenzimmer*
1933
Red Fox
224
PB
3.50

**Little Man**
1994
*Der kleine Mann*
Red Fox
286
PB
3.50

**Lottie and Lisa**
1995
*Das doppelte Lottchen*
1949
Red Fox
144
PB
2.99

**Salzburg Comedy, A**
1950
*Der kleine Grenzverkehr oder Georg und die Zwischenfalle*
1938
Brooks, C
Weidenfeld & Nicolson
115
HB
OP

**Till Eulenspiegel the Clown**
1967
*Till Eulenspiegel*
1939
Winston, R & C
Cape
70
HB
OP

KAUFMANN
Herbert
**Red Moon and High Summer**
1960
*Roter Mond und heiße Zeit*
1957
Humphries, S
Methuen
209
OP

**Heaven Pays no Dividends**
1952
*Der Himmel zahlt keine Zinsen*
1951
Mosbacher, E
Jarrolds
287
OP

**World is Full of Doors, The**
1957
*Die Welt ist voller Türen*
1955
Fitzgerald, E
Hutchinson
319
HB
OP

**Curse of Maralinga & other Stories, The**
1959
Seven Seas (E.Berlin)
135
PB
OP

KEILSON
Hans
**Death of the Adversary, The**
1961
*Der Tod des Widersachers*
1959
Jarosy, I
Wolff
208
HB

OP
KEMPOWSKI
Walter
**Days of Greatness**
1982
*Aus großer Zeit*
1981
Vennewitz, L
Secker & Warburg
399
HB
OP

**Days of Greatness**
1983
*Aus großer Zeit*
1981
Vennewitz, L
Zenith
399
PB
OP

KEUN
Irmgard
**After Midnight**
1987
*Nach Mitternacht*
1937
Bell, A
Sceptre
150
PB
3.50

**After Midnight**
1985
*Nach Mitternacht*
1937
Bell, A
Gollancz
152
HB
OP

KIRCHGESSNER
Maria
**High Challenge**
1963
*Vier unter Hüttendach*
1962
Emerson, J
Maomillan
287
HB
OP

KIRCHHOFF
Bodo
**Infanta**
1993
*Infanta*
1990
Brownjohn, J
Flamingo
PB
6.99

**Infanta**
1992
*Infanta*
1990
Brownjohn, J

Harvill
424
HB
14.90

**KIRST**
Hans Hellmut
**20th of July, The**
1966
*Aufstand der Soldaten*
1965
Brownjohn, J.M
Collins
416
HB
OP
**20th of July, The**
1968
*Aufstand der Soldaten*
1965
Brownjohn, J M
Fontana
350
PB
OP
**20th of July, The**
1974
*Aufstand der Soldaten*
1965
Brownjohn, J M
Chivers large print
416
HB
OP
**Affairs of the Generals, The**
1979
*Generalsaffären*
Brownjohn, J M
Fontana
255
PB
OP
**Brothers in Arms**
1965
*Kameraden*
1961
Brownjohn, J.M
Collins
384
HB
OP
**Brothers in Arms**
1967(1965)
*Kameraden*
1961
Brownjohn, J M
Collins
383
PB
OP
**Camp 7 last stop**
1969
*Letzte Station Camp 7*
1966
Brownjohn, J M
Collins
320
HB
OP

**Camp 7 last stop**
1971
*Letzte Station Camp 7*
1966
Brownjohn, J M
Fontana
285
PB
OP
**Death Plays the Last Card**
1968
*Die letzte Karte spielt der Tod*
1955
Brownjohn, J M
Vienna
252
PB
OP
**Death Plays the Last Card**
1968
*Die letzte Karte spielt der Tod*
1955
Brownjohn, J M
Fontana
252
PB
OP
**Fox of Maulen, The**
1968
*Die Wölfe*
1967
Brownjohn, J M
Collins
479
HB
OP
**Fox of Maulen, The**
1968
*Die Wölfe*
1967
Brownjohn, J M
Collins
479
HB
OP
**Gunner Asch Goes to War**
1965
*Die seltsamen Kriegserlebnisse des Soldaten Asch*
1954
Kee, R
Collins
288
PB
OP
**Gunner Asch Goes to War**
1965
*Die seltsamen Kriegserlebnisse des Soldaten Asch*
1954
Kee, R
Fontana
287
PB
OP
**Gunner Asch Goes to War**
1978

*Die seltsamen Kriegserlebnisse des Soldaten Asch*
1954
Kee, R
Chivers large print
288
HB
OP
**Gunner Asch Goes to War**
1965
*Die seltsamen Kriegserlebnisse des Soldaten Asch*
1954
Kee, R
Collins
288
HB
OP
**Hero in the Tower**
1972
*Held im Turm*
1970
Brownjohn, J M
Collins
320
HB
OP
**Hero in the Tower**
1974
*Held im Turm*
1970
Brownjohn, J M
Fontana
287
PB
OP
**Heroes for Sale**
1983
*Ausverkauf der Helden*
Brownjohn, J M
Fontana
286
PB
OP
**Lieutenant Must Be Mad, The**
1951
*Wir nannten thn Galgenstrick*
1950
Winston, R & C
Harrap
283
HB
OP
**Lieutenant Must Be Mad, The**
1951
*Wir nannten ihn Galgenstrick*
1950
Winston, R & C
Harrap
283
HB
OP
**Lieutenant Must Be Mad, The**
1972

*Wir nannten ihn Galgenstrick*
1950
Winston, R & C
Morley Books
283
HB
OP
**Lieutenant Must Be Mad, The**
1974
*Wir nannten ihn Galgenstrick*
1950
Winston, R & C
Mayflower
253
PB
OP
**Night of the Generals, The**
1978
*Die Nacht der Generäle*
1962
Brownjohn, J M
Fontana
286
PB
OP
**Night of the Generals, The**
1963
*Die Nacht der Generäle*
1962
Brownjohn, J M
Collins
319
HB
OP
**Night of the Generals, The**
1981
*Die Nacht der Generäle*
1963
Brownjohn, J M
Ulverscroft largeprint
480
HB
5.00
**Nights of the Long Knives**
1978
*Die Nächte der langen Messer*
1965
Brownjohn, J M
Fontana
255
PB
OP
**Nights of the Long Knives**
1976
*Die Nächte der langen Messer*
1965
Brownjohn, J M
Collins
279
HB
OP
**No One Will escape**
1959
*Keiner kommt davon*
1957
Graves, R

Weidenfeld & Nicolson
414
HB
OP
**No One Will escape**
1960
*Keiner kommt davon*
1962
Graves, R
World Distributors
446
PB
OP
**Officer Factory**
1962
*Fabrik der Offiziere*
1960
Kee, R
Collins
576
HB
OP
**Officer Factory**
1974
*Fabrik der Offiziere*
1960
Kee, R
Fontana
574
PB
OP
**Party Games**
1980
*08/15 in der Partei*
Brownjohn, J M
Collins
249
HB
OP
**Party Games**
1982
*08/15 in der Partei*
Brownjohn, J M
Fontana
249
PB
OP
**Party Games**
1982
*08/15 in der Partei*
Brownjohn, J M
Ulverscroft large print
432
HB
11.82
**Return of Gunner Asch, The**
1966
*Bis zum Ende. Der gefährliche Endsieg des Soldaten Asch*
1955
Kee, R
Fontana
286
PB
OP
**Revolt of Gunner Asch, The**

1965
*Die abenteurliche Revolte des Gefreiten Asch*
1955
Kee, R
Collins
254
PB
OP
**Revolt of Gunner Asch, The**
1977
*Die abenteuerliche Revolte des Gefreiten Asch*
1955
Kee, R
Chivers
254
HB
OP
**Revolt of Gunner Asch, The**
1981
*Die abenteuerliche Revolte des Gefreiten Asch*
1955
Kee, R
Fontana
253
PB
OP
**Time for Payment, A**
1977
*Alles hat seinen Preis*
1974
Brownjohn, J M
Fontana
288
PB
OP
**Time for Payment, A**
1976
*Alles hat seinen Preis*
1974
Brownjohn, J M
Collins
280
HB
OP
**Time for Scandal, A**
1973
*Verdammt zum Erfolg*
1971
Brownjohn, J M
Collins
255
HB
OP
**Time for Scandal, A**
1975
*Verdammt zum Erfolg*
1971
Brownjohn, J M
Fontana
252
PB
OP
**Time for Truth, A**
1974

*Verurteilt zur Wahrheit*
1972
Brownjohn, J M
Collins
256
HB
OP
**Time for Truth, A**
1976
*Verurteilt zur Wahrheit*
1972
Brownjohn, J M
Fontana
252
PB
OP
**Twilight of the Generals**
1979
*Generalsaffären*
1977
Brownjohn, J M
Collins
252
HB
OP
**Undercover Man**
1970
*Kein Vaterland*
1968
Brownjohn, J M
Collins
253
HB
OP
**Undercover Man**
1972
*Kein Vaterland*
1968
Brownjohn, J M
Fontana
224
PB
OP
**What Became of Gunner Asch**
1966
*08/15 Heute*
1963
Brownjohn, J M
Collins
285
HB
OP
**What Became of Gunner Asch**
1964
*08/15 Heute*
1963
Brownjohn, J M
Fontana
285
PB
OP
**What Became of Gunner Asch**
1977
*08/15 heute*
1963
Brownjohn, J M
Chivers large print

286
HB
OP
**Who's in Charge here?**
1971
Brownjohn, J M
Collins
254
HB
OP
**Who's in Charge here?**
1973
Brownjohn, J M
Fontana
224
PB
OP
**Wolves, The**
1970
*Die Wölfe*
1967
Brownjohn, J M
Fontana
509
PB
OP
**Zero Eight Fifteen 2: Gunner Asch goes to war**
1956
*08-15*
Kee, R
Weidenfeld & Nicolson
335
HB
OP
**Zero Eight Fifteen 3: The return of Gunner Asch**
1957
Kee, R
Weidenfeld & Nicolson
288
HB
OP
**Zero Eight Fifteen 2: Gunner Asch goes to war**
1956
*08-15*
Kee, R
Weidenfeld & Nicolson
335
HB
OP
**Zero Eight Fifteen: The strange mutiny etc**
1955
*08-15*
1954
Kee, R
Weidenfeld & Nicolson
288
HB
OP

**KLEIN-HAPARASH**
Jacob
**He Who Flees the Lion**
1963
*Der vor dem Löwen flieht*
1961
Winston, R & C

Weidenfeld & Nicolson
654
HB
OP

**KLIER**
Henry
**Summer Gone, A**
1959
*Verlorener Sommer*
1954
Kirkup, J
Bles
255
HB
OP

**KOCH**
Werner
**Pontius Pilate Reflects**
1961
*Pilatus Erinnerungen*
1959
Fitzgerald, E
Putnam
252
OP

**KOEPPEN**
Wolfgang
**Death in Rome**
1956
*Der Tod in Rom*
1954
Savill, M
Weidenfeld & Nicolson
217
HB
OP
**Death in Rome**
1992
*Tod in Rom*
1954
Hofmann, M
H.Hamilton
202
PB
9.99
**Death in Rome**
1994
*Tod in Rom*
1954
Hofmann, M
Penguin
202
PB
6.99

**KOESTLER**
Arthur
**Darkness at Noon**
1940
*Sonnenfinsternis*
1940
Hardy, D
Cape
256
HB
OP
**Darkness at Noon**
1980

*Sonnenfinsternis*
1940
Hardy, D introduction by Bukovsky, V
Folio Society
267
HB
OP

**Darkness at Noon**
1959
*Sonnenfinsternis*
1940
Hardy, D
Landsborough Publications
192
HB
OP

**Darkness at Noon**
1968
*Sonnenfinsternis*
1940
Hardy, D
Longmans
249
HB
OP

**Darkness at Noon**
1973
*Sonnenfinsternis*
1940
Hardy, D
Hutchinson
276
HB
OP

**Darkness at Noon**
1994
*Sonnenfinsternis*
1940
Hardy, D
Vintage
211
PB
5.99

**Gladiators, The**
1965
*Die Gladiatoren*
1939
Simon, E
Hutchinson
319
HB
OP

**Gladiators, The**
1949
*Die Gladiatoren*
1939
Simon, E
Macmillan
382
HB
OP

**Gladiators,The**
1965
*Die Gladiatoren*
1939
Simon, E
Hutchinson
319
HB

OP

**KOKOSCHKA**
Oskar
**Sea Ringed with Visions, A**
1962
*Spur im Treibsand*
1956
Wilkins, E & Kaiser, E
Thames & Hudson
274
HB
OP

**KÖNIG**
Barbara
**Beneficiary, The**
1993
*Der Beschenkte*
1980
THEOBALD, R
Northwestern UP
117
HB
OP

**KÖNIG**
Karl
**Christmas Story, A**
1984
Camphill Press
31
PB
OP

**Christmas Story, A and: The story of Kaspar Hauser**
1977
Camphill (Whitby)
45
PB
OP

**KONSALIK**
Heinz G.
**Angel of the Damned**
1975
*Engel der Vergessenen*
1974
Gotfurt, D
A. Ellis
253
HB
OP

**Battalion 999**
1976
*Strafbatallion 999*
1963
Coburn, O
A. Ellis
238
HB
OP

**Certified Insane**
1980
*Entmündigt*
Bell, A
Aidan Ellis
213
HB
OP

**Changed Face, The**
1979
*Das geschenkte Gesicht*
1962
Gibbons, I R
A. Ellis
207
HB
OP

**Changed Face, The**
1979
*Das geschenkte Gesicht*
1962
Gibbons, I R
Star Books
207
PB
OP

**Damned of the Taiga, The**
1978
*Verdammten der Taiga, Die*
1974
Lewis, Ch
A. Ellis
214
HB
OP

**Damned of the Taiga, The**
1979
*Verdammten der Taiga, Die*
1974
Lewis, Ch
Star Books
214
PB
OP

**Damned of the Taiga, The**
1982
*Verdammten der Taiga, Die*
1978
Lewis, C
Ulverscroft large print
432
HB
9.95

**Desert Doctor, The**
1979
*Wüstendoktor, Der*
Bell, A
A. Ellis
218
HB
OP

**Desert Doctor, The**
1981
*Wüstendoktor, Der*
Bell, A
Pan
218
PB
OP

**Diagnosis**
1981
*Diagnose*
A. Ellis
224
HB
OP

**Doctor Erica Werner**
1979

*Doktor Med E Werner*
1962
Bell, A
A. Ellis
202
HB
OP

**Doctor Erica Werner**
1981
*Doktor Med E Werner*
1962
Bell, A
Pan
201
PB
OP

**Doctor of Stalingrad**
1975
*Der Arzt von Stalingrad*
1959
Whitman, H
A. Ellis
272
HB
OP

**Front-Line Theatre**
1978
*Front-Theater*
Lewis, Ch
A. Ellis
178
HB
OP

**Heart of the 6th Army, The**
1981
*Das Herz der 6. Armee*
Coburn, O
Macdonald Futura
298
PB
OP

**Heiress, The**
1980
*Erbin, Die*
Bell, A
A. Ellis
215
HB
OP

**Highway to Hell**
1976
*Die Rollbahn*
Vacha, R
A. Ellis
237
HB
OP

**Highway to Hell**
1981
*Die Rollbahn*
Vacha, R
Macdonald Futura
235
PB
OP

**I Confess**
1979
*Ich gestehe*

A. Ellis
224
HB
OP

**Last Carpathian Wolf, The**
1978
*Der letzte Karpatenwolf*
1978
Coburn, O
A. Ellis
HB
OP

**Last Carpathian Wolf, The**
1981
*Der letzte Karpatenwolf*
1978
Coburn, O
Ulverscroft large print
320
HB
6.95

**Last Carpathian Wolf, The**
1981
*Der letzte Karpatenwolf*
1978
Coburn, O
Macdonald Futura
177
PB
OP

**Love on the Don**
1980
*Liebe am Don*
1970
Lewis, Ch
A. Ellis
250
HB
OP

**Love on the Don (part 2) Against the Tide**
1980
*Liebe am Don (2)*
Lewis, Charles
A. Ellis
255
HB
OP

**Mask my Agony**
1964
*Das geschenkte Gesicht*
1962
Gibbons, I R
Gibbs & Phillips
207
HB
OP

**Naked Earth, The**
1961
*Der Arzt von Stalingrad*
1959
Whitman, H
Gibbs & Phillips
327
HB
OP

**Naked Earth, The**
1962
*Der Arzt von Stalingrad*
1961

Whitman, H
Hamilton & Co
272
HB
OP

**Natasha**
1978
*Natascha*
1969
Coburn, O
A. Ellis
227
HB
OP

**Natasha**
1979
*Natascha*
1969
Coburn, O
Star Books
227
PB
OP

**Private Hell**
1979
*Privatklinik*
Bell, A
A. Ellis
217
HB
OP

**Ravishing Doctor, The**
1980
*Die schöne Ärztin*
1977
Bell, A
A. Ellis
218
HB
OP

**Ravishing Doctor, The**
1981
*Die schöne Ärztin*
1979
Bell, A
Pan
217p
PB
OP

**Ravishing doctor, The**
1981
*Die schöne Ärztin*
1979
Bell, A
Ulverscroft large print
384
HB
12.99

**Skies over Kazakstan**
1978
*Der Himmel über Kasakstan*
Lewis, Ch
A. Ellis
218
HB
OP

**Strafbattaillon 999**
1980
*Strafbattaillon 999*
Coburn, O

Futura Publications
238
PB
OP
**Strike Force 10**
1981
*Sie waren Zehn*
Bell, A
Macmillan
316
HB
OP
**Summer with Danica**
1979
*Ein Sommer mit Danica*
1973
Bell, A
A. Ellis
202
HB
OP
**Summer with Danica**
1981
*Ein Sommer mit Danica*
1973
Bell, A
Pan
201
PB
OP
**They Fell from the Sky**
1980
*Sie fielen vom Himmel*
Coburn, O
Futura Publications
221
PB
OP
**War Bride, The**
1979
*Die glückliche Ehe*
1969
Lewis, Ch
A. Ellis
211
HB
OP
**War Bride, The**
1979
*Die glückliche Ehe*
1969
Lewis, Ch
Star Books
211p
PB
OP
**War Bride, The**
1983
*Die glückliche Ehe*
1969
Lewis, Ch
Ulverscroft large print
432
HB
6.95
**Mask My Agony**
1964
*Das geschenkte Gesicht*
1962
Gibbons, I,R

Gibbs & Phillips
207
HB
OP
**Naked Earth, The**
1961
*Der Arzt von Stalingrad*
1956
Whitman, H
Gibbs & Phillips
327
HB
OP
**Naked Earth, The**
1962
*Der Arzt von Stalingrad*
1956
Whitman, H
Hamilton & Co
272
HB
OP

KORSCHUNOW
Irina
**Night in Distant Motion, A**
1984
*Er hieß Jan*
1983
Hafrey, L
Hodder and Stoughton
151
HB
OP
**Night in Distant Motion, A**
1986
*Er hieß Jan*
1983
Hafrey, J
Knight
160
PB
OP

KRAMER
Gerhard
**We Shall March Again**
1955
*Wir werden weiter marschieren*
1952
Powell, A G
Cape
383
HB
OP

KRAMP
Willy
**Prophecy, The**
1952
*Die Prophezeiung*
1951
Smith, K & Gregor, R
S.C.M.Press
124
PB
OP

KRÜGER
Hardy

**Upside-Down Tree, The**
1977
*Wer stehend stirbt lebt länger*
1973
Mainwaring, G A
W.H. Allen
222
PB
OP

KRÜGER
Michael
**End of the Novel, The**
1991
*Das Ende des Romans*
1990
Osers, Ewald
Quartet
106
HB
12.90
**Himmelfarb**
1994
*Himmelfarb*
1993
Wilson, L
Quartet
203
PB
10
**Man in the Tower, The**
1993
*Der Mann im Turm*
Wilson, L
Quartet
154
HB
13.90

KUBIN
Alfred
**Other Side, The**
1969
*Die andere Seite*
1909
Lindley, D
Gollancz
271
HB
OP
**Other Side, The**
1973
*Die andere Seite*
1909
Lindley, D
Penguin
300
PB
OP

KUBY
Erich
**Private Stefan**
1963
*Sieg! Sieg!*
1961
Lustig, T H
Cassell
389
HB
OP

**Rosemarie**
1960
*Rosemarie*
1960
Muller, R C J
Weidenfeld & Nicolson
224
HB
OP
**Rosemarie**
1961
*Rosemarie*
1960
Muller, R C J
Hamilton & Co
220
HB
OP

**KUPPER**
Heinz
**Simplicius 45**
1967
1963
Mosbacher, E
Panther
172
PB
OP
**Simplicius 45: a novel**
1966
1963
Mosbacher, E
Secker & Warburg
251
HB
OP

**KUSENBERG**
Kurt
**Restless Bullet, The**
1975
[Lion and Unicorn Press]
50
OP
**Sunflowers and other stories, The**
1972
Bird, G
Chatto and Windus
218
HB
OP

**KYBER**
Manfred
**Among Animals**
1967
*Unter Tieren*
1912
Fishwick, O
Centaur P.,
206
HB
14
**Three Candles of Little Veronica**
1990
Celestial arts
208
PB

7.99
**LAMPEL**
Rusia
**That Summer with Ora**
1967
*Der Sommer mit Ora*
1965
Humphries, S
Harrap
159
HB
OP

**LANIA**
Leo
**Foreign Minister, The**
1957
1956
Stern, J
P. Davies
221
OP

**LANSBURGH**
Werner
**Driftwood, an odyssey in our time**
1985
*Strandgut Europa*
Reinfrank, K
Wolff
183
PB
8.00

**LASKER-SCHÜLER**
Else
**Concert**
1994
*Konzert*
1932
Snook, J M
Nebraska UP: dist AUPG
162
HB

**LE FORT**
Gertrud
**Song at the Scaffold, The**
1953
*Die Letzte am Schafott*
1950
Marx, O
Sheed & Ward
110
HB
OP

**LEDERER**
Joe
**Late Spring**
1958
*Letzter Frühling*
1957
Hardie, D
Cape
253
HB
OP

**LEDIG**

Gert
**Brutal Years, The**
1959
*Faustrecht*
1957
Coburn, O & Lehrburger, U
Weidenfeld & Nicolson
192
HB
OP
**Naked Hill, The. A war book**
1957
*Die Stalinorgel*
1956
Savil, M
World Distributors
190
PB
OP
**Naked Hill, The**
1956
*Die Stalinorgel*
1955
Savill, M
Weidenfeld & Nicolson
190
HB
OP

**LEHMANN**
Marcus
**Count of Coucy & Vanished, The**
1964
Lehman
Honigson
118
OP
**Portrait of Two Families**
1981
*Saen und Ernten*
Feldheim Publishers,
Jerusalem
191
**Rabbi Joselman of Rosheim**
1974
*Rabbi Joselman von Rosheim*
494
OP
**Royal Resident, The**
1964
*Vergangenheit und Gegenwart*
Lehman
236
OP

**LEHNHOFF**
Joachim
**Homeward Run, The**
1957
*Die Heimfahrt*
1956
Wilson, L
Weidenfeld & Nicolson
224
HB

OP
## Homeward Run, The
1958
*Die Heimfahrt*
1956
Wilson, L
Hamilton & Co
192
HB
OP
___

## LENZ
Siegfred
### Exemplary Life, An
1976
*Das Vorbild*
1973
Parmée, D
Secker and Warburg
423
HB
OP

### German Lesson, The
1985
*Deutschstunde*
1968
Kaiser, E & Wilkins, E
Methuen
470
HB
OP

### German Lesson, The
1971
*Deutschstunde*
1968
Kaiser, E & Wilkins, E
Macdonald and Co.
471
HB
OP

### Heritage, The
1987
*Heimatmuseum*
1978
Winston, K
Methuen
458
PB
4.95

### Lightship, The
1987
*Das Feuerschiff*
1962
Bullock, M
Chivers large print
176
HB
8.95

### Lightship, The
1962
*Feuerschiff, Das*
1952
Bullock, M
Heinemann
153
HB
OP

### Training Ground
1991
*Exerzierplatz*

1985
Skelton, G
Methuen
425
HB
15.99
___

## LERNET-HOLENIA
Alexander
### Count Luns & Baron Bagge
1960
*Baron Bagge*
1936
Greene, J & Winston, R & C
Blond
252
HB
OP
___

## LETTAU
Reinhard
### Enemies
1973
*Feinde*
1968
Rook, A
Calder and Boyars
72
HB
OP
___

## LIND
Jakov
### Ergo
1967
*Eine bessere Welt*
1966
Manheim, R
Methuen
126
HB
OP

### Landscape in Concrete
1966
*Landschaft in Beton*
1963
Manheim, R
Methuen
151
HB
OP

### Soul of Wood
1985
*Eine Seele aus Holz*
1962
Manheim, R
Methuen
185
HB
OP

### Soul of Wood and other stories
1964
*Eine Seele aus Holz*
1962
Manheim, R
Cape
190
HB
OP

### Soul of Wood and other stories
1967
*Eine Seele aus Holz*
1962
Manheim, R
Panther
139
PB
OP

### Stove, The
1996
*Der Ofen*
1976
Menard
76
6.99
___

## LOEST
Erich
### Monument, The
1987
*Völkerschlachtdenkmal*
1984
Mitchell, I
Secker & Warburg
224
HB
10.95
___

## LOETSCHER
Hugo
### Noah: A novel
1970
*Noah*
1967
Gretton, G
Owen
140
HB
OP
___

## LORENZEN
Rudolf
### Anything but a Hero
1961
*Alles andere als ein Held*
1959
Bullock, M
Barrie & Rockliff
518
HB
OP
___

## LUDDECKE
Werner J
### Thursday at Dawn
1966
Dyrenforth, Dr H O
W.H.Allen
207
HB
OP
___

## LUNDHOLM
Anja
### Rainbow in the Night
1975
*Morgengrauen*
Sworder, M
Spearman

380
HB
OP
___

**MAASS**
Joachim
**Gabrielle**
1964
*Der Fall Gouffü*
1960
Bullock, M
Transworld
480
PB
OP
**Gouffü Case, The**
1960
*Der Fall Gouffü*
1958
Bullock, M
Barrie & Rockliff
481
HB
OP
**Magic Year, The**
1964
*Das magische Jahr*
1945
Meyer, E
Barrie & Rockliff
315
HB
OP
___

**MAETER**
Hans
**Sergeant Chung Ming**
1962
*Sergeant Chung Ming*
1958
Coburn, O
Hale
255
HB
OP
___

**MAHR**
Kurt
**Galactic Alarm**
1974
Mahr, K & Shols, W W
Futura Publications Ltd
PB
OP
**Ghosts of Gol, The**
1976
Ackerman, W
Futura Publications
126
PB
OP
**Menace of the Mutant Master**
1976
*Mutanten im Einsatz*
Futura Publications
124
PB
OP
**Planet of the Dying Sun, The**
1976
*Planet der Sterbenden Sonne*
Ackerman, W
Futura Publications
126
PB
OP
**To Arkon!**
1978
*Vorstoß nach Arkon*
Ackerman, W
Futura Publications
115
PB
OP
**Venus in Danger**
1976
*Venus in Gefahr*
Ackerman, W
Futura Publications
127
PB
OP
___

**MALTZ**
Albert
**Cross and the Arrow, The**
1958
Seven Seas (E.Berlin)
491
PB
OP
___

**MANN**
Heinrich
**Blue Angel, The**
1959
*Professor Unrat*
1904
Hamilton & Co
160
HB
OP
**Man of Straw**
1984
*Der Untertan*
1918
Penguin
295
PB
7.99
**Man of Straw**
1972
*Der Untertan*
1918
Sphere Books
320
PB
OP
___

**MANN**
Klaus
**Mephisto**
1995
*Mephisto. Roman einer Karriere*
1936
Smyth, R
Penguin
263

PB
6.99
**Pious Dance, The.
Adventure story of a young man**
1988
*Der fromme Tanz*
1926
Senelick
Gay Men's Press
181
PB
3.95
___

**MANN**
Thomas
**Black Swan, The**
1954
*Die Betrogene*
1953
Trask, W R
Secker & Warburg
128
HB
OP
**Buddenbrooks**
1992
*Buddenbrooks*
1901
Everyman's Library
640
HB
OP
**Buddenbrooks**
1996
*Buddenbrooks*
H. T. Lowe-Porter
Minerva
604
PB
8.99
**Buddenbrooks. The decline of a family**
1989
*Buddenbrooks. Verfall einer Familie*
1901
Lowe-Porter, H T
Folio Society
541
HB
OP
**Buddenbrooks. The decline of a family**
1957
*Buddenbrooks. Verfall einer Familie*
1901
Lowe-Porter, H T
Penguin Books / Secker & Warburg
591
PB
OP
**Buddenbrooks. The decline of a family**
1975(1971)
*Buddenbrooks. Verfall einer*

*Familie*
1901
Lowe-Porter, H T
Penguin
587
PB
OP

**Buddenbrooks. The decline of a family**
1956
*Buddenbrooks. Verfall einer Familie*
1901
Löwe-Porter, H
Penguin
591
PB
OP

**Buddenbrooks. The decline of a family**
1994
*Buddenbrooks. Verfall einer Familie*
1901
Woods, J E
Everyman
731
PB
10.99

**Buddenbrooks. The decline of a family**
1996
*Buddenbrooks. Verfall einer Familie*
1901
Porter, H T L
Minerva
624
PB
8.99

**Confessions of Felix Krull, confidence man**
1955
*Bekenntnisse des Hochstaplers Felix Krull*
1954
Lindley, D
Secker & Warburg
408
HB
OP

**Confessions of Felix Krull, confidence man**
1958
*Bekenntnisse des Hochstaplers Felix Krull*
1954
Lindley, D
Penguin & Secker & Warburg
347
PB
OP

**Confessions of Felix Krull, confidence man memoirs, part 1**
1977
*Bekenntnisse des*

*Hochstaplers Felix Krull*
1954
Lindley, D
Secker and Warburg
408
HB
OP

**Confessions of Felix Krull, confidence man memoirs, part 1**
1989
*Bekenntnisse des Hochstaplers Felix Krull*
1954
Lindley, D
Penguin
256
PB
6.99

**Confessions of Felix Krull,confidence man**
1955
*Bekenntnisse des Hochstaplers Felix Krull*
1954
Lindley, D
Secker & Warburg
408
HB
OP

**Death in Venice**
1996
*Der Tod in Venedig*
1912
Minerva
80
PB
4.99

**Death in Venice**
1971
*Der Tod in Venedig*
1912
Lowe-Porter, H T
Penguin
79
PB
OP

**Death in Venice (and other stories)**
1955
*Der Tod in Venedig*
1912
Lowe-Porter, H T
Penguin & Secker & Warburg
191
PB
OP

**Death in Venice; Tristan; Tonio Kroger; Doctor Faustus; Mario and the magician; A Man and his dog; The Black Swan; Confessions of Felix Krull**
1979
*Der Tod in Venedig*
n/a
Secker and Warburg

Octopus Books
809p
PB
OP

**Death in Venice and other short stories**
1996
*Der Tod in Venedig*
1913
Luke, D
Minerva
266
PB
5.99

**Death in Venice and other stories**
1991
*Tod in Venedig*
n/a
Lowe-Porter, H T
David Cambell
357
HB
8.99

**Death in Venice and other stories**
1983
*Tod in Venedig*
n/a
Heinemann
287
HB
OP

**Death in Venice, and two other stories**
1955
*Tod in Venedig*
1928
Lowe-Porter, H T
Penguin Books in association with Secker & Warburg
191
PB
OP

**Doctor Faustus**
1992
*Doktor Faustus*
1949
Lowe-Porter, H T
D. Campbell
523
HB
9.99

**Doctor Faustus**
1968
*Doktor Faustus*
1949
Lowe-Porter, H T
Penguin
491
PB
OP

**Doctor Faustus**
1991
*Doktor Faustus*
1949
Lowe-Porter, H T
Penguin
496

PB
7.99

**Doctor Faustus**
*Doktor Faustus*
**Doctor Faustus**
1997
*Doktor Faustus*
H. T Lowe-Porter
Minerva
510
PB
7.99

**Genesis of a Novel, The**
1961
*Die Entstehung des Doktor Faustus*
1949
Winston, R and C
Secker & Warburg
184
HB
OP

**Holy Sinner, The**
1952
*Der Erwählte*
1951
Lowe-Porter, H T
Secker & Warburg
280
HB
OP

**Holy Sinner, The**
1961
*Der Erwählte*
1951
Lowe-Porter, H.T
Penguin & Secker & Warburg
228
PB
OP

**Holy Sinner, The**
1972
*Der Erwählte*
1951
Lowe-Porter, H T
Penguin
228
PB
OP

**Joseph and his Brothers**
1956
*Joseph und seine Brüder*
1933-1942
Lowe-Porter, H T
Secker & Warburg
120
HB
OP

**Joseph and his Brothers**
1978
*Joseph und seine Brüder*
1933-1942
Lowe-Porter, H T
Penguin
120
PB
OP

**Joseph and his Brothers:Vol 1:The tales of**

**Jacob**
1968
*Die Geschichten Jakobs*
1933
Lowe-Porter, H T
Sphere
313
PB
OP

**Joseph and his Brothers:Vol 2: Young Joseph**
1968
*Der junge Joseph*
1934
Lowe-Porter, H T
Sphere
242
PB
OP

**Joseph and his Brothers:Vol 3: Joseph in Egypt**
1968
*Joseph in Ägypten*
1936
Lowe-Porter, H T
Sphere
483
PB
OP

**Joseph and his Brothers:Vol 4: Joseph the provider**
1968
*Joseph der Ernährer*
1943
Lowe-Porter, H T
Sphere
452
PB
OP

**Little Herr Friedemann, and other stories**
1972
*Der kleine Herr Friedemann*
1898
Penguin
208
PB
OP

**Lotte in Weimar**
1976(1968)
*Lotte in Weimar*
1939
Lowe-Porter, H T
Penguin
331
PB
6.99

**Lotte in Weimar**
1991
*Lotte in Weimar*
1939
Lowe-Porter, H T
Penguin
336
PB
6.99

**Magic Mountain, The**
1960
*Zauberberg, Der*
1924
Lowe-Porter, H T
Penguin & Secker & Warburg
716
PB
OP

**Magic Mountain, The**
1996
*Zauberberg, Der*
1924
Porter, H T L
Minerva
736
PB
8.99

**Magic Mountain, The**
1949
*Zauberberg, Der*
1924
Lowe-Porter, H T
Secker & W
716
HB
15.00

**Magic Mountain, The**
1996
*Der Zauberberg*
1924
Lowe-Porter, H T
Minerva
729
PB
8.99

**Mario and the Magician and other stories**
1997
*Mario und der Zauberer*
Lowe-Porter, H T
Minerva
365
PB
7.99

**Mario and the Magician, and other stories**
1975
*Mario und der Zauberer*
n/a
Penguin
368
PB
7.99

**Royal Highness**
1975
*Königliche Hoheit*
1909
Curtis, A C
Penguin
314
PB
OP

**Royal Highness**
1962
*Königliche Hoheit*
1909
Curtis, A C, revised by McNab, C
New English Library

298
PB
OP
**Selected Stories**
1993
*n/a*
Luke, D
Penguin
320
PB
6.99
**Stories and Episodes**
1955
*n/a*
1940
Dent;Dutton
359
HB
OP
**Stories of a Lifetime**
1961
Lowe-Porter, H T
Secker & Warburg
379
HB
OP
**Stories of a Lifetime (2)**
1985
Lowe-Porter, H T
Secker & Warburg
411
HB
OP
**Thomas Mann Diaries 1918-1939**
1984
*Tagebücher 1918-1939*
Winston, R & C
Robin Clark
471
OP
**Thomas Mann Diaries 1918-1939**
1983
*Tagebücher 1918-1939*
Winston, R & C
Deutsch
471
HB
OP

MANS
Adrienne
**On the Shores of Night**
1968
*An den Ufern der Nacht*
1965
Hogarth-Gaute, A
Harrap
190'
OP

MARNAU
Alfred
**Free among the Dead**
1950
*Der steinerne Gang*
1948
Harvill P
279

OP
**Guest, The**
1957
*Das Verlangen nach der Hölle*
1952
Thames & Hudson
234
HB
OP

MARON
Monika
**Defector, The**
1988
*Die Überläuferin*
1986
Marinelli, D N
Readers International
164
HB
9.95
**Flight of Ashes**
1986
*Flugasche*
1981
Marinelli, D N
Readers International
188
HB
8.90
**Silent Close no.6**
1993
*Stille Zeile Sechs*
Marinelli, D N
Readers International
HB
12.95
**Silent Close no.6**
1993
*Stille Zeile Sechs*
Marinelli, D N
Readers Internat.
192
PB
6.99

MARTELL
Gunter
**Hit and Run**
1967
*Das goldene Dreieck*
Long, D
Abelard-Schuman
157
OP

MASCHMANN
Melita
**Thirteenth, The**
1963
*Der dreizehnte*
Heller, R P
Abelard-Schuman
160
OP

MATRAY
Maria

**Liaison, The**
1975
Sharp, R
Cassell
346
OP

MAY
Karl
**Canada Bill, including The talking leather & One-Eye Joe Burkers**
1971
Gardner, F
Spearman
192
OP
**Captain Cayman**
1971
Gardner, F
Spearman
256
OP
**In the Desert**
1955
*Durch die Wüste*
1892
Billerbeck-Gentz, F
Ustad-Verlag; Willoughby; Pordes
318
OP

MECKEL
Christoph
**Snow Creatures and other stories. (Parallel Text)**
1990
*Schneetiere*
Bedwell, C
Mellen
85
HB
39.95
**Zünd and other stories. (Parallel Text)**
1990
*Der Zünd.*
Bedwell, C
Mellen
103
HB
39.95

MEICHSNER
Dieter
**Vain Glory**
1953
*Weißt du, warum?*
1952
Lloyd, C & A.L
Putnam
247
OP
**Vain Glory**
1960
*Weißt du, warum?*
1953
Lloyd, C & A.L

Hamilton
188
OP
**Duel in the Snow**
1979
*Alatna*
Pomerans, E
Mayflower
223
PB
OP

MEYRINK
Gustav
**Angel of the West
Window, The**
1994
*Der Engel vom westlichen
Fenster*
1927
Mitchell, M
Dedalus
421
PB
9.99
**Golem, The**
1985
*Der Golem*
1915
Pemberton, M
Dedalus
308
PB
3.50
**Golem, The**
1996
*Der Golem*
1915
Mitchell, M
Dedalus
262
PB
6.99
**Green Face, The**
1992
*Das grüne Gesicht*
1916
Dedalus
7.99
**Opal and other stories,
The**
1993
*n/a*
n/a
Raraty, M
Dedalus Sawtry
222
PB
7.99
**Walpurgisnacht**
1993
*Walpurgisnacht*
1917
Mitchell, M
Dedalus
169
PB
6.99

**White Dominican, The**
1994
*Der weiße Dominikaner*
1921
Mitchell, M
Dedalus, Sawtry
165
PB
7.99

MIEHE
Ulf
**Puma**
1978
*Puma*
1976
Talbot, K
Weidenfeld and Nicolson
278
OP

MITGUTSCH
Anna
**Punishment**
1988
*Die Züchtigung*
1985
Müller, L
Virago
216
HB
11.95

MONIKOVA
Libuse
**Façade, The**
1992
*Die Fassade*
1987
Woods, J E
Chatto & Windus
374
PB
9.99

MOOSDORF
Johanna
**Flight to Africa**
1955
*Flucht nach Afrika*
1952
Winston, R & C
Joseph
238
OP
**Flight to Africa**
1955
*Flucht nach Afrika*
1952
Winston, R C
M. Joseph
238
OP
**Next Door**
1963
*Nebenan*
1961
Glenny, M
Gollancz
224

OP

MÖRIKE
Eduard
**Mozart's Journey to
Prague**
1976
*Mozart auf Reise nach Prag*
1957
Loewenstein-Wertheim, L
Calder
93
OP

MORZFELD
Erwin
**He Flew by My Side**
1959
*Er flog an meiner Seite*
1957
Savill, M
Macdonald
336
OP

MÜHLENWEG
Fritz
**Big Tiger and Christian**
1954
*In geheimer Mission durch
die Wüste Gobi*
1950
MacHugh, F & I
Cape
557
OP

MÜLLER
Herta
**Passport, The**
1989
*Der Mensch ist ein großer
Fasan auf der Welt*
1986
Chalmers, M
Serpent's Tail
93
PB
5.95

MUNSTER
Thomas
**Sardinian Sheperdess, The**
1962
*Die sardische Hirtin*
1960
Fitzgerald, E
Muller
253
OP

MUSIL
Robert
**Confusions of young
Törleß**
1997
*Die Verwirrungen des
Zöglings Törleß*
1906
Aczel, R L

Panther
240
PB
5.99
**Man without Qualities,
The**
1953
*Der Mann ohne
Eigenschaften*
1930
Kaiser, E & Wilkins, E
Secker & Warburg
367
OP
**Man without Qualities,
The**
1960
*Der Mann ohne
Eigenschaften*
1930
Wilkins, E & Kaiser, E
Secker & Warburg
445
OP
**Man without Qualities,
The**
1996
*Der Mann ohne
Eigenschaften*
Wilkins, S
Picador
1,774
HB
40
**Man without Qualities,
The Vols 1-4**
*Der Mann ohne
Eigenschaften*
1930
Wilkins, E & Kaiser, E
Panther
4vols
**Man without qualities,
The. Vol. 1**
1995
*Der Mann ohne
Eigenschaften*
1930
Wilkins, E & Kaiser, E
Minerva
365
PB
7.99
**Man without Qualities,
The. Vol. 2**
1995
*Der Mann ohne
Eigenschaften*
1930
Wilkins, E & Kaiser, E
Minerva
454
PB
7.99
**Man without Qualities,
The. Vol. 3**
1995

*Der Mann ohne
Eigenschaften*
1930
Wilkins, E & Kaiser, E
Minerva
445
PB
7.00
**Posthumous Papers of a
living author**
1995
*Nachlass zu Lebzeiten*
Wortsman, P
Penguin
145
PB
6.99
**Precision and Soul. Essays
and addresses**
1990
Pike, B & Luft, S
University of Chicago Press
301
23.90
**Tonka and other stories**
1969
1924
Wilkins, E & Kaiser, E
Panther
173
PB
OP
**Tonka and other stories**
1965
1924
Wilkins, E & Kaiser, E
Secker & Warburg
222
OP
**Tonka and other stories**
1988
1924
Wilkins, E & Kaiser, E
Pan Bks
224
PB
3.99
**Tonka, and other stories**
1969
1924
Wilkins, E & Kaiser, E
Panther
173
OP
**Young Törleß**
1955
*Die Verwirrungen des
Zöglings Törleß*
1906
Kaiser, E & E
Secker & Warburg
217
OP
**Young Törless**
1961
*Die Verwirrungen des
Zöglings Törleß*
1906
Wilkins, E & Kaiser, E

Secker & Warburg & Penguin
189
OP
**Young Törless**
1971
*Die Verwirrungen des
Zöglings Törleß*
1906
Wilkins, E & Kaiser, E
Panther
189
PB
OP

**MUSKE**
Irmgard
**India the Hungry**
1970
*Die Hungrigen und die Satten*
1966
Hopka, E
Concordia
189
PB
OP
**Roosters Loud in Africa**
1968
*Nirgends krähen die Hähne
so laut*
1965
Hopka, E
Concordia
126
PB
OP

**NADOLNY**
Sten
**Discovery of Slowness, The**
1987
*Die Entdeckung der
Langsamkeit*
1983
Freedman, R
Viking
325
PB
11.95

**NEUMANN**
Alfred
**Look upon this Man**
1950
*Der Pakt*
Taylor, R T
Hutchinson
231
OP

**NEUMANN**
Robert
**Festival**
1963
*Festival*
1962
Bullock, M
Barrie & Rockliff
215
OP
**Shooting Star (and Circe's**

**island)**
1954
Neumann, R
Hutchinson
224
OP

**NIEBELSCHÜTZ**
Wolf Von
**Badger of Ghissi, The**
1963
*Die Kinder der Finstenis*
1959
Mussey, B
Allen & Unwin
264
OP
**Badger of Ghissi, The**
1985
*Die Kinder der Finstenis*
1959
Barrows, M
Unwin Paperbacks
261
PB
OP

**NOGLY**
Hans
**Anastasia**
1959
1956
Hood, S
Landsborough Pub.,
192
OP
**Anastasia**
1957
1956
Hood, S
Methuen
252
OP

**NOLL**
Ingrid
**Hell Hath No Fury**
1996
*Der Hahn ist tot*
1991
Mitchell, I
HarperCollins
203
HB
14.99

**NOSSACK**
Hans Erich
**Impossible Proof, The**
1969
*Unmögliche Beweisaufnahme*
1956
Lebeck, M
Barrie & Rockliff (Cresset P.,)
218
PB
OP
**To the Unknown Hero**
1974
*Dem unbekannten Sieger*
1969

Manheim, R
Alcove Press
154
OP

**NOWOTNY**
Joachim
**Labyrinth without Fear**
1970
*Labyrinth ohne Schrecken*
Peet, J
Seven Seas (E.Berlin)
159
PB
OP

**OLIVIER**
Stefan
**I Swear and Vow**
1961
*Ich schwöre und gelobe*
1960
Sebba, H
Blond
358
OP
**Lost Sons**
1965
*Roman der verlorenen Söhne*
1958
Foster-Melliar, A
World Distributors
409
PB
OP
**Lost Sons**
1961
*Roman der verlorenen Söhne*
1958
Foster-Melliar, A
Blond
503
OP
**Rise up in Anger**
1963
*Jedem das Seine*
1961
Rock, S & Roloff, M
Blond
384
HB
OP

**OPITZ**
Karlludwig
**General, The**
1958
*Mein General*
1956
Fitzgibbon, C
Brown, Watson
159
OP
**General, The**
1956
*Mein General*
1956
Fitzgibbon, C
Muller
150
OP

**Patriot, The**
1962
Cleugh, J
Muller
150
OP
**Soldier, The**
1954
*Der Barras*
1953
Fitzgibbon, C
Muller
208
OP
**Soldier, The**
1957(54)
*Der Barras*
Fitzgibbon, C
World Distributors
191
HB
OP

**OTT**
Wolfgang
**Sharks and Little Fish**
1957
*Haie und kleine Fische*
1956
Coburn, O
Hutchinson
398
OP
**Sharks and Little Fish**
1960
*Haie und kleine Fische*
Coburn, O
Arrow
398
OP
**Sharks and Little Fish**
1977
*Haie und kleine Fische*
1957
Coburn, O
Corgi
448p
PB
OP
**Sharks and Little Fish**
1960
*Haie und kleine Fische*
1957
Coburn, O
Arrow Books
398
OP

**OTTO**
Herbert
**Time of the Storks**
1968
*Zeit der Storche*
Wulff, E
Seven Seas (E.Berlin)
246
PB
OP

**PALMER**

Lilli
**Face Value**
1986
*Um eine Nasenlänge*
Grafton
326
PB
OP
**Night Music**
1982
*Nachtmusik*
1981
Weidenfeld and Nicolson
323
OP
**Night Music**
1984
*Nachtmusik*
1981
Hamlyn Paperbacks
323p
PB
OP
**Red Raven, The**
1981
*Der rote Rabe*
1977
Hamlyn
265
PB
OP
**Red Raven, The**
1979
*Der rote Rabe*
1977
W.H.Allen
265
PB
OP
**Time to Embrace, A**
1980
*Umarmen hat seine Zeit*
1979
Harrison, C
Weidenfeld and Nicolson
342
HB
OP
**Time to Embrace, A**
1981
*Umarmen hat seine Zeit*
1979
Harrison, C
Macdonald Futura
400
PB
OP
**When the Nightbird Cries**
1989
*Wenn der Nachtragel schreit*
Talbot, Katherine
Grafton
256
PB
OP

**PARETTI**
Sandra
**Magic Ship, The**

1980
*Das Zauberschiff*
1977
Hein, R
New English Library
342
PB
OP
**Maria Canossa**
1982
*Maria Canossa*
Hein, R
Hodder and Stoughton
296
OP
**Rose and the Sword, The**
1968
*Rose und Schwert*
1967
Pomerans, A
Heinemann
320
PB
OP
**Rose and the Sword, The**
1971
*Rose und Schwert*
1967
Pomerans, A
Pan Books
333
OP

**PAUSEWANG**
Gudrun
**Fall-Out**
1995
*Die Wolke*
1987
Crampton, P
Viking
160
9.99
**Final Journey**
1996
*Auf einem langen Weg*
Crampton, P
Viking
160
10.99
**Last Children**
1990
*Die letzten Kinder von Schewenborn*
Watt, N W
Walker
128
2.99

**PEDRETTI**
Erica
**Stones, or, The destruction of the child Karl and other characters**
1982
*Veränderung*
1953
Black, J L
John Calder

186
6.95

**PELITZER**
Felix
**Maloja Wind**
1953
*Malojawind*
1950
Hagen, L
Hammond, Hammond
192
OP

**PERUTZ**
Leo
**By Night under the Stone bridge**
1989
*Nachts unter der steinernen Brücke*
1975
Mosbacher, E
Collins Harvill
208
HB
10.95
**By Night under the Stone Bridge**
1991
*Nachts unter der steinernen Brücke*
1975
Mosbacher, E
Harvill
198
PB
6.99
**Leonardo's Judas**
1989
*Der Judas des Leonardo*
1959
Mosbacher, E
Collins Harvill
208
10.95
**Little Apple**
1991
*Wohin rollst du, Äpfelchen*
1928
Brownjohn, J
Collins-Harvill
199
13.00
**Marquis of Bolibar, The**
1989
*Der Marques de Bolibar*
1920
Brownjohn, J
Collins Harvill
182
10.95
**Master of the Day of Judgement, The**
1994
*Der Meister des Jüngsten Tages*
1921

Mosbacher, E
Harvill
147
HB
14.99
**Master of the Day of
Judgement, The**
1994
*Der Meister des jüngsten
Tages*
1921
Mosbacher, E
Harvill
147
PB
8.99
**Saint Peter's Snow**
1990
*Sankt Petri-Schnee*
1934
Mosbacher, E
Collins-Harvill
148
11.95
**Swedish Cavalier**
1992
*Der schwedische Reiter*
1936
Brownjohn, J
Harvill
192
HB
13.90
**Swedish Cavalier**
1993
*Der schwedische Reiter*
1936
Brownjohn, J
Harvill
192
PB
7.99
**Turlupin**
1996
*Turlupin*
1924
Brownjohn, John
Harvill
160
HB
14.99
**Turlupin**
1996
*Turlupin*
1924
Brownjohn, John
Harvill
160
PB
8.99
_____
**PETERSEN**
Jan
**Our Street. A chronicle of
only yesterday.**
1961
*Unsere Straße*
Rensen, B
Seven Seas (E.Berlin)

292
PB
OP
_____
**PIDOLL**
Carl
**Eroica; Nikolaus
Zmeskallvon
Domanovetz's reminis-
cences of Beethoven**
1956
*Verklungenes Spiel*
1952
Powell, A
Methuen
218
OP
_____
**PIRINÇCI**
Akif
**Felidae**
1994
*Felidae*
Noble, R
Fourth Estate
270
PB
OP
**Felidae on the Road**
1994
Bell, A
Fourth Estate
246
PB
OP
_____
**PLIEVIER**
Theodor
**Berlin**
1969
*Berlin*
1954
Hagen, L
Panther
478
PB
OP
**Berlin**
1956
*Berlin*
1954
Hagen, L & Milroy, V
Hammond Hammond
446
OP
**Berlin**
1976
*Berlin*
1954
Hagen, L & Milroy, V
Mayflower
PB
447
OP
**Moscow**
1956
*Moskau*
1952
Hood, S
Hamilton & Co.,

319
OP
**Moscow**
1953
*Moskau*
1952
Hood, S
Muller
316
OP
**Moscow**
1976
*Moskau*
1952
Hood, S
Mayflower
PB
319
OP
**Moscow**
1953
*Moskau*
1952
Hood, S
Muller
316
OP
**Stalingrad: The death of
an army**
1956
*Stalingrad*
1945
Langmead Robinson, H
Hamilton & Co.,
351
OP
_____
**POLONSKY**
Abraham
**Season of Fear, A**
1959
Seven Seas (E.Berlin)
239
PB
OP
_____
**PUMP**
Hans
**Before the Big Snow**
1960
*Vor dem großen Schnee*
1956
Kee, R
World Distributors
PB
220
OP
**Before the Great Snow**
1959
*Vor dem großen Schnee*
1956
Kee, R
Deutsch
HB
240
OP
_____
**PUTZ**
Helmut
**Adventures of Good**

**Comrade Schweik**
1969
*Abenteuer des braven*
*Kameraden Schwejk*
1965
Gillespie, S & Bassauer, R.E
Muller
325
OP

**RÄBER**
Johannes
**Bach and the Heavenly**
**Choir**
1956
*Die Heiligssprechung des*
*Johann Sebastian Bach*
1954
Michael, M
Hart-Davis
176
HB
OP

**RANSMAYR**
Christoph
**Dog King, The**
1997
*Morbus Kitahara*
Woods, J
Chatto & Windus
357
HB
15.99
**Last World, The, with an**
**Ovidian repertory**
1990
*Die letzte Welt*
1988
Woods, J
Chatto & Windus
202
HB
12.95
**Last World, The, with an**
**Ovidian repertory**
1991
*Die letzte Welt*
1988
Woods, J
Paladin Grafton
202
PB
3.99
**Terrors of Ice and**
**Darkness, The**
1991
*Schrecken des Eises und der*
*Finsternis*
1984
Woods, J
Weidenfeld & Nicolson
228
HB
14.00
**Terrors of Ice and**
**Darkness, The**
1992

*Schrecken des Eises und der*
*Finsternis*
1984
Woods, J
Paladin
199
PB
5.99

**RASP**
Renate
**Family Failure, A**
1970
*Ein ungeratener Sohn*
1967
Figes, E
Calder & Boyars
126
OP

**RASP-NURI**
Grace
**Yusuf**
1957
*Jussuf der Türkenjunge*
1954
Maxwell-Brownjohn, J
Cape
224
HB
OP

**REHMANN**
Ruth
**Man in the Pulpit, The**
1997
1979
Lohmann, C & P
Nebraska UP: AUPG dist.
215
HB
32.95
**Man in the Pulpit, The**
1997
1979
Lohmann, C & P
Nebraska UP: AUPG dist.
215
PB
14
**Saturday to Monday**
1961
*Illusionen*
1959
Hutter, C
Heinemann
250
HB
OP

**REICHART**
Elizabeth
**February Shadows**
1988
*Februar-Schatten*
1984
Hoffmeister, D
Women's Press
103
PB
3.95

**REIN**
Heinz
**Finale Berlin**
1952
*Berlin*
1947
Porter, D
Laurie
288
OP

**REMARQUE**
Erich Maria
**All Quiet on the Western**
**Front**
1968
*Im Westen nichts Neues*
1929
Wheen, A W
Mayflower
192
PB
OP
**All Quiet on the Western**
**Front**
1987
*Im Westen nichts Neues*
1929
Wheen, A W
Pan
192
PB
5.99
**All Quiet on the Western**
**Front**
1966
*Im Westen nichts Neues*
1929
Wheen, A W
Folio Society
184
HB
OP
**All Quiet on the Western**
**Front**
1994
*Im Westen nichts Neues*
1929
Murdoch, B
Cape
216
HB
14.99
**All Quiet on the Western**
**Front**
1991
*Im Westen nichts Neues*
1929
Chivers large print
200
HB
OP
**All Quiet on the Western**
**Front**
1980
*Im Westen nichts Neues*
1929
Wheen, A W

Putnam
192
OP
**All Quiet on the Western Front**
1984
*Im Westen nichts Neues*
1929
Murdoch, B
Methuen Educational
285
PB
OP
**All Quiet on the Western Front**
1968
*Im Westen nichts Neues*
1929
Wheen, A W
Mayflower
192
PB
OP
**All Quiet on the Western Front**
1970
*Im Westen nichts Neues*
1929
Wheen, A W
Heinemann Educational
248
OP
**All Quiet on the Western Front**
1996
*Im Westen nichts Neues*
1929
Murdoch, B
Vintage
256
PB
5.99
**Arch of Triumph**
1961
*Arc de Triomphe*
1946
Sorbell, W & Lindley, D
Hamilton
352
HB
OP
**Arch of Triumph**
1972
*Arc de Triomphe*
1946
Sorel, I W & Lindley, D
Hutchinson
446
HB
OP
**Black Obelisk, The**
1957
*Der schwarze Obelisk*
1956
Lindley, D
Hutchinson
368
HB
OP

**Black Obelisk, The**
1961
*Der schwarze Obelisk*
1956
Lindley, D
Four Square
288
PB
OP
**Flotsam**
1961
*Flotsam*
1941
Lindley, D
Panther
287
PB
OP
**Flotsam**
1961
*Flotsam*
1941
Lindley, D
Hamilton & Co
287
HB
OP
**Heaven has no Favourites**
1961
*Der Himmel kennt keine Günstlinge*
1961
Winston, R & C
Hutchinson
254
HB
OP
**Night in Lisbon, The**
1964
*Die Nacht von Lissabon*
1963
Manheim, R
Hutchinson
288
HB
OP
**Night in Lisbon, The**
1979
*Die Nacht von Lissabon*
1963
Manheim, R
Mayflower
224
PB
OP
**Road Back, The**
1979
*Der Weg zurück*
1931
Wheen, A W
Mayflower
208p
PB
OP
**Shadows in Paradise**
1972
*Schatten im Paradies*
1971
Manheim, R
Hutchinson

305
HB
OP
**Spark of Life**
1952
*Der Funke Leben*
1952
Stern, J
Hutchinson
368
HB
OP
**Spark of Life**
1981
*Der Funke Leben*
1952
Stern, J
Granada
383p
PB
OP
**Three Comrades**
1961
*Drei Kameraden*
1937
Wheen, A W
World Distributors
403
PB
OP
**Time to Love and a Time to Die, A**
1954
*Zeit zu leben, Zeit zu sterben*
1954
Lindley, D
Hutchinson
336
HB
OP
**Time to Love and a Time to Die, A**
1961
*Zeit zu leben, Zeit zu sterben*
1954
Lindley, D
Panther
288
PB
OP
**Time to Love and a Time to Die, A**
1981
*Zeit zu leben, Zeit zu sterben*
1954
Lindley, D
Granada
366
PB
OP
**Time to Love and a Time to Die, A**
1961
*Zeit zu leben, Zeit zu sterben*
1954
Lindley, D
Hamilton & Co
288
HB
OP

**REZZORI**
Gregor Von
**Death of My Brother Abel, The**
1986
*Der Tod meines Bruders Abel*
1985
Neugroschel, J
Pan
632
PB
OP
**Hussar, The**
1960
*Ein Hermelin in Tschernopoll*
1958
Hutter, C
Deutsch
343
HB
OP
**Hussar, The**
1960
*Ein Hermelin in Tschernopol*
1958
Hutter, C
Deutsch
343
HB
OP
**Memoirs of an Anti-Semite**
1983
*Memoiren eines Antisemiten*
Pan
281
PB
OP
**Orient-Express, The**
1993
*Kurze Reisen übern langen Weg*
Chatto
181
HB
OP
**Orient-Express, The**
1994
*Kurze Reisen übern langen Weg*
Vintage
181
PB
OP
**Short Cut Home**
1993
*Kurze Reisen übern langen Weg*
Chatto
HB
OP
**Snows of Yesteryear, The (portraits for an autobiography)**
1990
*Blumen im Schnee*
1989

Broch de Rothermann, H F
Chatto & Windus
290
HB
16.99
**Snows of Yesteryear, The (portraits for an autobiography)**
1991
*Blumen im Schnee*
1989
Broch de Rotherman, H F
Vintage
290
OP

**RICHTER**
Hans Werner
**Beyond Defeat**
1960
*Die Geschlagenen*
?1949
Panther
PB
OP
**They Fell from God's Hand**
1956
*Sie fielen aus Gottes Hand*
1951
Sainsbury, G
Harrap
335
OP
**They Fell from God's Hand**
1957
*Sie fielen aus Gottes Hand*
1951
Sainsbury, G
World Distributors
320
PB
OP

**RICHTER**
Hans, Peter
**I Was There**
1987
*Wir waren dabei*
Kroll, E
Puffin
204
PB
OP

**RILKE**
Rainer Maria
**Cornet, the manner of loving and dying of the Cornet Christoph Rilke, The**
1958
*Weise vom Leben und Tod des Cornets Christoph Rilke*
1903
Fitzgibbon, C
Wingate
32

**Cornet, the manner of loving and dying of the Cornet Christoph Rilke, The**
1958
*Weise von Liebe und Tod des Cornets Christoph Rilke*
1903
Fitz Gibbon, C
Wingate
32 ,21
OP
**Ewald Tragy**
1958
*Ewald Tragy*
1944
Gruenthal, L
Vision P.,
104
HB
OP
**Notebook of Malte Laurids Brigge**
1984
*Die Aufzeichnungen des Malte Laurids Brigge*
1910
Mitchell, S
Oxford University Press
243p
PB
OP
**Two Stories of Prague: King Bohush; The Siblings**
1994
Esterhammer, A
New England UP dist Estover
109
HB
18.95

**RINSER**
Luise
**Jan Lobel from Warsaw**
1991
*Jan Lobel aus Warschau*
1948
Hulse, M
Polygon
93
PB
6.99

**RISSE**
Heinz
**Earthquake, The**
1953
*Wenn die Erde bebt*
1950
Eldon, R
Secker & Warburg
254
HB
OP

**ROEHLER**
Klaus
**Dignity of Night, The**

1960
*Die Würde der Nacht*
1958
Mander, J N
Barrie & Rockliff
143
OP

ROSENDORFER
Herbert
**Architect of Ruins**
1992
*Der Ruinenbaumeister*
1969
Mitchell, M
Dedalus
368
PB
8.99

**Architect of Ruins, The**
1991
*Der Ruinenbaumeister*
1969
Mitchell, M
Dedalus
HB
18.90

**German Suite**
1979
*Deutsche Suite*
1972
Pomerans, A
Quartet
205
HB
OP

**Night of the Amazons, The**
1991
*Die Nacht der Amazonen*
1969
Mitchell, M
Secker & Warburg
247
HB
13.99

**Night of the Amazons, The**
1992
*Die Nacht der Amazonen*
1969
Mitchell, M
Minerva
246
PB
5.99

**Stephanie or A previous existence**
1995
*Stephanie und das vorige Leben*
1987
Mitchell, M
Dedalus
153
PB
7.99

ROTH

Gerhard
**Autobiography of Albert Einstein, The**
1997
*Die Autobiographie des Albert Einstein*
Green, M
Atlas
91
PB
7.99

ROTH
Joseph
**Confessions of a Murderer**
1985
*Berichte eines Mörders*
Vesey, D. I.
Chatto
224
HB
11.90

**Emperor's Tomb, The**
1984
*Die Kapuzinergruft*
1938
Hoare, J
Hogarth
157
HB
OP

**Flight without End**
1977
*Die Flucht ohne Ende*
1927
Le Vay, D & Musgrave, B
Owen
144
13.95

**Flight without End**
1984
*Die Flucht ohne Ende*
1927
Le Vay, D with Musgrave, B
Dent
140
PB
OP

**Hotel Savoy**
1986
*Savoy Hotel*
1924
Hoare, J
Chatto &
183
HB
OP

**Job. The story of a simple man**
1983
*Hiob, Roman eines einfachen Mannes*
1930
Thompson, D
Chatto & Windus
238
HB
OP

**Legend of the Holy**

**Drinker, The**
1989
*Die Legende vom heiligen Trinker*
1939
Hofmann, M
Chatto & Windus
49
HB
OP

**Legend of the Holy Drinker, The**
1990
*Die Legende vom heiligen Trinker*
1939
Hofmann, M
Pan in association with
Chatto & Windus
49
PB
OP

**Radetzky March, The**
1984
*Radetzkymarsch*
1938
Tucker, E & Dunlop, G
Penguin
318
PB
OP

**Radetzky March, The**
1974
*Radetzkymarsch*
1932
Tucker, E, based on Dunlop, G
Allen Lane
319
PB
OP

**Radetzky March, The**
1995
*Radetzkymarsch*
1938
Neugroschel, J
Penguin
352
PB
7.99

**Radetzky March, The**
1997
*Radetzkymarsch*
Neugroschel, J
Everyman
331
HB
9.99

**Right and Left**
1991
*Rechts und Links*
1929
Hofmann, M
Chatto & Windus
235
HB
OP

**Silent Prophet, The**
1979
*Der Stumme Prophet*

1969
Le Vay, D
Owen
220
HB
14.95
**Spider's Web, The**
1988
*Das Spinnennetz*
1923
Hoare, J
Chatto & Windins
245
OP
**Tarabas a Guest on Earth**
1987
*Tarabas, ein Gast auf dieser*
*Erde*
1934
Katzin, W
Chatto & Windus
311
HB
OP
**Weights and Measures**
1982
*Das falsche Gewicht*
1937
LeVay, D
Peter Owen
150
13.95
**Weights and Measures**
1983
*Das falsche Gewicht*
1937
Le Vay, D
Dent
150
PB
OP

RUTHERFORD
Dorothea
**Threshold, The**
1955
*Vor Tag*
1954
Budberg, M & Alexander, T
Hart-Davis
236
HB
OP

SACHER-MASOCH
Leopold Von
**Master Masochist, The.**
**Tales of Sadistic Mis-**
**tresses**
1968
Randall, E L
Tallis P
190
OP
**Master Masochist, The**
1968
Lemuel Randall, E
Tallis P.,
190
OP

**Venus in Furs**
1969
*Venus im Pelz*
1870
Sphere
160
PB
OP
**Venus in Furs and selected**
**letters**
*Venus im Pelz*
1870
Blast Books
210
PB
7.99
**Venus in Furs, together**
**with The black Czarina**
1965
*Venus im Pelz*
1870
Stenning, H J
Luxor P
191
OP
SAID
Kurban
**Ali & Nino**
1970
*Ali und Nino*
1937
Graman, J
Hutchinson
237
HB
OP
**Ali & Nino**
1971
*Ali und Nino*
1937
Graman, J
Arrow Books
237
PB
OP
**Ali & Nino**
1991
*Ali und Nino*
1937
Graman, J
Clark, R.
237
PB
5.95
SALTEN
Felix
**Florian the Lipizzaner**
1963
*Das Pferd des Kaisers*
1933
Gullick, N
J.A.Allen
287
OP
SANDER
Helke
**Three women K, The**

1991
*Geschichten der drei Damen*
*K*
Petzold, H
Serpent's Tail
142
PB
7.99
SCHÄFER
Georg
**In the Kingdom of Mescal:**
**a fairy tale for adults**
1969
*Im Reiche des Mescal*
1968
Livingstone, D
Macdonald
40
HB
OP
SCHAMONI
Ulrich
**Their Fathers' sons**
1963
*Dein Sohn läßt grüssen*
1962
Bullock, M
Barrie & Rockliff
184
OP
SCHAPER
Edzard
**Dancing Bear, The**
1960
*Das Tier*
1958
Denny, N
Bodley Head
224
HB
OP
SCHAUB
Franz
**Great Piece of**
**Krassnikova, The**
1960
*Der Große von Kraßnikowa*
1948
Dutfield, K T
Holborn Publishing Co
117
OP
SCHEER
Karl Herbert
**Enterprise Stardust**
1974
*Unternehmen Stardust*
Scheer, K. H & Ernsting, W
Futura Publications
189
PB
OP
**Enterprise Stardust**
1977
*Unternehmen Stardust*
Scheer, K H & Ernsting, W

Severn House [Distributed by Hutchinson]
189
OP
**Fortress of the Six Moons**
1975
*Der Festung der sechs Monde*
Ackerman, W
Futura Publications
124
PB
OP
**Immortal Unknown, The**
1976
*Der Unsterbliche*
Ackerman, W
Futura Publications
127
PB
OP
**Radiant Dome, The**
1974
Scheer, K H & Ernsting, W
Futura Publications Ltd
188
PB
OP
**Radiant Dome, The**
1977
Scheer, K H & Walter, E
Severn House [Distributed by Hutchinson]
188
OP
**Vega sector, The**
1975
*Raumschlacht im Vega-Sektor*
Scheer, K H & Mahr, K
Futura Publications
189
PB
OP

SCHIRMBECK
Heinrich
**Blinding Light, The**
1960
*Ärgert dich dein rechtes Auge*
1957
Denny, N
Collins
447
HB
OP

SCHMELTZER
Kurt
**Long Arctic Night, The**
1951
*Die Hütte im ewigen Eis*
1947
Brommer, E
Oxford U P
194
HB
OP

SCHMIDT
Arno

**Collected Novellas**
*n/a*
432
HB
17.99
**Egghead Republic, The. A short novel from the Horse latitudes**
1979
*Die Gelehrtenrepublik*
1957
Horovitz, M edited by Kraweh, E & Boyars, M
Boyars
164
13.95
**Egghead Republic, The. A short novel from the Horse latitudes**
1982
*Die Gelehrtenrepublik*
1957
Horovitz, M edited by Kraweh, E & Boyars, M
Boyars
164
PB
6.95
**Evening Edged in Gold**
1988
*Abend mit Goldrand*
Boyars
216
HB
60
**Nobodaddy's Children; Scenes from the life of a faun. Brand's Heath. Dark Mirrors.**
1995
*Nobodaddys Kinder*
1963
Woods, J E
Dalkey Archive
236
HB
10.99
**Nobodaddys Children; Scenes from the life of a faun. Brand's Heath. Dark Mirrors.**
1983
*Nobodaddys Kinder*
1963
Woods, J E
M. Boyars
160
PB
6.95
**Scenes from the life of a faun. A short novel**
1983
*Aus dem Leben eines Fauns*
1953
Woods, J E
Boyars
159

OP

SCHNABEL
Ernst
**Voyage Home, The**
1958
*Der sechste Gesang*
1958
Lindley, D
Gollancz
184
HB
OP

SCHNEIDER
Peter
**Wall Jumper, The**
1984
*Der Mauerspringer*
1982
Hafrey, L
Allison & Busby
139
OP

SCHNEIDER
Rolf
**Bridges and Bars**
1969
*Brücken und Gitter*
1965
Bullock, M
Panther
156
PB
OP
**Bridges and Bars.**
1967
*Brücken und Gitter: Ein Vorspruch und sieben Geschichten*
1965
Bullock, M
Cape
189
HB
OP
**Deep Waters**
1968
*Die Tage in W.*
Peet, J
Seven Seas (E.Berlin)
194
PB
OP
**November. A novel**
1981
*November*
1979
Bullock, M
Hamilton
235
HB
OP

SCHNELL
Robert Wolfgang
**Bonko**
1969
Wilkon, J
Dobson

30
HB
OP

## SCHNITZLER
Arthur
**Casanova's Homecoming**
1959
*Casanovas Heimfahrt*
1918
Paul, E & Cedar, M
World Distibutors
128
PB
OP

**Casanova's homecoming**
1954
*Casanovas Heimfahrt*
1918
Paul, E & Cedar,M
Weidenfeld & Nicolson
130
HB
OP

**Plays and stories**
Continuum
302
PB
14.99

**Road into the Open, The**
1992
*Der Weg ins Freie*
1908
Byers, R
University of California Press
297
HB
24.00

**Vienna 1900 - games with Love and Death**
1973
Penguin
365
PB
OP

## SCHÖNTHAN
Gaby Von
**Madame Casanova**
1971
*Madame Casanova*
Pellkan, M
W.H. Allen
309
PB
OP

**Madame Casanova**
1973
*Madame Casanova*
Pelikan, M
Sphere
315
PB
OP

**Roses of Malmaison, The**
1968
*Die Rosen von Malmaison*
1966
Pol, T
Cassell

309
HB
OP

## SCHROBSDORFF
Angelika
**Men, The**
1963
*Die Herren*
1961
Bullock, M
Collins
383
HB
OP

## SCHROEDER
Binette
**Wonderful travels and adventures of Baron Münchhausen as told by himself in the company of his friends, and washed down by many a good bottle of wine. The adventures on land**
1979
*Wunderbaren Reisen und Abenteuer des Freiherrn von Münchhausen*
1977
Buchanan Taylor, E
Chatto and Windus
56
HB
OP

## SCHULLER
Victor
**Sky Ablaze, The**
1958
Savill, M
Kimber
256
OP

## SCHWAB
Gunther
**Dance with the Devil**
1963
*Des Teufels Küche*
1959
Battershaw, B
Bles
271
OP

## SEBALD
W.G.
**Emigrants, The**
1997
*Die Ausgewanderten*
Harvill
256
HB
14.99

**Emigrants, The**
1996
*Die Ausgewanderten*

Harvill
256
PB
8.99

## SEGHERS
Anna
**Benito's Blue & nine other stories**
1973
*Das wirkliche Blau*
Seven Seas (E.Berlin)
dist.Collets
270
PB
OP

**Revolt of the Fishermen of Santa Barbara + A Price on his head**
1960
*Der Aufstand der Fischer von St. Barbara*
1928
Mitchell, J & R, Walff, E
Seven Seas (E.Berlin)
dist.Collets
295
PB
OP

## SEIPOLT
Adalbert
**All Roads Lead to Rome**
1962
*Alle Wege führen nach Rom*
1958
Harryman, A
Barrie & Rockliff
144
OP

## SELINKO
Annemarie
**Désirée**
1959
*Désirée*
1951
Bender, A & Dickes, E.W.
Pan
538
PB
OP

**Désirée**
1968
*Désirée*
1951
Bender, A & Dickes, E.W
Heinemann
674
HB
OP

**Désirée**
1974
*Désirée*
1951
Benders, A & Dickes, E W
Fontana
512
PB
OP

SENTJURC
Igor
**Prayer for an assassin**
1960
*Gebet für den Mörder*
1959
Schaeffer, C
Longmans Green
240
OP
**Thou Shalt not Kill**
1963
*Der unstillbare Strom*
Mosbacher, E
Constable
353
HB
OP

SIMMEL
Johannes Mario
**Affair of Nina B, The**
1979
*Affäre Nina B*
1858
Hutter, C
Hamlyn
349
PB
OP
**Affair of Nina B, The**
1980
*Affäre Nina B*
1958
Hutter, C
Piatkus Books
349
OP
**Berlin Connection, The**
1980
*Bis zur bitteren Neige*
1961
Mays, R
Hamlyn
512
PB
OP
**Cain Conspiracy, The**
1979
*Alle Menschen werden Brüder*
1967
Mays, R
Hamlyn
507p
PB
OP
**Dear Fatherland**
1969
*Lieb Vaterland magst ruhig sein*
1965
Winston, R & C
Deutsch
403
HB
OP
**Dear Fatherland**
1971

*Lieb Vaterland magst ruhig sein*
1965
Winston, R & C
Panther
383
OP
**Double Agent - Triple Cross**
1980
*Lieb Vaterland magst du ruhig sein*
1965
Winston,R & C
Hamlyn
477
PB
OP
**It Can't always Be Caviar**
1968
*Es muß nicht immer Kaviar sein*
1960
Clough, J
Mayflower
415
PB
OP
**It Can't always Be Caviar**
1965
*Es muß nicht immer Kaviar sein*
1960
Clough, J
Blond
447
PB
OP
**Sibyl Cipher, The**
1982
*Gott schützt die Liebenden*
Hutter, C
Hamlym
220
PB
OP

SPENGLER
Tilman
**Lenin's Brain**
1993
*Lenins Hirn*
1991
Whiteside, S
Hamish Hamilton
266
PB
9.99

SPERBER
Manès
**God's Water Carriers**
1987
*Die Wasserträger Gottes*
1974
Neugroschel, J
Holmes & Meier
174
12.95

**Like a Tear in the Ocean: A trilogy, v.1 The burned bramble**
1987
*Wie eine Träne im Ozean. Der Verbrannte Dornbusch*
1950
Fitzgibbon, C
Holmes &
432
25.00
**Like a Tear in the Ocean: v.2 The Abyss**
1987
*Wie eine Träne im Ozean. Tiefer als der Abgrund*
Fitzgibbon, C
Holmes&
272
17.50
**Like a Tear in the Ocean: v3 Journey without end**
1987
*Wie eine Träne im Ozean*
Fitzgibbon, C
Holmes&
272
17.95
**Lost Bay, The**
1956
*Die verlorene Bucht*
1955
Fitzgibbon, C
Deutsch
304
HB
OP
**To Dusty Death**
1952
Fitzgibbon, C
Wingate
264
OP
**Wind and the Flame, The**
1951
*Wie eine Träne im Ozean*
1950
Fitzgibbon, C
Wingate
416
OP

SPERLING
Robert Helgi
**Tigress of the Pearl River**
1955
Webber, R P
Hutchinson
191
HB
OP

SPRINGENSCHMID
Carl
**Miss Nobody**
1961
*Signorina N.N.*
1960
Dixon, C

Ward Lock
189
OP

**STACHOW**
Hasso, G.
**If this Be Glory**
1983
*Der kleine Quast*
Brownjohn, J M
Granada
288
PB
OP

**STEGER**
Hans, Ulrich
**Travelling to Tripiti**
1967
Crawford, E D
Bodley Head
48
OP

**STEPHAN**
Hanna
**Long Way Home, The**
1967
Goodall, D M
Heinemann
151
OP

**STERCHI**
Beat
**Blösch**
1988
*Blösch*
1985
Hofmann, M
Faber
353
OP

**STIFTER**
Adalbert
**Brigitta and other tales**
1997
*Brigitta*
Watanabe-O'Kelly, H
Penguin
247
PB
6.99
**Brigitta with Abdias,
Limestone & The Forest
Path**
1990
*Brigitta, Abdias etc*
Watanabe-O'Kelly, H
Angel Books: dist. Airlift
248
PB
7.95
**Brigitta with Abdias,
Limestone & The Forest
Path**
Watanabe-O'Kelly, H
Angel Books: dist. Airlift
248

HB
13.95

**STOIBER**
Rudolph, Maria
**Secret of Channel Six**
1962
*Das Geheimnis auf Kanal 6*
1961
Long, D
Abelard-Schuman
200
OP

**STRAUSS**
Botho
**Devotion**
1980
*Die Widmung*
1977
Wilkins, S
Chatto and Windus
120
OP
**Devotion**
1996
*Die Widmung*
1977
Wilkins, S
Hydra Books
dist.:Turnaround
120
PB
8.99
**Tumult**
1984
*Rumor*
1980
Hulse, M
Carcanet
136
OP

**STREIT**
Kurt
**Airline Captain Brand**
1966
*Flugkapitän Brand*
1963
Humphries, S
Blackie
118
OP

**STRITMATTER**
Erwin
**Ole Bienkopp**
1996
*Ole Bienkopp*
Mitchell, J & R
Seven Seas (E.Berlin)
393
PB
OP

**STRITMATTER**
Thomas
**Raven**
1994
*Raabe Baikal*

1990
Vintage
PB
5.99
**Raven**
1993
*Raabe Baikal*
1990
Chatto
HB
OP

**SÜßKIND**
Patrick
**Maitre Mussard's Bequest**
1996
Bloomsbury
PB
1.00
**Perfume, the story of a
murderer**
1986
*Das Parfüm. Die Geschichte
eine Mörders*
1985
Woods, J E
Hamilton
186
9.95
**Perfume, the story of a
murderer**
1987
*Das Parfüm. Die Geschichte
eines Mörders*
1985
Woods, J E
ISIS Large Print
361
8.95
**Perfume, the story of a
murderer**
1987
*Das Parfüm. Die Geschichte
eines Mörders*
1985
Woods, J E
Penguin
263
PB
3.95
**Perfume, the story of a
murderer**
1994
*Das Parfüm. Die Geschichte
eineMörders*
1985
Woods, J E
Bloomsbury
284
10.95
**Pigeon, The**
1988
*Die Taube*
1987
Woods, J.E.
Hamilton
77

9.95
**Pigeon, The**
1996
*Die Taube*
Woods, J.E.
Bloomsbury
335
HB
10.95
**Pigeon, The**
1989
*Die Taube*
1987
Woods, J.E.
Penguin
96
PB
3.50
**Story of Mr. Sommer**
1994
*Die Geschichte von Herrn Sommer*
1991
Hofmann, M
Bloomsbury
PB
7.99
**Story of Mr. Sommer**
1992
*Die Geschichte von Herrn Sommer*
1991
Hofmann, M
Bloomsbury
HB
12.99
**Three Stories and a Reflection**
1996
Howarth, Peter et al
Blo1omsbury
87
HB
10.99

TESSIN
Brigitte Von
**Bastard, The**
1958
*Der Bastard*
1957
Savill, M
Barrie
724
OP
**Bastard, The (Vol 1&2)**
1968
*Der Bastard*
1957
Savill, M
Corgi
284
PB
OP
**Bastard, The**
1958
*Der Bastard*
1957
Savill, M

Barrie
724
OP

TRAVEN
B
**Bridge in the Jungle, The**
1975
*Die Brücke im Dschungel*
1929
Penguin
176
OP
**Carreta, The**
1995
*Der Karren*
1932
Allison & Busby
264
7.99
**Cotton-Pickers**
1979
*Die Baumwollpflücker*
1931
Allison and Busby
200
OP
**Death Ship**
1980
*Das Totenschiff*
1926
Panther
304
PB
OP
**General from the Jungle**
1985
*Ein General kommt aus dem Dschungel*
1940
Vesey, D
Allison & Busby
280
HB
OP
**Government**
1994
*Regierung*
1931
Allison & Busby
231
PB
5.99
**Government**
1980
*Regierung*
1931
Allison & Busby
231
HB
OP
**Kidnapped Saint, The & other stories**
1978
*n/a*
1975
Lujan, R E et al
Allison and Busby
198

PB
OP
**March to the Montería**
1982
*Der Marsch ins Reich der Caoba*
Allison & Busby
227
HB
OP
**March to the Montería**
1996
*Der Marsch ins Reich der Caoba*
Allison & Busby
240
PB
8.99
**Rebellion of the Hanged, The**
1984
*Die Rebellion der Gehenkten*
1936
Allison & Busby
248
HB
OP
**Rebellion of the Hanged, The**
1970
*Die Rebellion der Gehenkten*
1936
Duff, C
Penguin
268
OP
**To the Honourable Miss S and other stories**
1981
Silcock, Peter
Cienfuegos Press: Sanday, Orkney
151
HB
OP
**Treasure of the Sierra Madre, The**
1980
*Der Schatz der Sierra Madre*
1927
Granada
222
PB
OP
**Treasures of B. Traven, The**
1980
*n/a*
Cape
627
OP
**Trozas**
1994
*Trozas*
1959
Young, H
Allison & Busby
265

PB
5.99
**White Rose, The**
1980
*Die weiße Rose*
1929
Allison & Busby
209
HB
OP

TUCHOLSKY
Kurt
**Castle Gripsholm, a
summer story**
1985
*Schloß Gripsholm*
1931
Hofmann, M
Chatto & Windus
128
8.95
**Germany? Germany!: A
Tucholsky reader**
1989
*n/a*
n/a
Zohn, H
Carcanet
320
18.95

TURPITZ
Erika
**Oberammergau's first
Christ**
1959
*Der erste Christus von
Oberammergau*
1959
Bailey & Swinfen
128
OP

UHSE
Bodo
**Lieutenant Bertram**
1961
*Leutnant Bertram*
1943
Hutter, C
Seven Seas; Collet's
468
OP

ULRICH
Max
**Bank Robbery**
1967
*Raub in der Münchner
Lombard-Bank*
1965
Constable
191
OP

VOLLMOELLER
Karl
**Last Miracle, The**

1950
Salm, L
Cassell
706
OP

WAGNER
Richard
**Exit, a Romanian story**
1990
*Ausreiseantrag*
Hoare, Q
Verso
111
HB
24.95

WALEWSKA
**Dearest Mama**
1956
*Meine schöne Mama*
1956
Fitzgibbon, C
Barrie
159
OP
**Dearest Mama**
1960
*Meine schöne Mama*
1956
Fitzgibbon, C
Brown, Watson
159
OP

WALSER
Martin
**Breakers. A novel**
1987
*Brandung*
1985
Vennewitz, L
Deutsch
305
12.95
**Gadarene Club, The**
1960
*Ehen in Philippsburg*
1957
Eigen, F
Longmans
273
OP
**Inner Man, The. A novel**
1987
*Seelenarbeit*
1979
Vennewitz, L
Methuen
276
PB
OP
**Inner Man, The. A novel**
1986
*Seelenarbeit*
1979
Vennewitz, L
Deutsch
288
HB

9.95
**Rabbit Race and Detour**
1966
*Jagd*
Boyars
HB
10.95
**Rabbit Race and Detour**
1966
*Jagd*
Boyars
PB
6.95
**Runaway Horse. A novel**
1980
*Ein Fliehendes Pferd*
1978
Vennewitz, L
Secker and Warburg
113
OP
**Swan Villa, The**
1983
*Das Schwanenhaus*
1927
Vennewitz, L
Secker & Warburg
247
HB
OP
**Unicorn, The**
1971
*Das Einhorn*
1966
Ellis-Jones, B
Calder and Boyars
283
7.95

WALSER
Robert
**Institute Benjamenta**
1995
*Jakob von Gunten*
1909
Middleton, C
Serpent's Tail
154
PB
8.95
**Jakob von Gunten**
1969
*Jakob von Gunten*
1909
Middleton, C
University of Texas (Austin,
Lon.,)
154
OP
**Masquerade & other
stories**
1993
*Gesamtwerk*
1978
Bernofsky, S
Quartet
202
PB

7.95
**Selected Stories**
1982
*n/a*
n/a
Middleton, C et al
Carcanet
194
OP
**Walk and other stories, The**
1957
*Der Spaziergang*
1917
Middleton, C
Calder
104
OP
**Walk, The**
1992
*Der Spaziergang*
1917
Middleton, C
Serpent's Tail
190
PB
9.99

**WALTER**
Otto Friedrich
**Mute, The**
1962
*Der Stumme*
1959
Bullock, M
Deutsch
207
OP

**WANDER**
Fred
**Seventh Well, The**
1976
*Der siebente Brunnen*
Linder, M
Seven Seas (E.Berlin)
146
PB
OP

**WASSERMANN**
Jakob
**Caspar Hauser: Enigma of a century**
1983
*Caspar Hauser*
1908
Newton, C
Floris Classics
467
PB
OP
**Caspar Hauser or the inertia of the heart**
1992
*Caspar Hauser oder die Trägheit des Herzens*
1908
Hulse, M

Penguin
381
PB
OP

**WEISENBORN**
Günther
**Fury, The**
1956
*Die Furie*
1937
Graves, R & C
Hutchinson
264
OP
**Pursuer, The**
1962
*Der Verfolger*
1961
Selver, P
Heinemanns
230
OP

**WEISKOFF**
Franz Carl
**Firing Squad, The**
1961
*Himmelfahrtskommando*
1945
Galston, J A
Seven Seas ; Collet's
336
PB
OP

**WEISS**
Ernst
**Aristocrat, The: Boetius von Orlamunde**
1994
*Der Aristocrat*
1928
Chalmers, M
Serpent's Tail
202
PB
8.99
**Eyewitness, The**
1978
*Ich der Augenzeuge*
1963
McKee, E R W
Proteus
206
OP

**WEISS**
Peter
**Conversation of the Three Walkers,The & The shadow of the coachman's body**
1972
*Der Schatten des Körpers des Kutschers (1965) & Gespräch der drei Gehenden (1963)*
1965
Cupitt, S M

Calder &n Boyars
167
PB
OP
**Leavetaking & Vanishing point**
1966
*Abschied von den Eltern & Fluchtpunkt*
1961
Levenson, C
Calder & Boyars
275
OP

**WEISS-SONNENBURG**
Hedwig
**Plum-Blossom and Kai Lin**
1958
*Pflaumenblüte und Kai Lin*
1955
Emerson, J
University of London P
128
OP

**WEITZER**
Horst
**Genocide at St-Honor**
1981
Hirst, G
New English Library
155
PB
OP
**Panzergrenadier**
1981
Hirst, G
New English Library
157
PB
OP
**Sonderkommando**
1982
New English Library
160
PB
OP

**WELLERSHOFF**
Dieter
**Winner Takes All**
1986
*Der Sieger nimmt alles*
1983
Knigh, P
Carcanet
388
9.95

**WERFEL**
Franz
**Song of Bernadette, The**
1977
*Das Lied von Bernadette*
1942
Lewisohn, L
Mayflower
446
PB
OP

**Song of Bernadette, The**
1950
*Das Lied von Bernadette*
1942
Lewisohn, L
Pan Books
424
OP
**Song of Bernadette, The**
1958
*Das Lied von Bernadette*
1942
Lewisohn, L
Collins
445
OP

**WERNER**
Bruno Erich
**Slave Ship, The**
1953
*Die Galeere*
1949
Wilkins, E
Heinemann
416
OP

**WESTPHALEN**
Joseph Von
**Diplomatic Pursuits**
1995
*Im diplomatischen Dienst*
Richter -Bernburg, M
Catbird Press
distr. Turnaround
300
9.99

**WICKERT**
Erwin
**Heavenly Mandate, The**
1964
*Der Auftrag*
1961
Kirkup, J
Collins
383
OP

**WIECHERT**
Ernst
**Earth is Our Heritage, The**
1951
*Die Jeromin-Kinder*
1946
Maxwell, R
Nevill
393
OP
**Missa Sine Nomine**
1953
*Missa sine nomine*
1950
Heynemann, M & Ledward, M B
Nevill
314
OP
**Simple Life, The**
1994

*Das einfache Leben*
1939
Heynemann, Marie
Quartet
342
PB
10
**Simple life, The**
1954
*Das einfache Leben*
1951
Heynemann, M
Nevill
295
OP

**WINSLOE**
Christa
**Child Manuela, The**
1994
*Das Mädchen Manuela*
1934
Scott, A N
Virago (Lesbian Landmarks)
295
PB
5.99

**WINTERFELD**
Henry
**Detectives and Togas**
1957
*Caius ist ein Dummkopf*
1953
Sheppard, K
Constable
199
HB
OP
**Star Girl**
1963
*Es kommt ein Mädchen
geflogen*
1957
Schabert, K
Lutterworth P
168
OP

**WODIN**
Natascha
**Interpreter, The**
1986
*Die gläserne Stadt*
1983
Brownjohn, J M
Harcourt Brace Jovanovich
326
**Once I lived**
1992
*Einmal lebte ich*
Galbraith, I
Serpent's Tail
210
PB
8.99

**WOLF**
Christa
**Accident, a Day's News**

1989
*Störfall*
1987
Schwarzbauer, H & Takvorian, R
Virago
176
PB
OP
**Cassandra: A novel and
four essays**
1984
*Voraussetzungen einer
Erzählung: Kassandra*
Van Heurck, J
Virago
288
PB
6.99
**Fourth Dimension, The.
Interviews with Christa
Wolf**
1988
Pilkington, H
Verso
220
HB
28.00
**Model Childhood, A**
1995
*Kindheitsmuster*
1976
Molinaro, U & Rappolt, H
Virago
407
PB
8.99
**No Place On Earth**
1995(1983)
*Kein Ort, nirgends*
1979
Van Heurck, J
Virago
129
PB
8.99
**Quest for Christa T, The**
1982
*Nachdenken über Christa T,*
1968
Middleton, Ch
Virago
192
PB
8.99
**Quest for Christa T, The**
1971
*Nachdenken über Christa T.*
1968
Middleton, C
Hutchinson
185
OP
**Reader and the Writer,
The**
1977
*Lesen und Schreiben*
Becker, J
Seven Seas (E.Berlin)

229
PB
OP
**What Remains and other stories**
1993
*Gesammelte Erzählungen*
1980
Schwarzbauer, H & Takvorian, R
Virago
295
PB
8.99

**WOLKOWSKY**
Maria
**Australian Adventure**
1968
*Australisches Abenteuer*
1961
Atlantic Book Pub.,
124
PB
OP

**WURTHLE**
Fritz
**Prince of Fergana, The**
1962
*Schwarz ist der Himmel in Turkestan*
1958
Crampton, P
Abelard Schuman
189
OP

**ZADOR**
Heinrich
**Hear the Word**
1962
*Die Erfüllung*
1958
Fenn, R W
S.C.M.Press
286
OP

**ZAND**
Herbert
**Last Sortie, The. The story of the cauldron**
1955
*Letzte Ausfahrt*
1953
Woodhouse, C M
Hart-Davis
271
OP
**Well of Hope, The**
1957
*Der Weg nach Hassi el Emel*
1956
Denny, N
Collins
159
OP

**ZECH**
Paul

**Birds in Langfoot's Belfry**
1994
*Die Vögel des Herrn Langfoot*
1954
Odio, Elena B
Camden House,: Columbia,
SC dist UK Boydell & Brew
105
23.50

**ZIEMANN**
Hans, Heinrich
**Explosion, The**
1978
*Die Explosion*
1978
Neugroschel, J
New English Library
288
PB
OP

**ZUCKMAYER**
Carl
**Carnival Confession**
1961
*Die Fastnachtsbeichte*
1959
Mander, J & N
Methuen
152
OP

**ZÜRN**
Unica
**House of Illness, The**
1997
Green, M
Atlas
64
PB
5.50
**Man of Jasmine, The**
1997
Green, M
Atlas
199
PB

**ZWEIG**
Arnold
**Bit of Blood and other stories, A**
1959
Seven Seas; Collet's
184
PB
OP
**Case of Sergeant Grischa, The**
1961
*Der Streit um den Sergeanten Grischa*
1959
Sutton, E
Panther (Hutchinson)
347
PB
OP

**Case of Sergeant Grischa, The**
1986
*Der Streit um den Sergeanten Grischa*
1959
Sutton, E
Penguin
449
PB
OP
**Case of Sergeant Grischa, The**
1961
*Der Streit um den Sergeanten Grischa*
1947
Sutton, E
Hutchinson
347
HB
OP
**Time is Ripe, The**
1962
*Die Zeit ist reif*
1957
Banerji, K & Wharton, M
Gibbs & Phillips
396
HB
OP

**ZWEIG**
Stefan
**Autobiography of Stefan Zweig Shadows Born of Light**
1992
Allborough Publishing
485
PB
OP
**Beware of Pity**
1985
*Ungeduld des Herzens*
1989
Blewitt, P & T
Penguin
353
PB
OP
**Beware of Pity**
1982
*Ungeduld des Herzens*
1989
Blewitt, Ph&T
Cape
353
HB
OP
**Beware of Pity**
1953
*Ungeduld des Herzens*
1939
Phyllis & Blewitt, T
Cassell
418
HB
OP

**Kaleidoscope One**
1949
*Kaleidoskop*
1936
Eden, P & Cedar, M
Cassell
294
HB
OP
**Kaleidoscope Two**
1951
Cassell
290
HB
OP
**Royal Game & other stories, The**
1981
Sutcliffe, J
Cape
250
HB
OP
**Royal Game & other stories, The**
1984
Sutcliffe, J
Penguin
250
PB
OP
**Stories and Legends**
1955
Paul, E & C & Fitzgibbon, C
Cassell
343
OP

Hutchinson
167
OP

ZWERENZ
Gerhard
**Little Peter in War & Peace**
1971
*Casanova od. der kleine Herr in Krieg und Frieden*
Whitman, W
Cape
339
HB
OP
**Little Peter in War and Peace**
1975
*Casanova oder der kleine Herr in Krieg und Frieden*
1966
Whitman, W
Panther
301
PB
OP
**Remembrance Day: Thirteen attempts in prose.etc.**
1966
*Heldengedentag. Dreizehn Versuche in Prosa...*
1994
Mosbacher, E

---

Babel Guides on Disk:

This Fiction in English Translation Database is available to bona fide Researchers and Libraries on 3½ inch diskettes in DOS.txt or DBF format, £50 post free. Regular updates to include titles and reviews entered since publication date can be provided to subscribers.

## Editors

*Ray Keenoy* founded the Babel Guides series and runs
Boulevard Books, a publishing house dedicated to
contemporary world literature
*Maren Meinhardt*, from Germany, works in London publishing
& journalism
*Dr Mike Mitchell* is a leading translator of Austrian fiction,
including works by Meyrink & Rosendorfer.

## Additional Contributors

*Mark Axelrod* is a novelist & screenwriter and teaches
Comparative Literature at Chapman University in Southern
California
*Petra M. Bagley* lectures at the University of Central
Lancashire
*Simonetta Castello* writes and works in the City of London
*Dr Clara Corona* teaches German and Italian Language and
Literature in Treviso, Italy
*Dr Robert Gillet* teaches German Literature at Queen Mary &
Westfield College (University of London)
*Charles Hills* reviews for *The Daily Telegraph* and *The Tablet*
amongst others
*Nick Jacobs* is the publisher of Libris books, specializing in
German classics
*Brian Murdoch* is Professor of German, Stirling University and
recently translated *All Quiet on the Western Front* (Remarque)
*Margaret B. Sargent* (Stirling University) is researching World
War Two as a theme in international literature

*for the traveller with literary inclinations...*

The Babel Guides are a new series of illustrated guides in a lively, accessible style to *world fiction available in English*. Each Guide has around 100 reviews of novels or short story collections and each review is an enjoyable 'trailer' for the book, with a long quote as a taster. As well as reviews there is a unique *database* with the original titles and current prices of all the 20th Century fiction from the country published since 1945.

*'Absolutely wonderful, accessible and fun'*
**British Centre for Literary Translation**
*'A brilliant idea'*
**BBC Radio 3**
*'A novel way to travel'*
**The Observer**
*'intelligent, comprehensible and entertaining'*
**Library Review**

Babel Guide to Italian Fiction in Translation
ISBN 1899460004 £7.95/$14.95
Babel Guide to the Fiction of Portugal, Brazil & Africa in
Translation
ISBN 1899460055 £7.95/$14.95
Babel Guide to French Fiction in Translation
ISBN 1899460101 £9.95/$18.95
Babel Guide to German Fiction in Translation
ISBN 1899460209 £9.95/$16.95
Babel Guide to Latin American Fiction in Translation
ISBN 1899460152 £12.95/$24.95 [Oct '98]

[Spanish, Jewish, Modern Greek, Dutch, Arab and other Babel
Guides to be announced.]


Available in bookshops or from the publisher, post and packing
free in the European Union, elsewhere please add 10%, US$ or
UK£ cheques/eurocheques accepted.

Boulevard Books 8 Aldbourne Road London W12 OLN UK
Tel/Fax 0181 743 5278 email: raybabel@dircon.co.uk

UK & Europe Trade orders & Credit Card orders from
Central Books 99 Wallis Road London E9 5LN tel 0181 986 4854
fax 0181 533 5821 email: bill@centbks.demon.co.uk

*US & Canada:* Paul & Co. Publishers Consortium Inc.
c/o PCS Data Processing Inc, 360 West 31 St, NY, NY 10001
212-564-3730 ext. 295 Fax 212-967-0928.

# German fiction from **Libris**

## Georg Heym *The Thief and Other Stories*

'The reader is in thrall . . . a book for those who like their fiction strange but free of the pretentiousness this sort of *noir* fiction easily attracts.' *European*

'. . . Heym's violent and hallucinatory Expressionist images of murder, madness, plague and revolt vibrate with apocalyptic prescience.'
*The Times Literary Supplement*

106pp. 1 870352 48 3 (paperback)

## Erich Kästner *Fabian: The Story of a Moralist*

'. . . crisp, elegant and ironic . . . both funny and painful . . . nowhere else have I read such a chillingly accurate prefiguration of Belsen and Auschwitz.' *Independent*

'I am a great admirer of *Fabian* and have read it at least twice.'
Graham Green

212pp. 1 870352 45 9 (hardback)

## Hans Fallada *Little Man – What Now?*

'a passionate sociological denunciation of a world in which greed has taken over from humanity . . . we need a Fallada to be living and writing in Britain today.' *Jewish Chronicle*

'This private novel is clearly a window onto very public matters . . . the novel of a time in which public and private merged even for those who wanted to stay at home . . .' *The Times Literary Supplement*

356pp. 1 870352 15 7 (hardback, not available in the USA)

## Hans Fallada *The Drinker*

'This is an heroic book, brave, fearless and honest. It is necessary reading.'
*Sunday Times*

'. . . to read it as observers drawn on to the stage of degradation is an opportunity not to be missed.' *Daily Telegraph*

'psychologically compelling . . . a brilliant portrait and a disturbing confession.' *Literary Review*

'Fallada joins Malcolm Lowry with this magnificent, minatory work.'
Candia McWilliam

306pp. 1 870352 50 5 (hardback)

## Available from all good bookshops

# BabelMail

is a new free service for anyone interested in writing from the wider world.

Join BabelMail and receive

— book news on translated novels, short stories, drama, poetry and literary reference.

— invitations to book launches and other literary events in and outside London and in the USA

— access to promotional offers on books of interest to you

BabelMail is operated by Boulevard Books/The Babel Guides on behalf of publishers, distributors, individuals and institutions interested in world literature.

To join simply send your name and address on a postcard to;

Boulevard Books (BabelMail)
8 Aldbourne Road
London W12 OLN
or leave your details on
tel/fax 0181 743 5278
or email: raybabel@dircon.co.uk

QM LIBRARY
(MILE END)